Mr Speaker

The Office and the Individuals since 1945

MATTHEW LABAN

Biteback Publishing

First published in Great Britain in 2013 by
Biteback Publishing Ltd
Westminster Tower
3 Albert Embankment
London SE1 7SP
Copyright © Matthew Laban 2013

ISBN 978-1-84954-222-7

10 9 8 7 6 5 4 3 2 1

A CIP catalogue record for this book is available from the British Library.

Set in Baskerville and Bulmer

Printed and bound in Great Britain by
CPI Group (UK) Ltd, Croydon CR0 4YY

Contents

Foreword

It is now more than a decade since I retired from the Speakership of the House of Commons and yet still people come up to me and ask about my time in office. This shows just how much the level of public interest in the Speaker has increased since I first became a Member of Parliament back in the early 1970s. Radio and television broadcasting of the House of Commons, introduced in 1978 and 1989 respectively, undoubtedly brought the Speakership to the forefront of British political life. It is, therefore, surprising that no one has written about the Speakership in any depth since Philip Laundy's book *The Office of Speaker* which was published almost fifty years ago. Well, 'time's up', as I used to say. Matthew Laban's history of the post-war Speakership has now filled that gap and I am pleased to be able to write the foreword to his book.

The Speakership is now a much bigger job than when I first entered Parliament. Not only is there the visible work chairing the debates in the chamber, there are now all the increasing number of administrative duties behind the scenes. One aspect of the role I was particularly keen to enhance was the representational duty. As Speaker, I was invited to visit legislatures across the world where I was pleased to talk about the importance of parliamentary democracy on behalf of the House of Commons. It seems that nowadays the Westminster Parliament is more highly regarded abroad than it is in our own country. The Speaker is first and foremost the servant of the House but, as its spokesperson, he or she must ensure that the good reputation of Parliament is upheld both at home and abroad. This is certainly an important role and Matthew Laban examines how this ambassadorial function has grown during the post-war period in his study.

Being Speaker is the best job in the world. I enjoyed every minute of my time in that role. Anyone who has been Speaker has added their own personality to the job and I am glad that Matthew Laban has looked at how the individuals who have occupied the Speaker's Chair have stamped their mark on that great parliamentary office. Charting the development of the Speakership from the end of the Second World War right up to the present day, this is an essential read for anyone interested in the history of the Speakership and of Parliament.

Rt Hon. The Baroness Boothroyd OM;
Speaker of the House of Commons,
1992–2000
House of Lords
December 2012

Introduction

The Speakership of the House of Commons: A Pre-Eminent But Understudied Parliamentary Office

Excepting only the Sovereign herself, no personage throughout the structure of British parliamentary government occupies a higher pinnacle of prestige than the Speaker of the House of Commons.

– Philip Laundy, *The Office of Speaker*, 1964[1]

Thanks to the introduction of sound broadcasting in the House of Commons in 1978 and then television broadcasting in 1989, the Speakership of the House of Commons has largely been defined in the eyes of the public by the five most recent holders of the office. Before the late 1970s, recognition of the Speakership was confined to an elite of fellow parliamentarians, officials, political journalists, visitors to the public gallery of the House of Commons and those who read newspaper parliamentary reports. The post-war period has, therefore, witnessed the holder of the office of Speaker become someone who is now worthy of much wider attention and scrutiny. Despite this high profile, the Speakership of the House of Commons is a public role in the United Kingdom which has seen very few books written on the subject. The aim of this book is to bring any previous research right up to date and look at how the Speakership has been executed and shaped by its holders since 1945.

The Speaker of the House of Commons is one of the oldest public offices in the United Kingdom and can trace its origins back to 1258 when Peter de Montfort presided over 'The Mad Parliament' of that year. It was not until 1376, however, that Peter de la Mare was elected as Parliament's first official spokesman with Sir Thomas Hungerford following in 1377 as the first person to be given the title of Speaker. The Speaker now ranks seventh in the official order of precedence after the Queen and members of the Royal Family. This status also means that the Speaker resides in Speaker's House, the palatial grace and favour apartments within the Palace of Westminster, for the duration of his or her period in office.

The office of Speaker has continually evolved over its 750 years. Until the seventeenth century, the Speaker was considered to be the agent of the King and was often blamed if he delivered news from Parliament that the King did not like. The Speakership was a precarious job and nine former Speakers were either beheaded on the orders of the King or met similarly violent deaths during the Middle Ages and Tudor period.[2] The fact that so many were executed is why newly elected Speakers follow the tradition of showing reluctance and are 'dragged' to the Chair. In 1642 it was Speaker William Lenthall who established the fact that he was the servant of the Commons and not of the King. When King Charles I entered the House of Commons chamber and tried to arrest five Members of Parliament, he asked Lenthall where they were. Lenthall dropped to his knees before the King and replied:

May it please Your Majesty, I have neither eyes to see, nor tongue to speak in this place, but as the House is pleased to direct me, whose servant I am here; and I humbly beg Your Majesty's pardon that I cannot give any other answer than this to what Your Majesty is pleased to demand of me.[3]

Having severed its subservience to the monarch, it was up to Speaker Arthur Onslow, who was Speaker between 1728 and 1761, to break the office's links with the executive. Before Onslow, who was the longest serving Speaker in history, it was common for Speakers to hold other political appointments which associated them with the ministry of the day. In 1742, Onslow decided to resign from the lucrative post of Treasurer of the Navy in order to safeguard his independence and impartiality as Speaker. From then on, the qualities and standards that Arthur Onslow brought to the office have defined the modern Speakership and his legacy can still be felt today.

The powers of the office morphed again in 1796, when Speaker Henry Addington established the convention that the Speaker's casting vote should always opt for the path which would mean further discussion such as another reading of a bill. In the 1860s, Speaker John Evelyn Denison took Addington's ruling even further and established more principles governing the use of the Chair's casting vote. Denison, who seems to have been called upon to use his casting vote on more occasions than any other modern Speaker, set down that if the Chair could not apply Addington's ruling on keeping discussion open then the Speaker should always vote to maintain the *status quo*. The way in which the post-war Speakers have applied the rules and conventions established by Addington and Denison will also be examined in this book.

I first became interested in the Speakership of the House of

Commons as far back as October 2000 when Michael Martin was elected to the Chair. I was amazed to discover that there have been very few books written about the office in the post-war period. The seminal work on the subject, *The Office of Speaker*, was written by the Librarian of the Southern Rhodesian Legislature, Philip Laundy, as long ago as 1964. A further book by Laundy called *The Office of Speaker in the Parliaments of the Commonwealth* was published twenty years later in 1984. Other than a few other publications, there are only the biographies and autobiographies of some of the Speakers who have held the post since 1945. Of these, only Selwyn Lloyd, George Thomas and Betty Boothroyd have published memoirs of their time as Speaker. Horace King wrote a short book on Parliament intended for schoolchildren but his memoirs were never published and the manuscript is now housed in the Parliamentary Archives. Biographies have been written on Speakers Lloyd, Thomas, Boothroyd and Bercow. There is, however, nothing for Speakers Clifton Brown, Morrison, Hylton-Foster, Weatherill or Martin. There is even a scarcity of primary material because there is no archive for Clifton Brown, Hylton-Foster or, as yet, Martin.

Why has so little been written on the Speakership? To use a sporting analogy, people are usually more interested in the players than they are in the referee and that has been the case with the Speakership. The Speaker is now, of course, far more than a referee and he or she exercises great administrative authority comparable to any government minister. With this comes financial responsibility so the Speaker's use of public money has also become of interest.

I shall cover the following occupants of the Chair and their execution of the role of Speaker:

Speaker	Political Party	Period in the Chair
Colonel Douglas Clifton Brown	Conservative	1943–51
William Shepherd Morrison	Conservative	1951–9
Sir Harry Hylton-Foster	Conservative	1959–65
Dr Horace King	Labour	1965–71
Selwyn Lloyd	Conservative	1971–6
George Thomas	Labour	1976–83
Bernard Weatherill	Conservative	1983–92
Betty Boothroyd	Labour	1992–2000
Michael Martin	Labour	2000–2009
John Bercow	Conservative	2009–

I will examine the functions and powers of the Speaker but concentrate much more on how each of the individuals have put their own mark on an office which evolves through precedent and previous incumbents' personal style.

This book would not have been possible without the help of all those who have allowed me to interview them about their thoughts on Speakers and the Speakership. Unless otherwise stated, material quoted has been sourced especially for this book. The late Sir Robin Maxwell-Hyslop, a veritable fountain of knowledge on the procedures of the House of Commons, was an invaluable source of guidance in the early days of my research. I have also been very fortunate to have had the help of the former Speaker, Baroness Boothroyd, and the current Speaker, John Bercow. I also count myself extremely lucky to have met the former Speaker, the late Lord Weatherill, who was determined to help with my research even though he was very ill at the time. Interviewing three of the post-war Speakers has really helped to see what a personal job it is to hold that office.

I am grateful to the following for granting me permission to quote from archives, oral history seminars and personal papers: Anthony Clifton Brown, Baroness Boothroyd, the Gloucestershire Archives and Mrs A. Young, the Institute of Contemporary British History, the Labour Party, Lord Tebbit, Lady Weatherill, The Churchill Archive Centre and the family of Selwyn Lloyd, The National Archives, the National Army Museum, The National Library of Wales, the Open University Library, the Parliamentary Archives and Mr J. Wilson, the Southampton City Archives and the University of Kent Special Collections.

I would also like to thank Professor the Lord Hennessy of Nympsfield and Dr Peter Catterall for their encouragement and help with my research. I have also been very lucky to have had the support of Patricia Sowter, the Chief Executive of Cuckoo Hall Academies Trust, who has encouraged me with this book despite the fact that I have been busy setting up and opening a Free School as one of her headteachers. I am also grateful to Sean Magee, Sam Carter and Hollie Teague of Biteback Publishing for their patience and help to publish this research. Finally, as always I would like to thank my family who have supported me throughout the ups and downs of putting together this study.

Matthew Laban
December 2012

One

In and Out of the Chair: The Speaker's Powers and Responsibilities

You have to gauge the mood of the House, you have to gauge the mood of the country because you are not a political person as a Speaker but nevertheless you are there, that is what your job is to do, to gauge the mood of everything. The clerks will advise you on the procedures but when they've done that the buck stops with you.

– Baroness Boothroyd

O nce a Speaker is elected, he or she is formally initiated into the role. The Speaker-Elect is marched off to a ceremony in the House of Lords and declares that he or she has been chosen by the Commons as their new Speaker. The Lords Commissioners, who represent the Queen, tell the Speaker-Elect that Her Majesty gladly approves the choice. From that moment, he or she becomes Mr or Madam Speaker and is invested with all the ancient rights, privileges and powers of the office.

The Speaker receives a salary in line with that of a Cabinet minister although recent changes have meant that Speaker Bercow receives just £1,000 less than the Prime Minister. The Speaker is supported in his work by the Speaker's Office and the head of this office is the Speaker's Secretary, a post first created in 1735. There have also been Assistant Speaker's Secretaries as well as the

Trainbearer, who is responsible for carrying the Speaker's train and escorting him to meetings and functions. The Speaker now has a Diary Secretary to organise the busy schedule of engagements both inside and beyond Westminster. The Speaker also appoints a chaplain who says the prayers at the beginning of each sitting in the chamber. Although not part of the Speaker's Office, there is also the Speaker's Counsel. He or she does not give advice on procedure because that is the role of the Clerk of the House. Instead, the Speaker's Counsel is there to give the Speaker and other officers of the House legal advice. All these people are there to help the Speaker carry out his duties and responsibilities.

The Speaker is also supported by the three Deputy Speakers who up until 2010 were chosen by the party managers in the House. The Deputy Speakers are now elected by secret ballot by MPs and the first ever election took place on 8 June 2010. Since 1855, the senior Deputy Speaker has been the Chairman of Ways and Means, a title which comes from his former role of chairing the Ways and Means Committee, the body responsible for proposing changes in taxation to the government, which was abolished in 1967. The other Deputy Speakers are the First Deputy Chairman and the Second Deputy Chairman whose roles were introduced in 1902 and 1971 respectively. The Chairman of Ways and Means is also responsible for chairing the Speaker's Panel of Chairmen, the group of MPs who chair the standing committees which examine legislation. Until 2010 these committee chairmen were chosen by the party managers but now they are also elected by the House. Since 1999, the Deputy Speakers and the members of the Speaker's Panel of Chairmen have also chaired the debates held in Westminster Hall. These MPs all form part of the overall office of Speaker and assist him or her in chairing the House whether it is in full session or in committee.

When asked what he thought was the most important element of the Speakership, the former Speaker, Lord Weatherill, answered:

Total impartiality. The Speaker has no political party. On becoming the Speaker he gives up party politics for life. I always make the point in saying that there's absolutely nothing wrong with party politics because that gives us choice but as far as the Speaker's concerned he must always be totally impartial and that continues for the rest of his time.

Moreover, on becoming Speaker all party affiliations must be renounced to forego questions of bias. Even on retirement, a Speaker does not return to party politics because he or she immediately stands down as a Member of Parliament and, on receiving the customary peerage, sits as a crossbencher in the House of Lords. Betty Boothroyd recalls that when she took up her seat in the House of Lords, the former Labour Cabinet minister Baroness Castle suggested she should sit on the Labour benches. Boothroyd did not entertain the idea determined as she was to remain above the political fray.[4]

It is this total impartiality and obligation to quit party politics for life which sets the Westminster Speakership apart from presiding officers in other Parliaments. Even the Commonwealth Parliaments which have sought to emulate the United Kingdom Speakership have not managed to achieve this degree of neutrality. The former Speaker of the New Zealand House of Representatives, Jonathan Hunt, explains how, in his country, the Speaker does not cut all links to the party in the House to which the Speaker was affiliated at time of election and may attend caucus meetings. This is also true in Australia and even in Canada, which is the closest parliamentary system to the Westminster model, the Speaker does not resign from his or her

political party. Even the presiding officers of the devolved parliament and assemblies in the United Kingdom retain membership
of their political party. Lord Elis-Thomas, who was the first
Presiding Officer of the National Assembly for Wales, stated that
he was 'still a member of the [Plaid Cymru] group but kind of
at a distance'. The impartiality of the Westminster Speakership is
one that has built up and become imbedded over many years and
is not something that other legislatures can copy quickly or easily.

The analogue of the Speaker in local government terms is
the old-style mayor rather than the newly introduced directly
elected mayors. The mayor represents the Council on official
visits in the same way that the Speaker represents the House
of Commons. Both offices support charities and voluntary
organisations by hosting functions. During a councillor's term as
mayor, he or she is supposed to be independent when chairing
Council meetings in the same way that the Speaker is neutral
when presiding over the House of Commons. In closely divided
local authorities, however, the mayor often has the casting vote
and this is used in a partisan way. In addition, when a mayoral
year is up, the person returns to his or her party benches in the
Council chamber.

Roger Sands believes that 'the Speakership is definitely the last
job of a political career' although Speaker Morrison went on to
become Governor-General of Australia and Speaker Weatherill
became Convenor of the cross-bench peers. These two exam-
ples, although important positions, are not overtly political
because being a governor-general is supposed to be above party
politics and being Convenor of the cross-bench peers is really an
administrative rather than a political role.

Following John Bercow's official statement in September 2012
announcing his decision not to take his pension until he is sixty-
five, it will be interesting to see what he will do once he stands

down from the Speakership; he will be too young to retire into obscurity like many of his predecessors. Unlike those in the post-war period who retired from office when they were in their sixties or seventies, John Bercow was only forty-six when he was elected. If he serves for nine years as he said he will then this will only take him to fifty-five. Indeed, the official statement on the Speaker's pension, which points out that Speakers have usually taken up office around retirement age and are, therefore, unlikely to seek employment once they have retired, announced that in Bercow's case 'these historical assumptions do not hold'.[5]

The overall notion of impartiality is taken very seriously and, in his short book on the Speakership, Lord Maybray-King makes the point that, once elected to the Chair, the Speaker should treat everyone equally. A Speaker lives a lonely life because he is not allowed to mix with his old friends and colleagues in the tea rooms or bars of the House of Commons lest he invite accusations of favouritism.[6]

Speaker Michael Martin, however, chose not to distance himself too much. On retiring from the House in 2001, Tony Benn stated that: 'In my opinion, you [Michael Martin] are the first Speaker who has remained a Back Bencher. You have moved the Speaker's Chair on to the Back Benches. You sit in the Tea Room with us. You are wholly impartial, but your roots are in the movement that sent you here.'[7]

Betty Boothroyd believes that her successor's decision to go into the tea rooms was 'breaking with a long-established and wise custom'. The impartiality of the Speakership is paramount and removal from the intrigue of the tea room is one way in which the Speaker can demonstrate detachment from party politics.

Moreover, MPs could, in effect, sack a Speaker who is not deemed to be fair and neutral. A Member can ask the Speaker to change his ruling and try to persuade him but if that same

MP is still dissatisfied then he can put down a motion criticising
the Speaker. If the motion is carried then the Speaker would
be deemed to have lost the confidence of the House because a
majority of MPs would have voted against him. On that basis
the Speaker would be obliged to resign.

Michael Martin got into trouble again over the question of
impartiality when he broke with tradition and made a political
point from the Chair on 29 October 2001. At the conclusion
of questions on asylum seeker vouchers to the Home Secretary,
David Blunkett, Martin said: 'The Home Secretary knows of
my interest in the matter that the House has been discussing.
I welcome vouchers being abolished because, as I know from
experience in my constituency, they take away people's dignity.'[8]

The press was quick to pick up on the point that the Speaker
had compromised his neutrality with the political journalist,
Melissa Kite, writing in *The Times* that:

> Michael Martin, the Speaker of the House of Commons, shat-
> tered centuries of parliamentary tradition yesterday when he rose
> not to call MPs to order but to voice his own political opinions
> [...] Veteran parliamentarians said it was the only time in living
> memory, and possibly in the history of Parliament, that the
> Speaker has expressed an opinion.[9]

It is certainly true that there is no other example of a Speaker
making a comment in the chamber on a policy issue during the
post-war period. Martin clearly realised that he had made a
mistake because the following day he made a statement to the
House in which he said:

> I wish to assure the House that I am wholly committed to main-
> taining the long-standing tradition that the Speaker stands aside

from politics. The remark I made yesterday stemmed from my personal experience with constituents in my Glasgow, Springburn constituency, particularly in the community of Sighthill. Members may be aware that there was a particularly tragic murder of a young asylum seeker in that area during the summer recess. If, contrary to my intention, my remark was subject to the interpretation that has been placed on it, I seek the indulgence of the House.[10]

The Conservative MP Sir Patrick Cormack immediately rose to thank Martin for his statement and for 'upholding the impartiality of the Chair'.[11] Despite criticism by the press, the House of Commons rallied to the Speakership's defence, helping to prevent more harm coming to the office. Roger Sands has said that: '[Speaker Martin] acknowledges that it was an error [...] it was a natural reaction but he's apologised to the House for it and so it's not a precedent.'

Even though Speakers do sometimes make mistakes, and MPs even put down motions against certain rulings, Maybray-King made the point that not once in 150 years have any of the motions of no confidence in the Chair been carried. MPs are prepared to tolerate mistakes made by the Speaker thanks to the dignity of the office and the tradition of fair play to which every incumbent has adhered.[12]

According to Baroness Boothroyd, it is the job of the Speaker to ensure that 'most Members, and that means minority groups as well as minorities within major parties [...] get a fair share of time'. Indeed, bearing in mind that so many Members from different parties had voted for her, Boothroyd has said on the question of impartiality, 'How could I let those people down?' Clearly, ensuring that Members all have a fair chance of participating in a debate also makes sure that the Speaker retains

the support of the House and so an even-handed approach
is essential.

Selecting MPs to speak is probably the most important task the
Speaker has to undertake in relation to the role in the Commons
chamber and is also the greatest test of his or her impartiality.
Selwyn Lloyd kept his 'Blue Book' which listed every Member's
name and when, and for how long, he or she last spoke. In this
way Lloyd was able to ensure that each and every MP was given
a fair chance of being called to speak. In a BBC Television
documentary broadcast in 1991 called *Mr Speaker, Sir*, the former
Speaker, Lord Weatherill, admitted that: 'Everything that the
Members do here [in the Commons chamber], even when they
stand and are not called, gets recorded in my computer.'[13]

Weatherill's computer, therefore, replaced the 'Blue Book'
system and enabled the Speaker to have accurate records on
who had spoken and for how long so that he could ensure that
all MPs had an even chance of being allowed to participate
in a debate.

A former Deputy Speaker, Baroness Fookes, explained how
Betty Boothroyd used her deputies to assist her with deciding on
whom to speak:

> I would take what was then the government side and Geoffrey
> [Lofthouse] would take the opposition side. We would have the
> letters or [...] telephone messages that would come through
> to the Speaker's Office and that would be put together by the
> Speaker's staff together with a list, not in order, but a list of all
> those who put their names in by a given time. It was our task to,
> as I say, prepare a preliminary batting order for the meeting [...]
> we would then go through the list of people and the Speaker
> would comment on order, perhaps query it, accept it, and then
> she [Boothroyd] would then write down the final batting order.

We worked to quite a useful system. In looking at names we would look first to see whether there were any Privy Counsellors who usually get to be first on the list [thanks to their seniority]. We would look at anyone who had some special interest or expertise or position in relation to the debate so, for example, if the Chairman of the Select Committee wished to speak or a member of the Select Committee for the relevant subject, let's say it's Foreign Affairs, so the Chairman of the Foreign Affairs Select Committee, we would give those a higher priority. Or, maybe, there's something where there's a special local interest and we would make sure then that if the local MP wished to speak he or she would be fairly high up the list. All other things being equal, we would then look at the number of times someone had spoken and the priority would go to those who had spoken less. There was also a penalty system because the staff would keep a list of those who had spoken for longer than a certain time. It might have been in order but I think it was twenty minutes and twenty-five. Twenty minutes would be one star and twenty-five minutes would be two stars. They would be given less priority if they had spoken too long in a previous debate.[14]

Whilst MPs will be aware of the pecking order for being called to speak, they will nevertheless try to 'catch the Speaker's eye' and see whether they can get called to participate in a particular debate. Stanley Baldwin, Conservative Prime Minister in the 1920s and 1930s, once called the Speaker's eye, 'the most elusive organ that Nature has ever yet created'.[15] The preparation outlined by Fookes explains why sometimes it is difficult for other MPs to be called during a debate because the Speaker knows that other Members have a greater claim to the floor and so they must be given precedence.

Of course, in order to be able to call MPs to speak, the Speaker has to undertake the huge task of learning the names of all the

more than 600 MPs. This gives him or her the necessary knowledge to ensure they are given a fair crack of the whip when it
comes to being called to speak in the Commons chamber. Lord
Weatherill pointed out the impact of television on Parliament:

> Television has made this difference that Members of Parliament
> now not only do they wish to be heard but they wish to be seen
> to be heard so the pressures on the Chair are very considerably
> greater than they were because they want to get on when the
> television cameras are actually running.[16]

This is a very important point and shows that Speakers who
have served since the introduction of televised broadcasting of
the proceedings of the Commons in 1989 have had a tougher
job than their predecessors. Clearly, the demand from MPs to
be called is greater for 'prime time' debates and so the Speaker
has to try to accommodate as many Members as possible whilst
maintaining fairness.

The Speaker cannot vote in a division but he or she does cast
the deciding vote in the event of a tie which makes the issue of
impartiality even more vital. The latest edition of the parliamentary rule book, *Erskine May*, states that:

> In the performance of this duty to give a casting vote, the
> Speaker is at liberty to vote like any other Member, according to
> his conscience, without assigning a reason; but, in order to avoid
> any imputation upon his impartiality, it is usual for him, when
> practicable, to vote in such a manner as not to make the decision
> of the House final.[17]

In his memoirs, Speaker Thomas wrote that, 'Fortunately a
Speaker's greatest ally is precedent and there is very little that

happens which has not happened before at some time in the long history of Parliament'.[18] *Erskine May* records:

1. that the Speaker should always vote for further discussion, where this is possible, e.g. Mr Speaker Addington's decision of 1796;
2. that, where no further discussion is possible, decisions should not be taken except by a majority, e.g. Mr Speaker Denison's decisions of 1861 and 1867; and
3. that a casting vote on an amendment to a bill should leave the bill in the existing form.[19]

Both Speakers Thomas and Boothroyd were in the Chair at a time when the government of the day did not enjoy a Commons majority which meant that the casting vote had to come into play. On 27 May 1976, a Conservative amendment to the Aircraft and Shipbuilding Industries Bill resulted in a tie of 303 to 303. It was necessary, therefore, for Thomas to use his casting vote and vote with the Noes so that the original bill was left in its existing form.

Betty Boothroyd was forced to use the casting vote on 22 July 1993 when Labour put forward a wrecking amendment restoring the Social Chapter to the Maastricht Treaty. The House divided with a result of 317 to 317 and so Boothroyd announced that:

The numbers being equal, it is my duty to cast my vote. It is not the function of the Chair to create a majority on a policy issue where no majority exists among the rest of the House. In accordance with precedent, I therefore cast my vote with the Noes.[20]

The casting vote is, therefore, an important function of the Speaker, to be exercised carefully in order not to compromise the impartiality of the office.

Whilst it is true, however, that the Speaker has to interpret the rules, it is also the case that he or she does not create them.

> The Speaker has not the powers that, maybe, a number of members think he has [...] The power lies with you; it lies with the House of Commons; it lies with the members. The Speaker is the servant of the House. The Speaker can do nothing unless you give that Speaker authority.[21]

Thus it is the House of Commons as a whole that decides upon the Standing Orders and it is up to the Speaker to uphold them.

As guardian of the rules, the Speaker has to take Points of Order each day. This is when an MP asks the Speaker to rule on whether something that has happened in the chamber was within in the rules. This can be a real test of the Speaker's knowledge of parliamentary procedure and, although he or she is assisted by the clerks at the Table, the occupant of the Chair has to respond quickly and give a fair ruling. This task is one which the Speaker has to be ready to respond to all the time he is in the Chair and can sometimes mean that he has to set his wits against veteran MPs who have extensive knowledge of the rules of the House. For example, a Point of Order from the former Conservative MP for Tiverton, Sir Robin Maxwell-Hyslop, was certain to be a challenge for any Speaker. In April 1980, George Thomas rejected one of them with the retort that he had checked in *Erskine May*, 'which I know the hon. Gentleman takes to bed with him'. When Maxwell-Hyslop accepted the Speaker's ruling, Thomas told him: 'I shall sleep a lot better tonight.'[22]

In his memoirs, Selwyn Lloyd asserts that the Speaker 'has wide powers' when it comes to ensuring that debates are managed properly and do not break down into disorderly slanging matches.[23] Standing Order 42 empowers the Speaker to order a Member who persists in irrelevance or tedious repetition to discontinue his speech. Standing Order 43 gives the Speaker the power to order an MP whose conduct is grossly out of order to withdraw from the House for the remainder of the day's sitting or, if deemed necessary, coupled with Standing Order 44, the Speaker can 'name' an unruly Member. This is the most severe sanction the Speaker can exercise and calls on the House as a whole to divide and vote on whether the MP concerned should be suspended for five sitting days if it is a first offence, twenty sitting days for a second offence or a period for Members to determine for repeated incidents. If the whole House is behaving in a disorderly fashion then Standing Order 46 enables the Speaker to suspend the sitting.

George Thomas wrote in his memoirs that 'whereas Selwyn Lloyd had boasted that he had not named or suspended anyone throughout his Speakership', the policy was no good for him.[24] Indeed, thanks to the increasingly unruly nature of the Commons, caused by the fact that there was a Labour government which eventually lost its overall majority between 1974 and 1979, Thomas decided that he 'would have to take firm action very soon or the House could easily spin out of control and Parliamentary business become impossible'.[25] Almost from the outset Thomas was true to his word because he had to suspend the sitting on 27 May 1976 when the Conservative MP Michael Heseltine seized the Mace following a breakdown in pairing arrangements.

Speaker Boothroyd also had to exercise her disciplinary authority early on in her period in the Chair. On 2 July 1992, veteran Labour MP Dennis Skinner described the Minister for Agriculture, John Gummer, as 'a little squirt'.[26] Boothroyd required Skinner to withdraw the remark which led to a short exchange about the word 'squirt' not being in *Erskine May*. Whilst Boothroyd admitted that this remark was not mentioned in *Erskine*

May she nevertheless ruled it as unparliamentary and so ordered Skinner to leave the chamber after he had refused to back down. The Speaker's powers to maintain order are essential in order to uphold the dignity of Parliament and to ensure that the business of the House is allowed to proceed unhindered.

However, the Speaker has no power over deciding the business to be debated in the House, such as Tony Blair's early decision to consolidate the twice-weekly fifteen-minute Prime Minister's Questions into one thirty-minute session on Wednesdays, announced through a press release rather than on the floor of the House. In her memoirs Betty Boothroyd states that she 'was neither forewarned nor consulted – merely informed'.[27] Roger Sands has pointed out that the most important powers the Speaker has when it comes to determining what goes on in the Commons chamber are the selection of amendments and the right to rule on granting Urgent Questions, previously known as Private Notice Questions. Urgent Questions are particularly important because they require a minister to come to the House and answer a question on a subject that he or she might not want to talk about and at a time that is not convenient.

The Speaker has the power to grant an emergency debate if a Member so requests. This debate can either be held for three hours from the commencement of public business the following day or, if deemed urgent by the Speaker, from 7 p.m. until 10 p.m. the same day. This is clearly an important power because it certainly enables the House to debate topics which are of immediate concern to the public.

The Speaker also has the power to limit the length of backbench debates to a minimum of eight minutes. He can also intervene to prevent deliberate time wasting by MPs who are either speaking repetitiously or calling for unnecessary votes.[28] At any time a Member may rise and ask that a debate be finished by moving 'that the question now be put'. The Speaker has the power both to accept this motion and allow it to be put. Sometimes this task can prove somewhat tricky as the Speaker has to make sure the debate is neither too long for those who wish it to end, nor too short for those wanting to continue. As Lord Maybray-King noted, this is often a difficult decision to make but the House accepts the decision regardless.[29]

The clerks of the House of Commons advise the Speaker over which Standing Orders to use and which precedents apply. In his diary entry for 26 October 1993, Tony Benn suggested that the Speakership was run by the Clerk of the House because Speakers are neither interested in procedure nor history.[30]

Speakers are very conscious of the rich history of the office to which they have been elected. More modern Speakers have had less reason to be interested in procedure because that is the way that the House of Commons has gone. MPs are now far more concerned with becoming community champions within their constituencies than learning all the rules of the House and so more recent Speakers have not needed the procedural knowledge that their predecessors might have had. The reason why Benn made this point, however, is explained in a much earlier diary entry he wrote when he wanted to remain in the Commons rather than take up his late father's peerage. Benn recalls that he would go to see Sir Edward Fellowes, the Clerk of the House, and ask his advice on raising a matter with Speaker Hylton-Foster. Fellowes would give the necessary advice and then he would be called upon by the Speaker to respond to Benn's letter containing his own advice.[31]

Of course, this might be a reflection on the Speaker of the time rather than of the Speakership in general. Indeed, on this point, Baroness Boothroyd has said that:

The Clerk of the House is asked for advice and the Speaker does exactly what she wants to do if you've got a Speaker who's got spirit and determination [...] I always asked for advice like you ask your solicitor for advice, but you don't always follow what your solicitor wants to do.

It would seem that whether or not a Speaker relies heavily on the advice of the clerks is down to the character of the individual concerned. Boothroyd often did not take the advice of the Clerk of the House, especially when determining whether to allow a Private Notice Question, and explains why:

I remembered once, many times, going against the advice of the Clerk of the House but I remember one Clerk saying to my secretary afterwards, 'You know, she was right.' Because they wouldn't advise on policy, they would just advise on structures and on standing orders. Of course, that is their job but you, the Speaker, have to determine whether an issue is of such urgency or importance [...] and very often I went against the will of the Clerk of the House [...] but I do recall on one occasion particularly when, it was Clifford Boulton who said to my secretary, 'You know she was right to accept that PNQ'.

Lord Naseby, as Michael Morris is now styled, remembers a particular occasion when he did not take the advice of the Clerk when Dennis Skinner insisted on taking formal votes rather than nodding orders through late one evening:

I gently nudged the Clerk and said to him there is a standing order that allows one to do standing and sitting [to vote], please find it. He found it, and then suggested that I did not use it as it had not been used for the best part of twenty plus years and, furthermore, the Speaker had gone to bed. So, I decided to use it, it was used, and we finished off the remaining votes and the rebellion collapsed.

Having been an MP for twenty years at that point, Morris had a keen knowledge of the rules of the House and so was able to use his own judgement to resolve the problem.

The Speaker now has to rule on whether matters relating to Scotland, and to a lesser extend Wales and Northern Ireland, should be discussed by the House of Commons since the creation of the devolved legislatures in the late 1990s. Baroness Boothroyd remembers that:

> I had to rule on it because it was such a new procedure and Members were still raising questions about Scottish affairs and making points in general debate on issues that were not the responsibility of the Westminster Parliament. My rulings did have an impact for a while, but I could not allow matters to be raised or discussed in debate which was outside our area of responsibility.

Although this is relatively new, Speaker Whitley made a similar ruling in 1923 with regard to the Stormont Parliament in Northern Ireland which sat until 1972. On 3 May 1923, Whitley ruled that:

> With regard to those subjects which have been delegated to the government of Northern Ireland, questions must be asked of Ministers in Northern Ireland and not in this House [...] The policy of voting money here in aid of Irish services may be discussed here, but [...] this right does not cover matters of administration for which a Minister in Northern Ireland is responsible.[32]

The former veteran Conservative MP, Sir Teddy Taylor has put a different slant on the issue:

> most of the cutting down is done by the clerks. They tell you what you can ask about and what you can't ask about and, to that extent, the questions are usually in order before you start. If someone in a supplementary stretches it a bit then the Speaker could, if he wanted to, curb them but you'll find he [Speaker Martin] doesn't really because he feels if they've got an opinion to express then good luck to them and what ministers often do is say, well, this is actually a matter for the Scottish Executive so I'd say, if anything, it's ministers who do it rather than the Speaker.

The Speaker is also guardian of Members' privileges 'to freedom of speech in debate, to freedom from arrest, and free access to Her Majesty whenever the occasion shall require'.[33] Whilst these privileges are ancient, the Speaker has had to assume the guardianship role in order to reassert the authority of the House. On 5 April 2000 Speaker Boothroyd reprimanded the Blair government for announcing a sports policy change through the media rather than at the despatch box on the floor of the House.[34] This was, however, only a request as the Speaker has no power to demand that a government announce new initiatives in the Commons chamber. Despite Boothroyd's statement being to no avail it does show that the Speaker is a key figure in fighting for the rights of the legislature in what Peter [now Lord] Hennessy has called 'the executive's constitution'.[35] Indeed, the Speaker has the duty of being the voice of the House and so must make sure that that voice is heard if the Commons is not being respected in the way that it should. Rogers and Walters have made the argument that: 'if Parliament is to be the focus of national attention, then, whether the news is momentous or not, the principle that the nation's representatives in Parliament are told first is an important one; and the Speaker must be its main advocate'.[36]

This is a new role that has come about thanks to the development of round-the-clock broadcast media during the second half of the post-war period. Governments want to get their message across but it is up to the Speaker to try to ensure that the House of Commons is not left out.

One of the most important discretions entrusted to the Speaker is the power to select the amendments to be discussed. This is indeed an important task because it is crucial in enabling the opposition to bring the government to account and in ensuring debate. Rogers and Walters highlight the importance of selecting amendments and give the example of when, in February 2003, the government put down seven free-standing motions as choices for the future composition of the House of Lords. On this occasion there was no option for abolishing the House of Lords altogether and so a Labour backbencher put down identical amendments to each option, declining approval as 'it does not accord with the principle of a unicameral parliament'. Speaker Martin selected the amendment allowing it to be debated and voted upon. Even though it was easily defeated, it nevertheless allowed those in favour of abolition to make their point.[37]

The Speaker can use this power to ensure that views from across the House are heard. Selecting amendments is all part of the judicial nature of the office of Speaker because he must decide which one warrants debate. Not only does the Speaker have the power to rule on the admissibility of bills, motions and amendments as well as determine whether an emergency adjournment motion meets the necessary criteria but he or she must also interpret the *sub judice* convention. *Erskine May* states that 'matters awaiting the adjudication of a court of law should

not be brought forward in debate'.[38] Speakers must not allow
MPs to discuss anything, no matter how topical, which could
prejudice the outcome of a court case.

Another of the Speaker's duties is to declare a seat vacant
in the event of a Member dying, being diagnosed as mentally
insane or having been convicted of a criminal offence. Under
the terms of the Lunacy (Vacating of Seats) Act 1886, the
Speaker has the power to authorise medical examinations
to determine whether a Member is suffering from mental
illness. If this Member is found to be in the same state of
health after a six-month gap then the Speaker is obliged to
declare the seat vacant thus making a by-election necessary.[39]
Speaker Boothroyd declared a seat vacant following the
conviction of Fiona Jones, the Labour MP for Newark, for
fraud over election expenses. The conviction was, however,
quashed by the Court of Appeal and so Mrs Jones was allowed
to resume her seat. In these instances the Speaker does
perform an important task in ensuring that constituencies are
represented adequately.

The Speaker is also responsible for deciding which political
party forms the official opposition, although this has not been
exercised during the post-war period. The last time it came
into play was in 1940, following the formation of the coalition
government led by Winston Churchill. Speaker FitzRoy rejected
the tiny Independent Labour Party's claim to official opposition status. However, following the collapse of the Conservative
Party at the 1997 general election, several Liberal Democrat MPs
occupied the opposition front bench. This usurpation did not
go unnoticed and the Speaker reminded them of their rightful
place – as the minority party – below the gangway, rather than
above it opposite the despatch box, where the opposition are
allowed to take their seat.[40]

What is clear is that if an election resulted in a coalition government and no obvious opposition because several smaller parties had a similar number of seats then this power could come into play.

The Speaker must also decide whether a Bill should be forced into law against the wishes of the House of Lords under the terms of the Parliament Acts. *Erskine May* describes the procedure:

> A bill which is passed by the House of Commons in two succes-sive sessions (whether of the same Parliament or not), and which, having been sent up to the House of Lords at least one month before the end of the session, is rejected by the House of Lords, in each of those sessions, shall, on its rejection for the second time by the House of Lords, unless the House of Commons directs to the contrary, be presented to Her Majesty and become an Act of Parliament on the Royal Assent being signified to it.[41]

Speaker Martin used this power twice during his time in the Chair. The first time was just a month after his election when he used the procedure to force into law the Sexual Offences (Amendment) Act 2000 which lowered the age of homosexual consent to sixteen. The second occasion was over the banning of fox hunting in November 2004 when Martin certified the Hunting Bill after it had been rejected by peers in successive parliamentary sessions. Laundy states that the Speaker's 'certifi-cate is conclusive and may not be questioned in a court of law'.[42] All money bills, that is a bill whose only purpose is to authorise expenditure or taxation, must be certified by the Speaker. Again, this adjudication means that the House of Lords' powers of delay are severely restricted and, in this case, they can only hold up the passage of the bill by a month. This is an important power although the Speaker has very little discretion in such matters as the 1911 Parliament Act clearly specifies the circumstances in which a Bill should be deemed a money bill.

The Speaker can recall the House of Commons during recess if there is an urgent matter to debate. On 20 July 2011, Speaker Bercow recalled Parliament in order to debate public confidence in the media and police in relation to the phone-hacking scandal. Under Speaker Martin the Commons was recalled on three separate occasions: following the attacks in the USA on 11 September 2001, on 3 April 2002 following the death of the Queen Mother and again on 24 September 2002 to debate possible military action against Iraq. The Speaker can also give permission to hold a debate on a Saturday and this was granted by George Thomas at the time of the Falklands War in April 1982.

The Speaker also has a role to play at the time of the death of the monarch, both in the Chair of the House and behind the scenes. When King George VI died on 6 February 1952, Speaker Morrison attended a meeting of the Cabinet that morning at 11.30 a.m. At this meeting the following was agreed:

> The Cabinet agreed that the meeting of the Privy Council to proclaim the Accession of the new Sovereign should be held at 5 p.m. that day. When the House of Commons met at 2.30 p.m. they would be informed of the Demise of the Crown. The sitting would then be suspended until the Accession Council had been held. Thereafter, the House would meet again for the sole purpose of enabling the Speaker to take the oath of allegiance and to swear in such other Members as were present.[43]

Morrison was clearly there to explain the parliamentary procedures that would have to take place because it is most unusual for a Speaker to attend a Cabinet meeting in the modern era. The most important duty for the Speaker at this time is to take the oath of allegiance to the new monarch. The former Clerk of the House, Roger Sands, has set out the format that would take place:

> Over the following days the Speaker presides and passes on to the House messages of condolence received. The Leader [of the House] announces future business, Members take the oath of allegiance to the new Sovereign, arrangements for the Lying-in-State are announced to the House and the House is asked to agree a motion for the House to attend the Lying-in-State. The modern precedent (1936 and 1952) is that normal business is suspended until after the State Funeral.

Moreover, the Speaker could well have to recall the House under Standing Order No. 13 if Parliament was in recess and so is central to all the formalities that go on when a monarch dies. The Speaker has to be fully aware of all these duties and Speaker Boothroyd recalls that 'certainly we had documents that came before me on what the role of the Speaker was'.

Although the Speaker is famous for his or her function in the Chair, he or she also has to perform duties and attend meetings behind the scenes that are out of the public eye. Indeed, in order to ensure the smooth conduct of business in the chamber, the Speaker meets with the Leader of the House, the government Chief Whip and the opposition Chief Whip on a regular basis. Boothroyd recalls:

> I met them all on a weekly basis. The Chief Whips of the respective parties would come and have a talk; they confided in me and told me of their problems. I would sympathise and offer some solution. The meeting with the Leader of the House was most important and something I always looked forward to. He would

let me know the government's forthcoming business, and the mid- to long-term business plans. It was important to keep in regular touch and good relations were formed. Not only was it good for a Speaker to listen, but in turn I could let them know my thoughts, and particularly let the Whips know my thoughts, and particularly let the Whips know of some of their Members who might be difficult to deal with and to remind them that I needed their help in disciplining and educating individual Members to ensure improved conduct.

These meetings, which are referred to as 'behind the Speaker's Chair', are crucial to the smooth running of the House of Commons and ensure that the Speaker is fully up to speed with what is going on.

The Speaker also has informal pastoral responsibilities and looks after Members of Parliament not only in their public duties but also with personal troubles. Lord Weatherill believed 'there must always be somebody in a position of authority to whom people can come and open their hearts and people used to come to me and open their hearts'.

Indeed, in his television documentary on the life of Betty Boothroyd, Michael Cockerell claims that 'Madam Speaker liked to keep a motherly eye on her MP charges'.[44]

The Speaker is also responsible for overseeing the administration of the House of Commons and is Chairman of the House of Commons Commission which employs all the staff. The Commission was established under the House of Commons (Administration) Act 1978 which replaced the House of Commons Services Committee set up in 1965. Roger Sands has explained how these administrative duties have increased since the time Laundy was writing:

It was recognised first of all in the House of Commons Administration Act 1978, but it had pre-existed that and it's become, just as the role as the Clerk of the House has become much more significant in those directions, so the role of the Speaker has since, well I've dated it from 1992 roughly, when the House of Commons took over managerial and financial responsibility for a whole number of basic services which previously had been provided for us by government agencies, principal among them being the building, management of the building and the building's budget.

Although the Speaker had administrative responsibilities before the 1978 Act and the further reforms in 1992, it is clear that this role has increased in its scope in more recent times and is one that has developed substantially over the post-war period. Michael Ryle, who was Clerk of Committees in the late 1980s, has stated that the 'present Commission did not exist before 1978. Speakers before then had no significant role or responsibility for staff employment'.[45] Roger Sands commented on the amount of administrative work a Speaker now has to do: 'Possibly the number of meetings that the House of Commission which he [the Speaker] chairs has not increased but the weight of the business has increased because of the growth in the House's budget and the matters which the Commission, therefore, has to deal with.'

The Speakership now comprises managerial aspects as well as traditional duties within the Commons.

A very new administrative task undertaken by the Speaker came into force during the Blair government. The Clerk of the House, Robert Rogers, explains:

Something the Speaker does himself, which he's never had to do before is signing off certificates under Section 34 and Section 36

of the Freedom of Information Act [2000] and satisfying himself
that he's signing them off properly. Now, of course, that is something that only Speaker Martin ever had to do. None of their
predecessors has had to do it.

Under the Act, the Speaker is allowed to sign a certificate exempt-
ing private information about the House or about Members
which, if released, would either breach parliamentary privilege
or prejudice the effective conduct of public affairs. This new
power was used by Martin in his attempts to shield MPs from
the expenses scandal towards the end of the Speakership. In the
end, the revelation he had used this power to try to protect MPs
contributed to his eventual resignation. Whilst a Speaker has a
duty to try to help the MPs who elected him, he now had a much
wider duty to the British public in upholding good standards in
the House.

Prior to this, Speaker Boothroyd campaigned to raise the
standard of debate and conduct in the House. Her call for
urgent action in 1996 prompted an inquiry into the conduct of
twenty-five MPs. The inquiry, led by Sir Gordon Downey, the
Parliamentary Commissioner for Standards, exonerated most of
the MPs but five were judged to have fallen below the standards
of the House.[46]

The Speaker is certainly influential and a call for action from
the Chair can indeed make things happen. It is the House of
Commons Commission, chaired by the Speaker, which employs
the Parliamentary Commissioner for Standards and since the
creation of this post there have been high-profile investigations
into the business activities of the former Paymaster-General,
Geoffrey Robinson and into a loan he gave to the former Cabinet
minister Peter Mandelson that was not declared in the register
of interests. In this sense, Members of Parliament now have a

'watchdog' who is completely independent of anyone else in the House of Commons. The creation of this office has meant that the Speaker does not have to get involved with investigating allegations against Members and so can be totally removed from the process and, therefore, remain completely impartial. The downside of this was exposed during the expenses scandal of 2009 when the public, the media and even MPs still expected the Speaker to step in and take personal action.

The Speaker is also responsible for the security of the House of Commons. The Conservative frontbench spokesman on Northern Ireland, Airey Neave, was killed in the Commons car park by a bomb planted by Irish Republican terrorists on 30 March 1979 and since that time the Speaker has overseen security. Roger Sands has pointed out that, in terms of the Speaker's security responsibilities 'the buck does stop with him' when it comes to day-to-day smaller scale measures. Larger systems would come under the remit of the Commission but of course the Speaker is the chairman of that body.

Speaker Martin was faced with responding to two very serious breaches of security during 2004. The first incident involved purple powder being thrown down from the gallery onto the government front bench and the second witnessed fox hunting supporters storming the chamber. Under pressure from senior ministers, the Speaker appointed Peter Mason, a top-ranking MI5 officer, to take over as security co-ordinator, to oversee the work previously undertaken by the Serjeant-at-Arms.

The Serjeant-at-Arms is an office dating back to 1415 when one of the King's bodyguards was appointed to attend upon Parliament. The holder is responsible for carrying the Mace in the Speaker's procession and he or she is in charge of the security of the House of Commons. The Serjeant heads up the Serjeant-at-Arms Department and meets with the Speaker, the Deputy Speakers and the Clerk at the daily meeting to discuss the forthcoming business of the House. He or she is responsible for all the arrangements and security surrounding an event hosted by the Speaker and is another key role that forms part of the overall office of Speaker.

Another role of the Speaker is that of ambassador for the House of Commons and he or she must host or attend international events. Indeed, the Speaker attends the Conference of Speakers and Presiding Officers of Commonwealth Parliaments which has met periodically since 1969. In this forum Speakers from the various lower and upper Houses of Parliament within the Commonwealth can exchange views on how to approach different issues of mutual interest. Baroness Boothroyd has recalled the following:

> I received a huge number of invitations from overseas Parliaments and spent a good deal of the recesses, summer, Easter and Christmas, travelling abroad to meet these requests [...] I addressed the Russian Duma, the Ukraine and Slovak Parliaments and many others as well as speaking to various Constitutional and Foreign Affairs Committees in the various countries visited. I also put in a regular attendance at the Commonwealth Speakers' Conference, European Speakers' Conference, and the Inter-Parliamentary Union Conference at the United Nations. There was a large agenda outside Westminster to be tackled. It was exhausting, not least for my staff, but I liked meeting people and representing the Commons in this way.

Since Boothroyd's time there has also been the introduction of the G8 Speakers' Conference which brings together the presiding officers of the Parliaments of eight of the world's wealthiest countries.

In addition to representing the Commons abroad, the Speaker also has to entertain foreign dignitaries in the grace and favour residence of Speaker's House. When Selwyn Lloyd was Speaker he entertained several visiting Heads of State including Queen Juliana of the Netherlands, King Zahir Shah of Afghanistan and President Heinemann of West Germany.[47] The very fact that the Speaker entertains foreign royalty and world leaders demonstrates the prestige and dignity that is associated with the office. Baroness Boothroyd believes that the Speaker should be seen on the international stage because:

> Many Parliaments are anxious to hear about the way we manage our affairs at Westminster. Westminster may not find the respect I believe it should have in many parts of this country, but it is held in the highest regard by overseas legislatures, many of whom are keen to examine our procedures and our ways and means of doing things.

The Speaker is also used by the Foreign and Commonwealth Office to improve relations with other countries by means of parliamentary diplomacy. Lord Weatherill explained that during his first month as Speaker, Geoffrey Howe, the Foreign Secretary came to see him and asked if he would go to Romania. The eastern European country was breaking away from the Soviet Union and Howe wanted Weatherill to speak to Ceaușescu, the Romanian leader, and gather information.

> And, thereafter, there was not a recess when I wasn't asked to go somewhere [...] Really not the job of the Speaker, but merely I think a 'visiting card' to get ambassadors in. I think that was probably new in my time.[48]

Today, the office of Speaker commands respect around the world and can be used to the British government's advantage when it comes to diplomatic relations and uncovering information about foreign countries. The former Clerk of the House, Sir Donald Limon, confirmed that Betty Boothroyd conducted similar diplomatic missions when she was Speaker and so this role has continued.[49] The Speaker is, therefore, a very useful tool when it comes to strengthening diplomatic relations with another country because he or she can make visits and be granted audiences thanks to the dignity of the office.

The Speaker also represents Parliament at national services, commemorations and state occasions. For example, the Speaker is always present at the Remembrance Sunday service at the Cenotaph in Whitehall. Indeed, the Speaker is seventh [sixth if you discount the defunct role of Lord High Treasurer] in the official order of precedence after the Royal Family and ahead of all peers except those who hold offices which outrank his own.

One ceremony that the Speaker does, of course, partake in every day the House is sitting is the Speaker's Procession. The Speaker leaves his residence preceded by the Bar Doorkeeper, the Serjeant-at-Arms carrying the Mace and followed by the Trainbearer, Chaplain and Secretary. The formal procession goes via the Library Corridor, the Lower Waiting Hall, Central and Members' Lobbies to the Commons chamber before every sitting. This route was adopted during the Second World War when MPs had to use the House of Lords chamber because the Commons had been destroyed by enemy bombing. It has been retained in preference to the shorter pre-war route because it allows visitors in the Central Lobby to witness the ceremony. This procession is the event around which the Speaker's day revolves. George Thomas's time in office was marked by an increase in the number of parties hosted in Speaker's House. 'In all my time in Parliament, Speaker's House had remained something of a mystery even to members, very few of whom had a chance to see it properly.'[50] Thomas was determined to change that and so Speaker's House has become a neutral meeting ground for politicians to meet, relax and chat informally away from the Commons chamber. Even before Thomas's time, Selwyn Lloyd wrote that he would regularly invite seven MPs to have lunch with him and believed that these occasions 'were extremely valuable to me for keeping in touch with the feelings of backbenchers, and for getting to know younger Members and their first impression of the House'.[51] However, this was not good enough for Lloyd's successor who decided that the state dining room should not just be used for formal official occasions. George Thomas not only entertained his friends but also a wide cross-section of society including policemen, trade union leaders, actors, the Archbishop of Canterbury and ex-President Nixon.[52]

Cockerell mentions in his television documentary that 'anyone who was anyone in politics would come to Betty Boothroyd's parties'.[53] Indeed, Boothroyd records in her memoirs that she continued with the formal dinners but she also added in buffet suppers, musical evenings and carol concerts into the social diary. She was determined that long-serving Commons staff, such as the cleaners, canteen and post office workers and policemen who had never seen inside Speaker's House were invited to one of her parties.[54]

The post-war period has witnessed the referral of questions concerning electoral reform to a conference of Members of Parliament chaired by the Speaker. The idea of cross-party talks dates back to 1869 when William Gladstone's bill to disestablish the Irish church became stalled in the House of Lords. Fifteen years later, the struggle over the Third Reform Act in 1884–5 also produced informal all-party talks and this set a precedent for such a meeting to negotiate electoral reform. In 1916, Prime Minister H. H. Asquith secured the consent of Speaker Lowther to preside over the first Speaker's Conference on Electoral Reform to examine reform of the franchise and the redistribution of seats. In the post-war era, Speaker King presided over an electoral reform conference which recommended lowering the voting age to twenty in 1968. Speaker Lloyd chaired a conference between 1973 and 1974 which proposed that the minimum age for a parliamentary candidate should be lowered from twenty-one to eighteen and Speaker Thomas presided over a conference which looked at the number of parliamentary constituencies in Northern Ireland. In his last year in office, Michael Martin chaired a Speaker's Conference to examine the under-representation of women and ethnic minorities in the House of Commons and this report was concluded by his successor in 2010. Whilst these electoral conferences do not happen all the time, they nevertheless are an extra responsibility that the Speaker has to undertake when the need arises.

Following the expenses scandal of 2009, the Speaker now chairs the Speaker's Committee for the Independent Parliamentary Standards Authority (IPSA). IPSA is the body which now administers the pay and allowances of Members of Parliament. The committee reviews IPSA's annual estimate of the resources it needs and ensures that this money enables IPSA to perform its functions in an efficient and cost-effective manner.

The Speaker has an enormous workload and actually the chairing of Commons proceedings is only a small part of what has to be done. The job of the Speaker is like an iceberg: the bit that everyone sees is the small part above sea level with that under the water being the huge amount of behind the scenes work that is undertaken. Baroness Boothroyd has described a typical day when she was Speaker:

I started work around half past seven in the morning with radio news, the newspapers and the daily Order Paper (that day's agenda). I needed to familiarise myself with all Parliamentary Questions of that day and to consider who might stand to be called for a supplementary Question, for example, Chairmen of Select Committees related to the subject matter. I also considered Questions that would not be reached that related to an earlier Question. I took the view that if a Member took the initiative to table a Question that was far down on the Order Paper and related to an earlier one, he/she had some right to be called for a supplementary. It was very detailed work, but I regarded it as essential.

Boothroyd's hands-on style was a feature of her Speakership and meant that all parties felt they were treated fairly. She continues:

At 9.30 my secretary and I would go through it all again. Then other staff would join us to go through correspondence, letter signing, faxes, lists for social gatherings, diary engagements and detailed, long-term planning for overseas visits and weekend engagements. There were security meetings and heads of various departments to see, but 12 noon was the crucial meeting of the day which no one was allowed to miss, with the three Clerks at the Table, Serjeant-at-Arms, my three deputies and secretary. I conducted a 'wash-up' session of the previous day, an examination of the current day's dossier and attempted to anticipate the hazards and pitfalls of that day and suggest how we might best deal with them. At twenty minutes to 1 o'clock a slot was kept available for visiting VIPs, ambassadors, High Commissioners who wished to pay a courtesy call or to say farewell. The House started at 2.30 p.m. and I would remain in the Chair for a couple of hours, or, as a matter of courtesy, until a Secretary of State had completed a Ministerial Statement and questions. From around 5 o'clock I would see Whips or the Leader of the House, or anyone who wished to see me as my door was always open to Members. And then of course at about 7 o'clock the receptions and dinners would commence in the Speaker's State Rooms.

The Speaker's is a busy schedule indeed, with only around three hours a day actually in the Chair. The rest of the time is filled with meetings and sacred preparatory time.

The post-war period has seen the Speakership's impartiality endure, with the office enjoying wide-ranging powers to regulate the debates in the House of Commons. Since the Second World War, Speakers have had to maintain order over an unruly House, particularly during parliaments with small-majority governments, but now the Speaker has to look after administrative affairs as well. They not only have to be a skilled presiding officer and guardian of the rules; he or she now has to be the chairman of the board, a keen entertainer and an international statesman. The Speaker is no longer confined to the corridors of Westminster; he or she must now represent the House of Commons at international events in a role that has developed and increased in the post-war era. Much is expected of the person who holds the office of Speaker. He or she must now be the embodiment of the House and convey its traditions to all those who wish to learn through its example.

Two

Divisions and Ballots: Electing and Re-Electing A Speaker

A convoluted parliamentary version of pub skittles.
– Robin Oakley, former BBC Political Editor, 2001[55]

T he electoral procedures surrounding the Speaker of the House of Commons have changed markedly during the post-war period. Many of these changes have been prompted by a greater degree of competition for the office. Becoming Speaker is not the only election he or she has to face. If the Speaker wants to remain in office beyond a general election then he or she must seek re-election in his or her constituency in order to be re-elected to the House and the Chair.

Electing a Speaker

The Conservative MP for Hexham, Colonel Douglas Clifton Brown, who had been elected as Speaker in 1943 following the death of Edward FitzRoy, faced re-election after the Labour landslide of July 1945. The first act of any new Parliament is to elect, or re-elect, a Speaker because without a chairman the business of the House cannot be conducted. Despite the historic Labour victory, Clifton Brown managed to retain his parliamentary seat. He did not, however, believe that he would be allowed to continue in the Chair because he assumed that the new government would want a Speaker from its own benches. Philip Laundy mentions that Lord Pannell, the former Labour MP for Leeds West, told him that 'Clifton Brown came to London with a pile of suitcases expecting to pack up'.[56] The new Prime Minister, Clement Attlee, did not see the need for a change, however, and at a meeting of the Parliamentary Labour Party he reported that the leadership supported the re-election of Colonel Clifton Brown.[57]

Clearly, Attlee did not want to break with the convention that allows the Speaker from the previous Parliament to continue in office if re-elected as an MP and it is reported that Clifton Brown wept at what he described as an act of 'amazing political generosity'.[58] The decision not to replace Speaker Clifton Brown set the standard for the rest of the post-war period.

When Clifton Brown retired at the 1951 general election, the new government, which saw Winston Churchill's return as Prime Minister, had to search for a replacement. Harold Macmillan, who had become Minister for Housing and Local Government in Churchill's new administration, wrote in his diary: 'But what about the Service Ministers? ... And then the Speaker? Shall it be W. S. Morrison or Hopkins Morris – both good men?'[59]

In the end, the former wartime Cabinet minister William Shepherd Morrison was selected as the candidate to be put forward as Speaker. Lady Dunrossil, Morrison's daughter-in-law, remembers that following the Conservative victory in 1951, her father-in-law 'didn't know what job he was going to get'. Dr Alasdair Morrison, Speaker Morrison's son, believed that it suited Churchill to offer his father the Speakership because it 'made use of his talents [he was an experienced parliamentarian and had been a recorder in Walsall] and kept him personally happy with something to do'.

Laundy argues that 'the consultative process broke down very badly' and, indeed, it resulted in the first contested election for the Speakership since William Gully was opposed in 1895.[60] Though the Labour leadership had agreed Morrison's nomination, some in the Parliamentary Labour Party believed that it was time that a Labour MP became Speaker. At the meeting of the Parliamentary Party on 31 October 1951, it was decided that Major James Milner would be put forward as the Labour nomination. The former Attorney General, Hartley Shawcross, had it agreed, however, that Milner's candidature would be withdrawn if the Conservatives agreed to replace Morrison with Sir Charles MacAndrew.[61] Both Milner and MacAndrew had been Deputy Speakers in the previous Parliament and so they had the experience of the Chair that Morrison, with his ministerial background, was lacking.

Churchill did not agree to change his candidate and so the aggrieved Labour backbenchers proposed Milner. In the end, Morrison was chosen by 318 votes to 251 but this election highlighted the difficulty of consulting the whole House in the choosing of its Speaker and not just leaving it up to the two front benches to decide.

Controversy returned to the issue of selecting a Speaker when Morrison retired in 1959.

The Prime Minister, Harold Macmillan, recorded in his diary on 18 October 1959 that, 'There is a problem – not yet resolved – about the Speakership. A strong "moderate" opinion has appeared, in the Party and in the Press, that we ought to have a "Labour" Speaker.'[62] He was, therefore, prepared to allow Sir Frank Soskice, the well-respected former Solicitor-General, to be put forward.

Rab Butler was despatched to see Hugh Gaitskell, the Labour leader, and discussions took place between the two parties.

Macmillan records, however, that: 'Gaitskell would not part with him [Soskice], and then tried to turn this act of generosity into a grievance, accusing us of trying to "dictate" a Labour choice. However, this proved very thin. The Press gave it no support.'[63]

Finally, the Conservatives proposed one of their own Members, the Solicitor-General Sir Harry Hylton-Foster. However, during the debate on 20 October 1959, Gaitskell voiced his dissatisfaction with the whole process and went on to say that:

> there are some objections in my opinion to a member of the Treasury Bench being selected for the post of Speaker. We were not enthusiastic when Mr Speaker Morrison was chosen, because he had been a Minister, but he was not at that time a Minister, nor had he held Ministerial office – I think I am right in saying – for some years. The right hon. and learned gentleman [Sir Harry Hylton-Foster] comes straight from a distinguished position on the Treasury Bench, and that, I think, is another difficulty.[64]

Despite this protest, the Labour Party did not put forward an alternative candidate and so Hylton-Foster was elected unanimously as Speaker. However, the issue of a former minister being elected to the Speakership was to become a recurring theme whenever the matter of electing a Speaker was discussed.

Hylton-Foster was re-elected as Speaker following Labour's narrow victory at the 1964 general election although Laundy states that Lord Pannell had written to him and told him that the continuity convention might have been breached had the government's majority been larger.[65]

This possibility of removing Hylton-Foster continued even after he had been re-elected. The convention which allows a sitting Speaker to continue in office until he or she chooses to retire was most definitely at risk. Sir Robin Maxwell-Hyslop, felt that Hylton-Foster was a weak Speaker:

> Eventually, I wrote to the Chairman of the 1922 Committee [Sir William Anstruther-Gray], during a Recess (1965?), telling him that I had little but contempt for Speaker Hylton-Foster's manifest cowardice, and that I would oppose his re-election next time round. The Chairman of the 1922 Committee replied in a letter saying that he agreed that Harry H-F must not be re-elected as Speaker, and must be told that his re-election was unacceptable.[66]

The death of Hylton-Foster on 2 September 1965 prevented this from happening and brought about the election of the first Speaker from Labour ranks. This episode is the most recent example of what happens when a sitting Speaker dies in office. On this occasion, the death of the Speaker occurred during the summer recess because otherwise the House of Commons would have had to have been adjourned until an election for a new Speaker was arranged. With the Commons unable to sit without a Speaker, the election was the first item of business when the House reconvened on 26 October 1965.

The former veteran Labour MP, Tony Benn, recounts in his published diaries that, during a dinner at 10 Downing Street on 4 September 1964, Marcia Williams, Harold Wilson's Personal Secretary, suggested that they make Desmond Donnelly Speaker.[67] Donnelly was a Labour rebel opposed to the renationalisation of steel and it might have suited the Wilson government to have removed this thorn from their side because, once in office, a Speaker cannot voice his or her political opinions.

The obvious choice for the Speakership was, however, the Chairman of Ways and Means and Deputy Speaker, the Labour MP for Southampton Itchen, Dr Horace King. Wilson recorded in his memoirs that 'the Conservatives immediately called for the election of Dr King, less, we felt, through admiration of his qualities than through voting arithmetic'.[68] Indeed, Labour had only been returned with an overall majority of four in October 1964 and so the election of the first Labour Speaker happened at a time when the government could not really afford to give up one of its number. Benn records in his diaries that, at a meeting of the Parliamentary Labour Party, Ted Short, the government Chief Whip, argued that the choice of Horace King had been forced on them by the Conservatives and the views of 5 per cent of Labour MPs regardless of the parliamentary consequences.[69]

Despite this warning, the Labour Party did not prevent King's candidature and so his election went through smoothly and unanimously. Ironically, the first Labour Speaker was elected at a time when his party would have preferred a Conservative in the Chair.

King's successor, the former Cabinet minister Selwyn Lloyd, did not enjoy a smooth election when he became Speaker in January 1971 thanks to the fact that the Conservatives had two potential candidates. Lloyd, who had been Foreign Secretary and Chancellor of the Exchequer, was approached by the Chairman of the 1922 Committee, Sir Vere Harvey, and asked whether he would like to become Speaker. Whilst this was happening, another former Conservative Cabinet minister, John Boyd-Carpenter, was also sounded out. When Boyd-Carpenter questioned whether Lloyd wanted the Speakership, he was told that Lloyd was out of the picture because he was going to be made ambassador to Washington. When Lloyd turned down Washington the Conservative leadership decided it would support whichever of the two candidates had the backing of the Labour shadow team. According to Boyd-Carpenter, Bob Mellish, the opposition Chief Whip, let it be known that the vast majority of the shadow Cabinet supported Selwyn Lloyd.[70]

Despite the fact that Roy Jenkins, who was deputy leader of the Labour Party at the time, told Boyd-Carpenter that this was not necessarily the case, Willie Whitelaw asked him not to stand in order to prevent a contest. Whitelaw even went as far as to say that he would have to resign if Boyd-Carpenter went for the Speakership and managed to win. On 30 December 1970, John Boyd-Carpenter put out a press statement saying that he was not going to put his name forward for the Speakership. Obviously Boyd-Carpenter thought that he could not prevail against the combined forces of the government and opposition front benches. Indeed, the future Speaker, Bernard Weatherill, recalled that: 'with a heavy heart I was put in as a junior whip to deliver Selwyn Lloyd as Speaker [...] when I think that left to its own devices or its own choice, John Boyd-Carpenter would have been their first choice'.

Trouble soon erupted because backbenchers on both sides of the chamber felt they had not been properly consulted. They were determined to make the point that choosing a Speaker was a matter for the whole House and not just the two front benches.

On 12 January 1971 the veteran Conservative MP Dame Irene Ward proposed Lloyd as Speaker, a motion which was seconded by the Labour MP Charles Pannell. Shortly afterwards the objections began with the dissatisfied Liberal MP John Pardoe announcing that he thought the Commons should question whether a former senior minister ought to become Speaker: 'The Speaker ought to be a protector of the rights of backbenchers, and can a man who is imbued with the rights of government ever throw off that mode of thinking entirely?'[71]

Robin Maxwell-Hyslop agreed with Pardoe and nominated the Labour MP for Kettering, Sir Geoffrey de Freitas, to become Speaker. The irony here is that de Freitas had been a junior Air and Home Office minister during the Attlee governments and had only just returned to the Commons having been made High Commissioner to Ghana in 1961. The argument was, however, more to do with the lack of consultation among backbenchers and so Maxwell-Hyslop's nomination was swiftly seconded by the Labour MP Willie Hamilton. Hugh Noyes, the parliamentary correspondent for *The Times*, wrote that this was 'a mini-revolution against the party establishments'.[72] This move was without the consent of de Freitas himself, who announced to the House that he would be voting for Lloyd. The House divided with the result being 294 for the Ayes and 55 against and so Lloyd was elected Speaker.

Clearly the issue of a former minister becoming Speaker was a factor in there being so many abstentions. The former Clerk of the House, William McKay also points out that Selwyn Lloyd was 'not just a minister but one involved in Suez'. Indeed, Lloyd had been Foreign Secretary during the Suez crisis of 1956 – a very senior member of a government that had misled the House over the collusion with Israel.[73] This undoubtedly associated him with executive power rather than defending the rights of the legislature. During the debate which finally elected Lloyd to the Speakership, Willie Hamilton made the point that:

> When Mr Speaker Morrison was elected in 1951, my party [Labour] objected at that time that it was a serious break with precedent, the precedent being that of electing a Speaker who had not held Ministerial office. Mr Morrison had held six Ministerial offices before he was called to the Speakership. In the previous hundred years, only two Speakers had been Ministers – Mr Speaker Peel in 1884 and Mr Speaker Lowther in 1905. If and when the right hon. and learned Member for Wirral [Selwyn Lloyd] is elected, he will be the third successive Conservative Speaker who has been elected after having held Ministerial office.[74]

Hamilton went on to argue that Speakers who had previously held ministerial office might have to preside over debates in which their actions when they were a minister were discussed and possibly criticised. Hamilton said that:

> The right hon. and learned Member for Wirral will, no doubt, if he is elected, be sitting in that Chair when we have foreign affairs debates in this House, and, no doubt, some of us on this side will have recourse to reminiscing and, no doubt, will bring up the part he played in 1956.[75]

Lloyd countered the argument against former ministers becoming Speaker because he believed that a Speaker who had had ministerial experience would know how Whitehall departments work and so could withstand blandishments from colleagues in the government.[76]

A former Clerk of the House, Sir Donald Limon, believes that there are 'some likenesses' between being a minister and being Speaker and so ministerial office might in fact be a good training ground. After all, the Speaker does have to balance being a constituency representative with his or her responsibilities in the House just as a minister has to divide his or her time between constituency and Whitehall.

Despite the arguments against having former ministers as Speaker, George Thomas, the Labour MP and a former Secretary of State for Wales, was elected unopposed to succeed Lloyd on 3 February 1976. For the second time in little over a decade, a Labour Speaker was elected at the time when a Labour government with a tiny majority could not really afford to lose one of its number.

The system for electing a Speaker was altered in 1972 following a Procedure Committee report, chaired by the Conservative

MP Sir Robin Turton. This enquiry followed criticisms made after the election of the Speaker on 12 January 1971. Rather than the Clerk of the House chairing the proceedings, it was decided that either the outgoing Speaker or the MP with the longest unbroken service in the Commons would oversee the Speakership election. William McKay believes this is a far better system: when his predecessors chaired the election, they were not allowed to speak in the chamber because only elected Members can speak. Instead, the Clerk had to point at MPs to call them. However, the method of putting forward a motion, and then an amendment if you oppose a candidate, was not changed in the 1972 reforms. Moreover, Sir Robin Maxwell-Hyslop wrote: 'Of the six recommendations which I made in my letter, and orally, to that Committee, five the Committee adopted in its Report. The sixth (a secret ballot, so that the Speaker elected does not know who voted for, and who against) was adopted by the House much more recently.'

Selwyn Lloyd presided over the election of his successor, George Thomas, although from then on the Father of the House, as the longest continuously serving MP has become known, has undertaken the duty. The reason for this move is that if a Speaker retires at the end of a Parliament then he or she is no longer a Member when the new House of Commons meets and so cannot take part. It is also the case that if a Speaker retires and resigns his or her seat during the summer recess, then he or she is not an MP when the Commons reconvenes.

On Thomas's retirement in 1983 there was again a difference of opinion between the front bench and the back bench over who should become the next Speaker. The Prime Minister, Mrs Thatcher, wanted either the former Foreign Secretary, Francis Pym, or the former Conservative Chief Whip, Sir Humphrey Atkins, to become Speaker. According to Douglas Hurd, who was a junior Foreign Office minister at the time, when Francis Pym retired from the government he was offered the Prime Minister's support for the Speakership, but it was not a position he wanted.[77]

Thus the Speaker was in the process of becoming the back-benchers' choice rather than being decided by the government and opposition front bench of the day. Indeed, the Conservative MP Bernard Wetherill, who was Deputy Speaker during George Thomas's time in the Chair, became Speaker thanks to a bold move from a Conservative backbencher.

The backbencher in question was Robin Maxwell-Hyslop, who remembered the events that took place as follows:

Prior to the Dissolution of the previous Parliament, I had discussed the matter with backbenchers of all (11?) parties, except Sinn Fein, and satisfied myself that Jack Weatherill was the Speaker that they wanted. Subsequent to that, both Jack and I were subjected to intense, and repeated, pressure from both the Conservative Whips, and No. 10, to give way in favour of the 'official' candidate: but we stood firm.

Indeed, Weatherill stated that he was summoned to No. 10 and offered a ministerial job in the Foreign Office by Mrs Thatcher a few days before the new Parliament met following the 1983 general election. However, Weatherill turned down ministerial office on the basis that there was 'no precedent for a Chairman of Ways and Means [as he had been in the previous Parliament] ever going back into party politics'. He went on to recall that he had 'literally thirty-six hours' notice' that he was going to be Speaker; the next day James Callaghan came to see him and told him that the Labour Party was going to support him and then so did David Steel and some of the younger members of the Conservative Party.

Weatherill himself believed that the reason why he enjoyed the support of the opposition was down to an episode which took place when he was Deputy Chief Whip in 1979. On the evening of 28 March 1979, before the crucial vote of no confidence which brought down the Callaghan government, Weatherill had offered not to vote in order to honour an agreement 'to pair sick with sick' due to that fact that the Labour MP Sir Alfred Broughton was too ill to get to the Commons. In the end, the Labour Deputy Chief Whip, Walter Harrison, did not put his Conservative opposite number in that position and so the government lost the motion of no confidence by one vote. Weatherill stated that: 'I am now told that it was that action of being prepared to honour my word that caused Jim Callaghan and the Labour Party to propose me as Speaker against the will of Mrs Thatcher.'

Betty Boothroyd records in her autobiography how Maxwell-Hyslop ensured that the backbenchers got their man: 'He nominated Jack in a recorded-delivery letter to Jim Callaghan, Father of the House, and at the same time told the BBC's *World at One* programme what he had done.'[78]

The nomination was now out in the open and the Whips' Office could do nothing about it. Maxwell-Hyslop recounted what happened on 15 July 1983 just before the Speakership election:

Twenty minutes before we all went into the Chamber to elect a Speaker, the Conservative Chief Whip (or his Deputy, I forget which) came up to me in the Members' lobby and said: 'The Prime Minister concedes defeat but, to save face, will you allow Cranley Onslow (Chairman of the 1922 Committee) to take over your nomination of Jack Weatherill?' I replied: 'Yes: but I never trust a Whip! In authorising the Father of the House to substitute Cranley's name for mine on the first Resolution put to the House,

I shall also instruct him that if Cranley attempts to double-cross me by nominating, instead, No. 10's candidate, he will immediately call me to move an Amendment thereto nominating Jack Weatherill. And, dear boy, you will realise that under the new procedure, MY AMENDMENT WILL BE TAKEN BEFORE THE MAIN QUESTION!'

In the end, it was actually Sir Humphrey Atkins, Mrs Thatcher's preferred candidate, and not Cranley Onslow who proposed Weatherill as Speaker, in order to show Conservative solidarity. Weatherill was, therefore, put forward and elected unopposed and so, as the 2000 Procedure Committee report into the election of a Speaker points out, 'even a Prime Minister at the height of her influence within her party, and who had just been returned to power with a majority of 144, was unable to secure the election of her preferred candidate for the Chair'. Julian Haviland, the Political Editor for *The Times*, commented:

> What seems to have clinched his [Weatherill's] election was the discovery by his fellow MPs that he did not have the Prime Minister's approval. For opposition MPs that would have been commendation enough, but Conservatives have also been affronted by the idea that Mrs Margaret Thatcher, or anyone in government, should have wished to dictate the decision of the House.[79]

The Speakership election of 1983 was the culmination of this gradual post-war move towards backbenchers finally getting the Speaker of their choice rather than just accepting what the leadership of the two main parties had agreed between them.

The other significance of Weatherill's election was, as Maxwell-Hyslop stated, that it broke 'the power of the Prime Minister to impose "a decayed ex-Minister" on the House of

Commons as its Speaker'. The recurring issue of concern that a Speaker should not have previously been a minister, which first arose in 1951 when Morrison took the Chair, seems to have been solved. Although Weatherill had been Deputy Chief Whip, he was not associated with high ministerial office in the way that Speakers Morrison, Hylton-Foster, Lloyd and Thomas had been.

Jack Weatherill stood down at the 1992 general election and so an election for a new Speaker was required as soon as the new Parliament met. On this occasion there was a contest for the post as once again backbenchers were not in favour of the government's candidate, the former Northern Ireland Secretary and Conservative MP Peter Brooke. Indeed, the then leader of the Labour Party, Neil Kinnock, is said by Betty Boothroyd to have held the view that it was Labour's turn to nominate Weatherill's successor.[80] Unlike the 1983 Speakership election, however, the government did not withdraw their candidate at the last minute; instead there was an open contest on the floor of the House.

Giles Radice, the former Labour frontbencher, recorded in his diary how he spent the Sunday before the election ringing round Conservatives, including his pair John Biffen. Boothroyd agreed to allow Biffen to propose her for the Chair and this proved crucial in gaining the support of a sufficient number of government backbenchers. Radice had also been promised the support of the Liberal Democrats and the other minority parties, and Harold Walker, the other Labour Deputy Speaker, had been persuaded not to stand.[81]

On 27 April 1992, the Conservative MP Sir Michael Neubert moved that 'Mr Peter Brooke do take the Chair of this House as Speaker'.[82] This motion was seconded by fellow Conservative, Sir Thomas Arnold. However, as Radice had arranged, John Biffen moved an amendment to the motion which deleted

Brooke and inserted the name 'Miss Betty Boothroyd'. This was seconded by Labour MP Gwyneth Dunwoody and so the House divided in order to decide the matter. The result of the vote was 372 to 238 in favour of Boothroyd. Radice commented that her victory lay in over seventy Tories breaking rank and voting for her.[83] Members from the government benches were prepared to vote for the candidate of their choice rather than one who was thrust upon them. The Prime Minister at the time, John Major, believes that it was the case of 'the House of Commons asserting its independence'. By defying the executive, the legislature not only consolidated on the position gained in 1983 but also elected the first female Speaker and the first not to come from the governing party.

During her speech indicating her willingness to become Speaker, Boothroyd noted that:

> I have been a Deputy Speaker, but always at heart I have been a Back Bencher, and, except for a period sixteen years ago when I was in the Whips' Office, that has been my position. I have never sought, and I have never expected, to occupy one of the great offices of government.[84]

Again, the Commons had rejected a former minister in favour of a backbencher to become its Speaker. Another first, as Boothroyd herself put it, was that, 'For a Tory Parliament to put a Labour nominee in the chair was as unprecedented as electing a woman'.[85]

It was the election following Boothroyd's retirement that provoked calls for further reform. The Speakership election held on 23 October 2000 was contested by an unprecedented twelve candidates from across the three major parties. Radice described the election in his diaries as 'a medieval jousting tournament' because each of the contestants for the Speakership had to knock out the other leaving the victor as the last man standing.[86]

The election, which was presided over by the Father of the House, Sir Edward Heath, lasted nearly seven hours. In the end, one of Boothroyd's deputies, the Labour MP for Glasgow Springburn, Michael Martin, was elected as Speaker. However, Martin failed to get an opposition Member to second his nomination and, in fact, eight Conservatives voted against him in the final division. The trend towards electing a Speaker who enjoyed widespread cross-party support had been reversed. Despite the fact that there were better qualified and more experienced candidates, the Labour backbenchers had used their vastly superior numbers to put in their own man. Indeed, they voted against the former Conservative Cabinet minister, Sir George Young, who had been the preferred candidate of the two front benches. Again, the legislature had asserted its independence from the executive and elected a Speaker of its own choosing who was a backbencher rather than a former minister. Michael Martin said during the debate that:

> My apprenticeship has been one of serving the House as a Chairman of Standing Committees, the Administration Committee and the Scottish Grand Committee. I have never sought to be a Whip, a Front-Bench spokesman or a Minister.[87]

Robin Maxwell-Hyslop had begun the move away from the front benches choosing the Speaker in 1971 and finally achieved it in 1983. This shift in power has been firmly established in all the subsequent Speakership elections.

The circumstances of the October 2000 Speakership contest resulted in calls for reform from both inside and outside the Commons. During the debate Tony Benn called for a ballot to decide which of the twelve candidates should become Speaker. The Conservative MP, David Davis, and the Labour Member, Paul Marsden, shot straight up to support what Benn had put forward. However, as the former BBC Political Editor, Robin Oakley, describes:

> To their shame, they [MPs] decided it wasn't worth the fuss. They let the Father of the House, Sir Edward Heath, who presided over the process, get away with refusing to allow a vote to change the procedure on the grounds that 'such a motion requires notice', and the day was won by the 'we've always done it this way so we'd better do it this way again' school.[88]

Controversially, Heath had complete power over the order in which the twelve candidates were presented when it came to voting. When questioned by the veteran Labour MP Tam Dalyell on how he had decided upon the order, Heath responded, 'It was done at my discretion'.[89] Dalyell has said that the 'sequence is all-important' because, of course, candidates who might have stood more of a chance if they came later on could be knocked out at an early stage.[90] Although Heath rejected the proposal, the Procedure Committee, which later looked into reform of the 1972 system, concluded that it 'be replaced by a ballot-based system' going on to 'recommend that the ballot be secret'.[91] These recommendations now form part of the Standing Orders of the House of Commons and were agreed on 22 March 2001.

These new rules were first used following Michael Martin's resignation as Speaker in June 2009. Martin announced his resignation on 19 May 2009, stating that he would relinquish the office on 21 June. The month in between gave MPs who wanted the Speakership time to campaign for the role. Peter Riddell explains that:

After nine years of the Michael Martin era, it was widely accepted at Westminster that the election after he resigned should be more public and open. As Chairman of the Hansard Society, it was my idea to hold a hustings of all the candidates. Initially, some people said, 'Well, can you do that?' And I said, 'Well, let's do it.' I happened to meet a couple of the potential candidates […] and set about organising this with the Hansard staff. Eventually, we had all the candidates.

It was a complete innovation to have ten candidates saying why they should become Speaker in a public forum before the formal election in the House of Commons, a symbol of the extent to which the Speakership had been given wider ownership and was no longer confined to the Commons chamber.

Out of the ten contenders, Sir George Young stood once again with the backing of most of the Conservative side. Margaret Beckett, the former Foreign Secretary and Labour MP, also threw her hat into the ring. The House demonstrated that it was still not keen on former Cabinet ministers becoming Speaker and John Bercow soon became favourite for the job. Bercow had moved from being on the right of the Conservative Party to someone with more liberal ideals. In addition, he was married to a Labour-supporting wife. This would have gained him support on the government benches though Bercow also admits that he had a campaign manager, Martin Salter. The former Labour MP has described how he conducted the campaign:

I have run a number of campaigns in parliament both within the PLP [Parliamentary Labour Party] and across the house. I recruited organisers within the regions, the intake groupings and in the other parties. Some of this was highly organised with canvass sheets and the like and in other cases it was more a case of supporters quietly talking to colleagues and making the case for JB.

The contest for the Speakership is now as fiercely and ruthlessly contested as any other post in Parliament. In the end, the new electoral system, which consists of rounds which knock out candidates who receive the fewest votes or less than 5 per cent of the votes cast, left only John Bercow and Sir George Young in the contest. The former Labour MP Chris Mullin recorded in his diary that Bercow 'has virtually no support on his own side, which is precisely why many of our lot are proposing to vote for him'.[92] Labour's superior numbers gave Bercow 322 votes to Young's 271 in the final round. Most of Bercow's support came from the Labour back benches with the vast majority of Conservatives having voted for Young. Mullin commented that the 'Tories have been well and truly shafted and they know it', with very few of them cheering or applauding when Bercow's victory was announced.[93] Again, Labour had put in their man in a partisan move rather than simply looking to see who would be best for the job.

On 18 May 2010, Speaker Bercow had to seek re-election to the Chair following the general election which resulted in David Cameron forming a Conservative and Liberal Democrat coalition government. The re-election of a sitting Speaker is usually a formality but, on this occasion, a few disgruntled Conservative backbenchers were determined to signal their disapproval of Bercow and attempt to force a vote. As it turned out, only Nadine Dorries and a few others shouted, 'No'. The new Prime Minister had decided to back Bercow and so his re-election was proposed by the former Foreign Secretary, Sir Malcolm Rifkind. With this support, the vast majority of Conservative MPs, along with the opposition parties, cried out 'Aye'. The Father of the

House, Sir Peter Tapsell, ignored the few dissenting voices and
concluded, 'I think the Ayes have it, the Ayes have it'.[94] Tapsell
could have called a division but, as Simon Carr, the parliamentary sketch writer for *The Independent*, put it, 'Sir Peter "collected
the voice of the House" and decided there was no need for a
vote'.[95] Whilst Bercow would have easily won, Tapsell's use of
his discretion prevented an unnecessary vote that could have
discredited the office of Speaker. Additional problems for the
Speakership following the fall of Michael Martin would have
further weakened Parliament in the eyes of the public.

The last two Speakership elections have been a case of one
side getting one over on the other. A quarter of a century before,
the backbenchers had seized the power to decide who their
Speaker should be but now they had turned it into a tribal struggle which looked to outdo political opponents. The front benches
no longer determine who the Speaker should be. It is now the
backbenchers of the majority party who seem to be able to get
their own way over who should chair the Commons.

The Speaker seeking re-election in his or her constituency

In order to continue in the Chair for more than one Parliament a
Speaker has to be re-elected in his or her constituency. After all,
the Speaker is first and foremost a Member of Parliament and
is only able to accede to the Chair because he or she has been
elected to the House of Commons. The convention by which
a sitting Speaker is not opposed in his or her constituency at a
general election was broken in 1935 by the Labour Party's decision to run a candidate against Speaker Edward FitzRoy in his
Daventry seat. Since that time, every Speaker has had to face
one or more opponents in his constituency when standing as
'Speaker seeking re-election'.

At the 1945 general election, Clifton Brown faced a Labour

opponent in his Hexham constituency because, as Laundy points out, Labour 'regarded itself as a struggling party which could not afford to miss any opportunity of gaining an extra seat'.[96] Despite Labour's landslide victory, Clifton Brown managed to hold on to Hexham by 4,645 votes and so the problem of a sitting Speaker being defeated at the polls was avoided. At the 1950 general election the Labour Party did not put up a candidate against Clifton Brown although he was opposed by an Independent Liberal who, in the words of Laundy, 'expressed the view that no candidate, not even the Speaker, should be allowed an unopposed return'.[97] On this occasion, Clifton Brown was returned with a far more comfortable 20,000 majority.

In 1955 Speaker Morrison was opposed in his Cirencester and Tewkesbury seat by a member of the local Labour Party, Douglas C. Cox, who stood as an Independent Socialist candidate. On this occasion, the Prime Minister, Sir Anthony Eden, wrote to the leaders of the Labour and Liberal parties urging them to write letters in support of the Speaker; both obliged. Eden wrote that anyone challenging a sitting Speaker in their constituency was 'contrary to tradition'.[98] At this stage, it was only twenty years since the convention to allow a sitting Speaker to be re-elected unopposed was broken although this break with tradition had happened on two subsequent occasions and it meant to continue. Morrison defeated Cox by 13,000 votes and so the continuity of the Speakership was once again preserved.

The next time that a Speaker wished to seek re-election to the House was at the 1964 general election. This time Speaker Hylton-Foster faced both Labour and Liberal opponents in the Cities of London and Westminster. This occasion established that if Labour decided to put up a candidate against the Speaker then the Liberals would follow suit. Hylton-Foster's majority fell by nearly 6,000 compared to the result he achieved when he

was elected as a Conservative in 1959. In this case, the swing
in favour of Labour at the 1964 general election clearly had an
impact on the Speaker's seat because Hylton-Foster had come
from the Conservative ranks.

The first Labour Speaker, Dr Horace King, was not opposed
by the Conservatives at either the 1966 or 1970 general elections.
The Conservatives therefore honoured the tradition that the
Speaker should not be opposed even though both Labour and
the Liberals had previously opposed Speakers drawn from their
side. In 1966, King was opposed by an Independent candidate
who described himself as a Democratic Non-Party Nationalist.
King won by a convincing 25,000 votes. In 1970 Dr King faced
two opponents neither of whom were drawn from the major
parties. At this election, Speaker King's vote dropped because of
the swing to the Conservatives that year and thanks to the fact
that two people had opposed him. He nevertheless achieved a
comfortable majority of almost 20,000.

Selwyn Lloyd was the next Speaker to be opposed by both the
Labour and Liberal parties. In his memoirs, Lloyd states that:
'Although most senior members of the Labour and Liberal Parties
at Westminster with whom I had discussed the matter told me
privately that they thoroughly disapproved of the Speaker being
opposed when seeking re-election in his constituency, I knew that
they could not overrule their local party organisations.'[99]

Lloyd was, therefore, opposed by Labour and Liberal candidates at both general elections held in 1974. In the February
election he secured a majority of nearly 16,000 over the Labour
opponent. At the general election held in October of the same
year, Lloyd records in his memoirs that the Liberal candidate
'placed much more emphasis on the issue that the electors of
Wirral were being disenfranchised by having the Speaker as
their Member'.[100] Whilst this campaign did nothing to boost

Liberal support, Selwyn Lloyd's vote dropped by nearly 3,000 at the October 1974 general election.

Speaker George Thomas was not opposed by the Conservative or Liberal parties in 1979 although a Welsh Nationalist and a National Front candidate did stand against him in Cardiff West. Thomas was, however, returned with an overwhelming majority of nearly 24,000. Despite being a Speaker from the Labour Party, the swing to the Conservatives in 1979 did not affect George Thomas because, as his successor in the Chair has pointed out, during the post-war period 'the Tory Party has given a free run to the sitting Speaker'.

The next time a sitting Speaker was to face opponents from the major parties was at the 1987 general election when Speaker Weatherill faced Labour and Social Democrat candidates. However, Weatherill managed to increase his majority in Croydon North East to 12,519 compared to the 11,627 margin he had achieved in 1983 when he had stood as a Conservative. Weatherill argued that 'it is a myth that the Speaker gets a free ride' and he recalls that it was not the Labour leadership in the House of Commons that decided to put up a candidate against him but the London Labour Party. This was the last occasion on which a sitting Speaker faced opponents from the main parties. Ever since, he or she has been opposed by candidates from smaller parties or by those who stand as independents. A tradition has, therefore, built up whereby the Speaker is never elected unopposed in his or her constituency.

This tradition continued when Betty Boothroyd faced two opponents in West Bromwich West at the 1997 general election. One of these candidates stood as an independent socialist Labour Change candidate and the other stood as a National Democrat. Despite this opposition, Boothroyd increased her majority by a massive 9,249 votes although she probably benefited from the

Labour landslide of that year thanks to the fact that she had been the Labour MP for the area since 1973.

At the general election held on 7 June 2001, Speaker Michael Martin faced four opponents in his Glasgow Springburn constituency, including a Scottish Nationalist. Whilst Martin was returned with a comfortable majority of 11,378, the Scottish Nationalists managed a swing of 2.91 per cent in their favour.

Speaker Martin fought the new seat of Glasgow North East at the 2005 general election. He was again opposed by a candidate from the Scottish Nationalist Party as well as by a host of smaller parties and an independent. Indeed, never before in the post-war period had the Speaker been faced by so many opponents, which perhaps demonstrates discontent with the fact that the Speaker's constituency is removed from normal party politics because he or she cannot raise matters on the floor of the House. On 11 May 2005, when Speaker Martin was re-elected as Speaker by the House, the leader of the Scottish Nationalists, Alex Salmond, said the following:

> On behalf of the Scottish Nationalist party and Plaid Cymru, I warmly congratulate you, Mr Speaker, on your second unanimous re-election by the House. I also congratulate you, despite the best efforts of my party, on your thumping majority in Glasgow North East. Your campaigning in a non-political way is perhaps, given your thumping majority, a tactic we should all employ.[101]

Indeed, Speaker Martin was returned with a convincing 10,134 majority at the 2005 general election (although the SNP again increased its vote). What is clear from this result is that, in order to preserve the convention whereby a sitting Speaker can remain in office despite a general election taking place, it is beneficial for the holder of the office to represent a 'safe' seat.

John Bercow certainly has what can be termed a 'safe' seat securing a majority of 18,129 in his Buckingham constituency at the 2005 general election. At the 2010 general election, John Bercow had to stand as the 'Speaker seeking re-election'. Bercow did not get a free run although, unlike previous post-war Conservative Speakers, he was not opposed by Labour or Liberal Democrat candidates. Nigel Farage resigned as leader of the United Kingdom Independence Party (UKIP) in order to concentrate on fighting Bercow in Buckingham. Farage states that: 'I was persuaded that Bercow's seat was there for the taking. Although he was nominally a Conservative, the huge majority of Conservative activists disliked him. After his prolonged flirtation with New-but-shop-soiled-Labour, they thought him a turncoat.'[102]

Fortunately for Bercow, the leader of the Conservatives, David Cameron, backed the sitting Speaker and so local members had to fall in line and not campaign for other candidates. This meant that Bercow was home and dry. The only thing that could have stopped his re-election as Speaker was the fact that Nigel Farage was in an aeroplane crash on polling day although fortunately he survived and the election in Buckingham took place as planned. Bercow did, however, face ten opponents at the 2010 general election which was even more than Speaker Martin had faced five years before. Although the main political parties respected the tradition of not contesting the Speaker's seat, the smaller parties still viewed it as fair game. Despite the ten other candidates, Bercow still achieved a massive 12,000 majority but his vote share did fall to 47.3 per cent.

These figures point to the fact that if a Member of Parliament who represents a more marginal seat were to be selected as Speaker then this might create difficulties. Indeed, Laundy does admit the following: 'The possibility of a Speaker one day losing

his seat must therefore remain. Should this happen there might
well be demands for a further inquiry into the method whereby
the Speaker is returned to Parliament at a general election.'[103]

Moreover, there has been debate over how to solve the potential problem of the Speaker losing his seat and on 24 April 1963
Labour MP Richard Marsh introduced a ten minute rule bill 'for
the creation of a constituency to be known as St Stephen's and
represented by Mr Speaker'.[104] This specially created constituency would mean that the Speaker would not have to face the
possibility of being defeated at the polls because it would contain
no electors. However, along with a very similar motion put
forward by Liberal MP Clement Freud on 26 January 1982, it
was defeated because the feeling was, as Lord Weatherill put it,
that the 'Speaker should be one of us'. More recently, in October
2011, the House of Commons Procedure Committee once again
looked at the creation of a special Speaker's seat.[105] This was
partly in response to a letter from Speaker Bercow who reported
that: 'There was a sizeable minority of my constituents who felt
disenfranchised by the convention that political parties do not
field candidates against the Speaker Seeking Re-election.'[106]

Despite this evidence, the committee did not support the
concept of a St Stephen's seat for the Speaker stating that:

> There are great benefits to the House and to the Speaker in the
> Speaker's retaining responsibility for a normal constituency and
> being thereby fully aware of the issues currently causing concern
> to constituents. The access that the Speaker, like Ministers who are
> unable to speak out in debates, gains to the government in order
> to raise matters relating to his or her constituents compensates in
> no small measure for the lack of a constituency voice on the floor
> of the House. We are also concerned that the proposal would
> remove the important democratic check on the re-appointment

of a Speaker by either the public or the House and would create
a new, separate, distinctive and privileged category of Member to
the detriment of the House.[107]

In his book on the Speakership, Selwyn Lloyd argued that if the
Speaker were given a special seat this would diminish his author-
ity and reduce his status to that of an official of the House.[108]
The Speaker needs to share the experiences of other Members if
he or she is to ensure that the office does not become even more
removed than it already is. Lloyd goes on to point out that other
MPs are confined by the nature of their offices such as Deputy
Speakers, government whips and members of the Chairmen's
Panel. He concludes that: 'If the Speaker is to be given a special
constituency, what about the Deputy Speaker, and these others?
Should they not have special seats? Where would it end?'[109]

For all these reasons the Speaker continues to represent a
constituency in the same way as other Members of the House
of Commons.

Lloyd raises an important issue when he mentions the position
of the Deputy Speakers. Indeed, William McKay, believes that
'being a Deputy Speaker is not a plus' when it comes to a general
election because the holder of this office is not allowed to raise
questions in the House and yet has to fight his or her seat on a
party ticket. McKay points to the fact that the Conservative MP,
Michael Morris, who was Deputy Speaker and Chairman of
Ways and Means under Betty Boothroyd, lost his Northampton
South seat to Labour at the 1997 general election. Indeed, Lord
Naseby, as Michael Morris is now styled, highlights the fact that
a Deputy Speaker 'can't go at an election time and campaign
until Parliament is prorogued' thanks to his duties in the House
and so is not in an advantageous position.

Another problem for a Speaker wanting to continue in office

beyond a general election is if a boundary review abolishes, or radically alters, the sitting Speaker's constituency. The former Speaker, Lord Weatherill, believed quite simply that 'my seat goes and I go too', adding that 'to do one parliament is no dishonour'. The former Deputy Speaker, Baroness Fookes, disagrees with this point and has stated that:

> My view is that one looks at the person concerned not as Speaker but as a Member of Parliament. There is no reason why a sitting MP should not seek to be a candidate in any other seat or part of his or her old seat. I do not see that the Speaker would be in any different position, since he or she is first and foremost a Member of Parliament and indeed in our system cannot be Speaker unless a Member of Parliament.

The former Speaker's Secretary, Sir Nicolas Bevan, agrees with Baroness Fookes although added the comment, 'Let us hope it never arises!' Perhaps Bevan agrees with Lord Weatherill that, in these circumstances, a Speaker 'would have to put themselves up for auction' in order to secure a new seat?

These circumstances have indeed arisen because the devolved settlement, as set out in the Scotland Act 1998, made reference to the electoral quota for English constituencies now applying in Scotland. The Boundary Commission, therefore, redrew the political map of Scotland and reduced the number of Scottish constituencies from seventy-two to fifty-nine. A result of this review was that Speaker Martin's Glasgow Springburn constituency disappeared as the number of Glasgow seats went from ten to seven. Clearly, some internal Labour Party discussions must have taken place in order to allocate Martin the new Glasgow North East constituency because Labour MPs would have had to have made room and given up their seats for him. As it was, Glasgow

North East took in all Speaker Martin's old Glasgow Springburn constituency plus three wards from the old Maryhill division of the city and so the move was not as controversial as perhaps it could have been if the seat had been altered dramatically.

Another possible scenario which could affect the office's tradition of continuity is if a sitting Speaker were prevented from being re-elected to the House of Commons and so could not be re-appointed to the Chair on the first day back after a general election. This could happen if one of the other candidates in the Speaker's seat dies before polling day, causing the election in that constituency to be delayed. If such an episode took place then the Speaker would not be present on the first day of the new session of Parliament and so could not be re-elected to the Chair. The Commons must have a Speaker in order to conduct its business. Therefore, the new House would either have to delay the new sitting or elect a new Speaker regardless of the fact that the old Speaker might well be back in the chamber within a few weeks once the constituency contest is resolved.

As hypothetical as this seems, the events in Staffordshire South in 2005, when the poll was delayed because the Liberal Democrat candidate died, and then in Buckingham in 2010, show that it is quite possible. Indeed, when asked about this, the former Clerk of the House, Roger Sands, responded by saying that: 'The same thought had occurred to me, and I spent the last few days of the [2005] general election campaign praying for the sustained good health of the candidates in Glasgow North-East.'

There is an example of such an occurrence taking place in the United Kingdom, although not in the Westminster Parliament. The incident involved the Speaker of the Northern Ireland House of Commons, Sir Norman Stronge, who had to resign the Speakership on 24 January 1956 because there was a possibility that he would be disqualified as a Stormont MP. The reason for the potential disqualification was that Stronge's membership of the Central Advisory Council on Disabled Persons, although voluntary and unpaid, could have been deemed to be an 'office of profit under Crown Law'.[110] On 25 January 1956, William Frederick McCoy was elected as the new Speaker to replace Sir Norman Stronge whilst his position was in question. The passing of the Validation of Election Act at Westminster, however, removed the legal question mark hanging over Stronge and enabled him to take up his seat once again at Stormont. William McCoy swiftly resigned on 24 April 1956 in order to allow Stronge to regain the Speakership. Stronge was re-elected as Northern Ireland Speaker on 26 April 1956 and in the Stormont Commons chamber he said: 'Today, through the interpretation of an ancient law, I find myself in the unique position of being twice elected to the office of Speaker during the life of one Parliament. I trust that no holder of this honourable office will ever find himself in a like position in the future.'[111]

In the end, the continuity of the Northern Ireland Speakership was upheld because Members allowed the old Speaker to return to office once his position was clarified and it was deemed that he was not disqualified from being an MP. This is a good example of what could happen at Westminster and also an interesting precedent that could be used if such an occurrence ever happened to the Speaker of the United Kingdom House of Commons.

Clearly, the events in South Staffordshire made the 'powers that be' surrounding the Speakership stop and think about the possibility that it could one day happen in the Speaker's seat and thus cause an unintentional break with continuity.

One tradition that evolved during the post-war period, but has since been broken, is the convention whereby the Speakership alternates between the two main political parties. Although the first three post-war Speakers were all from the Conservative ranks, after that there was a period in which the office alternated between the Labour and Conservative sides. Labour's Horace King was succeeded by the Conservative Selwyn Lloyd who was followed by Labour's George Thomas and then came Conservative Jack Weatherill.

So, in 1992, when Weatherill retired, there was a firm belief that a Labour MP should be elected. This is indeed what transpired when Betty Boothroyd was elected and so the concept of the Speakership alternating between the two main parties continued. The convention being established was nevertheless destroyed when Boothroyd was succeeded by a fellow Labour MP, Michael Martin, in 2000. The Labour front bench had wanted to continue with the idea of the Speakership alternating between the two main parties, favouring the former Conservative Cabinet minister, Sir George Young, for the job. However, this was not to be and so a recently created tradition was prevented from embedding itself into the unwritten codes of the House.

The Speakership is now seen as the pinnacle of the career of a long-serving backbencher who has worked his or her way up the ranks by first becoming a committee chairman or Deputy Speaker. It is no longer the swansong for a distinguished ex-minister it had been up until the 1970s.

Three

From the Second World War to Suez: Colonel Douglas Clifton Brown (1943–51) and William Shepherd Morrison (1951–9)

By common consent, the manner in which Clifton Brown steered the House of Commons through the difficult period of post-war transition was both efficient and admirable.

– Philip Laundy, 1964[112]

I think he [W. S. Morrison] was very well suited to being Speaker [...] he was by nature not a strongly partisan person. He very rarely quoted the Bible [...] and the one quotation which has stuck very firmly in my mind, which I've heard him use more than once, comes from the Book of Proverbs which is, 'A soft answer turneth away wrath' and that catches something very characteristic of him because he didn't like rows.

– Dr Alasdair Morrison, son of W. S. Morrison, 2004

The first of the post-war Speakers, Colonel Douglas Clifton Brown, was actually elected during the Second World War in 1943 following the death of Speaker Edward FitzRoy. To this military gentleman fell the task of presiding over a post-war House of Commons that was dominated by the Labour Party for the first time. On Clifton Brown's retirement in 1951, the Scottish barrister and former Cabinet minister, William Shepherd Morrison, was elected to take his place. Morrison faced the challenge of chairing the House during the unruly debates of the 1956 Suez crisis.

Douglas Clifton Brown was born on 16 August 1879 and was educated at Eton College and then Trinity College, Cambridge. He was commissioned in the Lancashire Royal Garrison Artillery in 1900 and transferred to the 1st Dragoon Guards in 1902 in which he later obtained his captaincy. In 1910 Clifton Brown joined the special reserve of his regiment and during the First World War he served in France and Belgium. In 1919 he was promoted to major and from 1925 to 1929 he was the lieutenant-colonel commanding The Northumberland Hussars Yeomanry and was awarded the brevet of colonel.

Despite his continuing military career, Clifton Brown was first elected to Parliament for Hexham in 1918 although he lost the seat at the 1923 general election. Clifton Brown swiftly regained Hexham in 1924 and soon became a member of the panel of Chairmen of Committees appointed by the Speaker. In 1938 he became Chairman of Ways and Means and Deputy Speaker which made him the natural choice to succeed Speaker FitzRoy when he died in office in 1943. Indeed, Conservative MP Sir Cuthbert Headlam recorded in his diary entry for 3 March 1943 that except for a few, almost everyone was in favour of Clifton Brown succeeding as Speaker.[113]

This is backed up by Harold Macmillan who, when writing down some thoughts on the Speakership of Clifton Brown, recorded in his diary entry for 12–17 March 1951 that when Clifton Brown had been made Speaker during the war it had been against the wishes of both Churchill and Eden following pressure from Conservative ranks. Macmillan explains that: 'Churchill, who then rode magnificently in the saddle of the state but uneasily in that of the party, gave in.'[114]

The reason that Clifton Brown did not have the backing of the Prime Minister was because, according to William Shepherd Morrison's widow, the job had been offered to her husband on the basis that some MPs were anxious that the elevation of the Chairman of Ways and Means to the Speakership should not become a precedent. Morrison declined Churchill's offer and so delayed becoming Speaker for another eight years.[115] Clifton Brown was, therefore, elected on 9 March 1943 thanks to the fact that Morrison did not take up the post and because he enjoyed the support of the Conservative parliamentary party.

Clifton Brown's obituary in *The Times* went as far as to say that he would 'probably be remembered as the most unconventional of Speakers',[116] the reason being that he was less austere than his immediate predecessors. A profile of Clifton Brown published in 1945 gives a good example. On the first occasion he took part in the formal procession to the chamber, 'Mr Speaker solemnly paused in his stride, bowed gracefully to a row of astonished MPs who were bowing to *him*, said with a twinkle, "Thank you very much!" and passed on'.[117]

Moreover, Clifton Brown, having been allowed to stay in office by the Attlee government, was the first Speaker to preside over a House of Commons which was totally dominated by the Labour Party. In order to maintain the support of the whole House, the Conservative Clifton Brown had to ensure that the Labour government was allowed to get its business through whilst at the same time maintaining strict impartiality.

However, the former Cabinet minister and Conservative MP John Boyd-Carpenter is of the opinion that the Speaker was the weakest in his time in Parliament.[118] Indeed, Boyd-Carpenter was very critical of Clifton Brown's Speakership and commented that he allowed MPs to argue with him and lacked dignity in the role.

'Sometimes when summoned to give a ruling during late sittings he arrived looking dishevelled and obviously having been in bed.'[119]

This obviously seemed unprofessional to Boyd-Carpenter. A Speaker is on constant watch when the House is sitting and must be on hand to come to the chamber very quickly if he is needed to make a ruling or to tackle unruly behaviour from MPs.

Boyd-Carpenter recalled in his memoirs an evening when Clifton Brown was summoned to close a debate but quite obviously wanted to get to bed. When Boyd-Carpenter insisted that he be allowed to speak and continue the debate, Clifton Brown responded, 'Very well, if you want to kill your Speaker'.[120]

The sheer workload had most definitely taken its toll!

However, Lord Renton, a Conservative MP between 1945 and 1979, recalled discussing Clifton Brown's Speakership with his friend John Boyd-Carpenter:

I remember he and I disagreeing about Clifton Brown. I quite agree Clifton Brown was not a very strong Speaker but there was no real need for a strong Speaker. The great thing was the Speaker should deal with outstandingly bad behaviour and there wasn't much.

On one occasion Speaker Clifton Brown did have to reprimand Winston Churchill who was Leader of the Opposition at the time. On 4 March 1947, the backbench Conservative MP William Shepherd and Winston Churchill both rose simultaneously to ask a supplementary question of the Chancellor of the Exchequer, Hugh Dalton, following on from an answer given to Shepherd's main question. Clifton Brown remarked that 'The Front Bench must not gatecrash on a backbencher' but when Churchill objected the Speaker ruled that:

It is always my custom that when an hon. Member asks a Question
he is entitled to the first supplementary, and if a Member of the
Front bench wants to get up, surely he can look round to see if
the hon. Member who put the Question has risen. Personally, I
do not see, if the right hon. Gentleman does not look round, what
the difference is between that and gatecrashing.[121]

Whilst Clifton Brown did not back down, he made the point
that if Churchill took offence at the term 'gatecrashing' then
he was sorry.[122] Clearly, Shepherd allowed his leader to continue
because Churchill put his supplementary question to Dalton.
Evidently, Speaker Clifton Brown was not afraid to rebuke even
the most senior of parliamentarians if he thought that they were
not respecting the etiquette of the House. In his obituary in *The
Times*, the remark was made that: 'He [Clifton Brown] always
remembered that it was the special duty of the Chair to see that
minorities were not brow-beaten and got a hearing in debate.'[123]

Towards the end of the Second World War, Clifton Brown
was the first Speaker to travel abroad and make diplomatic
tours on behalf of the House of Commons, a move that saw the
office grow beyond the confines of the Houses of Parliament. In
August 1944, he travelled to Normandy: 'It was a proud moment
for me to feel, when I landed back in Heston, that the Speaker
of the House of Commons had been in direct contact with our
fighting forces and those of our Allies.'[124]

In late November 1947, Clifton Brown was awarded the Grand
Croix de la Légion d'Honneur, the highest decoration in France,
for his personal visits to the theatres of war and the trouble he had
taken to talk to servicemen and civilians. In an article he wrote
for the local newspaper in Hexham, Clifton Brown recorded:
'This was the first time in history that the Speaker of the
House of Commons has been invited to visit officially a foreign

country, and I know of no case where, as chief representative of Parliament, a Speaker has received such a high honour.'[125]

As Speaker, he was the figurehead of the British Parliament and now acted as its ambassador abroad. The Second World War, and the more hands-on and adventurous nature of Clifton Brown, changed the office of Speaker from a purely official Westminster-based role into one which added overseas travel and representing Parliament abroad to its job description.

Towards the end of Clifton Brown's period in the Chair, however, it became clear he was finding the job a difficult task. Macmillan commented that 'Mr Speaker is clearly breaking up'. He was losing control of the House by allowing MPs to openly argue with his rulings. According to Macmillan, the Speaker 'alternates between weak appeals, and weaker threats'.[126]

Whilst Macmillan felt that the Speaker was losing control of the House, Laundy, when looking back at Clifton Brown's tenure in the Chair, does not indicate that this was so, arguing that the Speaker 'ruled with tact and patience rather than through force of personality'.[127]

However, Laundy does recognise the difficulties Clifton Brown faced during the short-lived parliament of 1950–51. With the parties so evenly balanced, sittings were long with frequent disputes; the Speaker was constantly required to mediate.[128]

Unlike Macmillan, Laundy does not believe that Clifton Brown lost command of the House and indeed he wrote that, 'The conscientious manner in which he [Clifton Brown] ensured fair play, often in circumstances which would have frayed the most placid temper, was a triumph of endurance'.[129] Moreover, one of Clifton Brown's successors in the Chair, Dr Horace King, who was the newly elected Labour MP for Southampton Test in 1950, wrote how 'a new Member, seeking to be called, waved his papers at the Chair. He was sent for by Speaker Clifton Brown who said to him that he must not do that, and, that because he had done so he would be moved down the list a number of places.'[130]

Clifton Brown was still not prepared to allow standards to slip during the 1950–51 parliament. He did not allow incidents to pass unnoticed and he even punished MPs concerned in order to ensure that such discourtesy to the Chair did not happen again.

Periods in which a government only enjoys a very slender majority are far more difficult for a Speaker because the tensions are greater and opposition Members want to do their utmost to outdo the other side. Macmillan and Boyd-Carpenter perhaps did not think Clifton Brown was particularly effective in the Chair because he ensured fair play and did not allow Conservative MPs to always get their own way. In contrast, Lord Renton was not critical of Clifton Brown's period in the Chair. Clifton Brown's last year as Speaker was most definitely a difficult one and it would have taken its toll as he himself admitted. Indeed, *The Times* wrote that:

> Clifton Brown was plagued during his later years in the Chair, with many complaints of breach of privilege and he had difficult decisions to take, often with very little time to consider them. He did his best in trying circumstances, but the heavy burden affected his health for a time.[131]

There was clearly great pressure on the Speaker during this period and, as always, it was crucial that the incumbent maintained the notion of impartiality and did not take decisions that risked this in any way.

The highlight of Clifton Brown's Speakership was the opening of the new House of Commons chamber, which replaced the one destroyed by bombing during the Second World War, on

26 October 1950. Sir Ralph Verney, who was Speaker's Secretary at the time, recorded some of the events of that day:

> It was a truly dramatic moment when we entered the new Chamber for the first time, in dead silence, in this packed House. Then followed the Prime Minister [Clement Attlee], moving his Motion of Welcome to all our visiting Speakers and Representatives from the Dominions and Colonies of the British Empire. This was seconded by Winston Churchill and supported by Clement Davies, the leader of the Liberal Party, and by Lord Winterton, the Father of the House.[132]

It fell to Clifton Brown to preside over this truly historic moment and to lead the grand procession of Commonwealth Speakers into Westminster Hall where the King (George VI) addressed the assembled gathering from the two Houses of Parliament. This ceremony was one of those where the Speaker was centre stage, entertaining dignitaries from across the world and wearing all the formal regalia. The dignity and importance of the office of Speaker would have been evident on that day and Colonel Clifton Brown was fortunate enough to be the incumbent.

Speaker Clifton Brown's obituary sums up his achievements whilst in the Chair; he realised his three ambitions: to lead the House of Commons into St Margaret's Church for the thanksgiving service at the end of the Second World War, to sit in the new Speaker's Chair in the new House of Commons chamber and to turn on the lantern on the top of Big Ben when peace came.[133]

Two of these ambitions came early on in his Speakership but Clifton Brown had to wait a bit longer until he could preside in the new chamber. As a result of his bad health, Clifton Brown would have liked to have retired at the 1950 general election but

he felt compelled to stay on in the knowledge that it was going
to be a tight contest. This great commitment was detrimental to
Clifton Brown's health, but the postponement of his retirement
did allow him to fulfil that last ambition of sitting in the new
Commons chamber. Clifton Brown retired at the 1951 general
election and was later elevated to the peerage as the Viscount
Ruffside of Hexham. He died seven years later on 5 May 1958
aged seventy-eight.

When the new Parliament met on 31 October 1951, the House
of Commons had to elect itself a new Speaker. Mavis, Lady
Dunrossil, daughter-in-law of Clifton Brown's successor, William
Shepherd Morrison, recalls that:

> He [Morrison] was invited obviously, he didn't know what job he
> was going to get when they [the Conservatives] got back in again
> and I remember the excitement when he was invited up. I'm not
> sure whether he was offered something else or not but, anyway,
> they were thrilled to accept the Speakership.

The Speakership was still in the gift of the Prime Minister in
1951 and treated very much like a Prime Ministerial appointment; one was summoned to No. 10 in the same way as if you
were going to become a minister and join the government. Lady
Dunrossil's use of the word 'they' also shows that Morrison and
his wife Allison were very much a team when it came to his
political career.

Speaker Morrison was elected to the Chair in October 1951,
following the first contested Speakership election for fifty-six
years. His son, Alasdair Morrison, remembered:

> There was a bit of a change of the guard when my father became
> Speaker because Clifton Brown, who'd been before him, was a

fairly solid country landowner, used to a fairly solid kind of existence, and he had a butler called Dover. Dover got the surprise of his life sharply because on the first morning within a couple of hours more or less of the announcement being made that he [Morrison] was going to be Speaker, or his taking up office, he got four calls from the four of us sons all asking to speak to our parents and reverse the charges please which showed things weren't going to be quite the same in future.

William Shepherd Morrison, known as 'Shakes' because he liked to recite Shakespeare, was born on 8 October 1893 in Torinturk, Argyll and Bute. His son, Alasdair Morrison, described his father's early life and how it affected his later career:

He was one of these people who had taken a terrific beating in World War One. He had been at Edinburgh University [reading law] for two years already when it broke out and, as a side interest, he had been doing what's called the 'Battery', which was the gunner section of the officer training corps there. So, in fact, he received his commission on October 14, I think it was, 1914 and he was in France very soon after serving most of the time as a forward artillery officer. He had what I call 'a good war'. He was mentioned in despatches, got a Military Cross, a wound and so on, a minor wound, and came out alive at the beginning of 1919. He would never talk about it at all afterwards, absolutely not at all, but I think it left a great impression on him that war was to be avoided at all costs.

Morrison completed his law degree and was called to the bar in 1923. He stood as the Unionist candidate for the Western Isles at both the 1923 and 1924 general elections but was unsuccessful. He finally entered Parliament in 1929 as Conservative MP for

Cirencester and Tewkesbury and soon rose through the ranks
becoming Financial Secretary to the Treasury in 1935. Alasdair
Morrison believed that his father was sidelined when Churchill
became Prime Minister in 1940 because:

> I think it's fair to say that he [W. S. Morrison] was also a fairly
> loyal Chamberlain supporter largely because he thought that
> Chamberlain was right to do everything he possibly could to
> avoid a recurrence of war and partly temperament because he
> was of a conciliatory disposition.

Nevertheless, Morrison was included in the ministerial team,
becoming Postmaster General on the creation of the wartime
coalition and in 1943 he became the first ever Minister for Town
and Country Planning. Morrison continued as a frontbench
spokesman with the Town and Country Planning portfolio whilst
the Conservatives were in opposition between 1945 and 1951. His
ministerial background was to prove controversial when he was
put forward for the Speakership in 1951 and was the main reason
why the election was contested. Despite this, on 31 October 1951,
Morrison became the 149th Speaker of the House of Commons
and the first Scot to be chosen since James Abercromby, later
Lord Dumfermline, in 1835.[134]

Morrison had to prove his worth when he first became
Speaker because of the process by which he arrived at the office.
He did not enjoy the support of the Labour benches and so had
to demonstrate his skills of impartiality and fairness so necessary
in a good Speaker. The Parliamentary Labour Party minutes of
April and May 1952, just six months after Morrison's election
to the Chair, record much criticism of his Speakership. On 24
April 1952 the minutes record that: 'Mr Harry Hynd [Labour
MP] referred to a Motion which had been tabled by Mr Sidney

Silverman [Labour MP] and three other Labour Members complaining about the conduct of the Chair.'[135]

At the next meeting on 29 April, it was also recorded that 'Mr R. Paget [Labour MP] referred briefly to complaints against actions by the Chair on a number of recent occasions, and suggested that some action ought to be taken with regard to this'.[136] There was clearly growing criticism of Morrison's Speakership from Labour backbenchers although the meeting agreed to refer this matter to the Parliamentary Committee. On 6 May 1952, Silverman's motion was again discussed but 'the Parliamentary Committee felt that the right thing was that this Motion should be taken off the Order Paper'.[137] When pressed on this 'the Chairman [Clement Attlee] stated that the Party would not support it as there was no adequate ground for censuring the Speaker'.[138] Whilst a small band of Labour backbenchers was probably still annoyed at the way Morrison had been installed, it is evident that the leadership of the Party had accepted his election as Speaker and was not prepared to attack the Chair at this early stage. The unfortunate business of the contested election had to be put behind them and the House of Commons' traditionally fierce protection of the office of Speaker had to be maintained.

Either Attlee's ruling quelled any further criticism or Morrison upped his game because, a few months later, a feature in the *Sunday Times* gave the following comment on his style in the Chair:

It might have seemed, then, that he lacked that touch of asperity so characteristic of our past Speakers. Nor has he developed it in the Chair, yet without it he commands the House. It might have seemed, too, almost cruelty to condemn so friendly a man to a life aloof and a little lonely.[139]

On the last point, Lady Dunrossil, who lived at Speaker's House with her husband, Morrison's eldest son John, and young family, remembers that:

> The Speaker's life is much more isolated. I mean, he couldn't, as he had all his life as a Member of Parliament, stroll into the smoking room or the library or just chat and relax and I think that was quite hard so he very much appreciated the contacts that came to him.

Speaker Morrison presided over the Commons at the time of the Suez Crisis towards the end of 1956. Indeed, Morrison and his wife Allison had a ring-side seat when the events at the Suez Canal unfolded. His son remembered that they were actually at Downing Street when the news came through and that the dinner had to be concluded early.

Morrison was, therefore, fortunate to learn straight away that an issue had arisen which would provoke lots of debate in the House of Commons. He rose to the occasion and proved that he could indeed command the House as the *Sunday Times* article stated. Indeed, Laundy has written that Speaker Morrison 're-established, in the opinion of Lord Tranmire, the discipline which had been slackened in the time of Clifton Brown'.[140]

This remark demonstrates the contrast between the styles of Clifton Brown and Morrison. Moreover, Speaker Morrison was not afraid of using his powers to maintain order in the House. On 1 November 1956, following the censure motion debate after a statement by Antony Head, the new Minister of Defence, that the RAF had bombed Egyptian targets and sunk a frigate, unruly behaviour abounded.

The Leader of the Opposition, Hugh Gaitskell, rose and asked the Prime Minister, Sir Anthony Eden, whether Britain had declared war on Egypt. Eden stated that Britain was not at war but in 'a state of armed conflict' with Egypt and went on to say that he would deal with the matter in more detail during the main debate. *The Times* describes what happened:

> It was then that there developed what the Speaker evidently interpreted as a defiance of the authority of the Chair. He asked whether it would be possible for all these matters to be raised during the debate. ('No' interrupted Opposition voices). The motion, he said, was in the widest possible terms and all these matters could be raised. Again there was an Opposition chorus of 'No, no,' in which Mr Bevan joined vehemently.[141]

Speaker Morrison attempted to read out the motion but was constantly interrupted by cries from the opposition benches. His warning that he would suspend the sitting if this behaviour continued was not heeded and so he had no choice but to carry out his threat. During that period Alasdair Morrison was staying with his parents at Speaker's House whilst he was convalescing from jaundice:

> I remember one particular moment involving my father because it got very lively; I was up there one afternoon [...] and I came down the passage and, to my surprise, I saw my father sitting in his usual chair, in his knee breeches with a pint of beer beside him doing *The Times* crossword in the middle of the afternoon and I said, big surprise, 'What are you doing here?' He said, 'Oh, they're making too much noise, I've shut them down for half an hour.' But he was completely relaxed about it and, apparently, I think it was Aneurin Bevan making a lot of noise and he came up and said afterwards, [...] very conciliatory, and said, 'That's quite all right I'm sorry I made a bit of a noise and you were quite

right to shut us down.' But I think it takes quite a lot of fuss in the House of Commons for that to happen. When he [Speaker Morrison] went back and they started up again of course they were much better behaved.

It was the first time since 1924 that a Speaker had suspended a sitting and so Morrison proved his mettle and showed that he would use all the powers at his disposal to maintain order.

Lord Renton stated that 'As far as I remember "Shakes" Morrison handled the Suez debate in 1956 very well [...] I've never heard of any criticism of "Shakes" Morrison on that'. Former Conservative MP Sir Richard Body agrees:

The Suez debates required very skilful handling and the temperature in the House was very high and several times he [Speaker Morrison] had to just adjourn and walk out. But he was very good. He had the gift of being able to allow the House just to raise its temperature to a certain height and then stop it. He had a great sense of humour but was very much liked by everyone and that made a lot of difference.

Sir David Price, Conservative MP between 1955 and 1992, concurs with Body and remembers that:

The House was very rowdy and potentially disruptive. The Speaker handled everybody with firmness but fairly. Emotions ran high, but he was able to keep control throughout a pretty tempestuous debate through his own personality.

Ulster Unionist MP for Londonderry between 1955 and 1974, Sir Robin Chichester-Clark, remembers just how heated the Suez debates were:

They were very alarming [...] I could never have believed that since the eighteenth century that politics could have been quite so rugged. It was only in the latter days where I felt that he [Speaker Morrison] was very rattled and it showed. You couldn't blame anyone for losing their nerve because people were looking for a way to get in and they weren't sparing anybody, there was no quarter given and they wouldn't have given any quarter to the Speaker either. He was given a very, very rough time. I thought at one time I saw him close to tears.

However, Lady Dunrossil has stated that her father-in-law was 'at the height of his powers' by that stage. With five years' experience in the Chair, Morrison was able to control a very heated House of Commons and ensure that proceedings did not break down. Sir David Price, whose turn it was to present BBC radio's *Week in Westminster* during the time of the Suez debates, remembers that he made Speaker Morrison his 'hero of the week' because he was so impressed at how he had managed the House.

The political journalist, Anthony Howard, when looking back, has made the point that, 'if ever there was a person absolutely cut out for television, it was probably Speaker Morrison. He had a wonderful voice; he had a wonderful head of hair.'[142] Unfortunately, Morrison's Speakership came thirty years before the televising of the House of Commons but Howard's comment does indicate that 'Shakes' was clearly a skilled performer whose voice and appearance made him very much suited to the part.

Morrison's obituary made reference to his qualities and physical attributes when it said that:

Physically he looked the part to perfection with his towering figure and finely modelled countenance so fitly framed in the wig [...] Morrison's voice never lost its native tones. It was a magnificent organ and he managed it superbly. The rolling 'r's' of his 'Order, Order,' could bring the House to its senses in a second.[143]

Alasdair Morrison commented that his father's qualities made him more successful in the Speakership than when he was a government minister. Dr Morrison said that, 'It was better for him to give up the idea of being a partisan minister because he was not by nature a particularly partisan person'. Clearly, the fact that Morrison was not strongly party political meant that he could easily uphold the notion of impartiality which is so vital to the Speakership. His physical attributes and his skills enabled him to make a success of the Speakership because he was able to maintain order when, particularly during the Suez debates, others might have failed.

Despite his skilful handling of the Suez debates, Speaker Morrison was criticised less than a year later for a ruling he gave and was subject to a motion of censure put forward by the Labour MP Tony Benn. On 22 July 1957, during a statement by the Foreign Secretary Selwyn Lloyd on disturbances in central Oman, Benn had asked the Speaker to move the adjournment of the House under Standing Order No. 9 so that Members could discuss 'the decision of Her Majesty's Government to offer British military assistance to the Sultan of Muscat and Oman'.[144] Morrison refused saying that, 'I think that this submission must fail on the ground of urgency. We have just heard that, at the moment, there are no British troops in Muscat.'[145] However, Morrison allowed Benn to come back and argue why he thought the matter was urgent. Labour MPs George Wigg and Reginald Paget joined in and supported Benn. Morrison did not back down and suggested to opposition MPs that they used one of the Supply Days that week to discuss the issue. Benn was still not happy and so he moved his motion of censure against

the Speaker on the afternoon of 29 July. After much debate,
when it was made quite clear that Members were not criticising 'Shakes' personally, Benn decided to withdraw his motion
having succeeded in having his grievance aired. What was clear
about the debate was that it was not a personal attack on Speaker
Morrison himself and there was no desire to even attempt to
remove him from office.

Morrison's Speakership happened to coincide with the death
of George VI and the accession of Elizabeth II and so, as Speaker,
he represented the House of Commons at both the King's State
Funeral on 16 February 1952 and the Queen's Coronation on
2 June 1953. As set out previously, Speaker Morrison played a
key role at the time of the King's death and attended a Cabinet
meeting to ensure that ministers were clear as to the parliamentary protocol on the occasion of the demise of a monarch.

Morrison was not keen on hosting or attending the banquets
and drinks parties which are seen so much as part of the Speaker's
job. Indeed, Philip Laundy has written that 'Speaker Morrison
maintained "it is the entertainment that kills" rather than the
work in the Chair' and that he refused to accept any invitations
for functions that he did not have to attend as Speaker unless
they came from Buckingham Palace.[146]

Whilst 'Shakes' was not keen to attend engagements in his
role as Speaker, he nevertheless hosted many events at Speaker's
House and represented the House of Commons at various functions. Brigadier Sir Francis Reid, who was Speaker's Secretary
during Morrison's period in the Chair, recorded in his diary the
many events which the Speaker had to attend. For example, on
31 March 1955, Speaker Morrison hosted a dinner at Speaker's
House for the Lebanon Delegation and on 12 July 1956, Speaker
and Mrs Morrison attended a dinner at Lambeth Palace.
Reid's diaries also show that, whilst Morrison refused various

engagements in his role as Speaker, he nevertheless continued to attend functions in his constituency in Gloucestershire. Reid recorded such events as Morrison attending the annual general meeting of the Cirencester Archaeology and History Society and when he opened the Cirencester Horticultural Society Show.[147] Morrison always made time for his constituency duties despite being extremely busy exercising the functions of Speaker.

In terms of the way in which Morrison conducted himself as Speaker, and particularly the manner in which he presided over the Commons chamber, his son made the following comment:

> He thought that very often rows achieved very little and that there had to be some better way round it. Now, this, I think, doesn't necessarily make for a good departmental minister in a strongly confrontational two-party system because you can't really be friends with the opposition whilst you're doing that sort of thing [...] I think probably, I've no doubt at all, that my father was a very good Speaker and he was temperamentally, and by experience, very well suited to it because at the same time as being conciliatory and not liking rows, he was a stickler for protocol. He could be relied upon to play the rules of the game, as far as the Speaker was concerned, very strictly on all occasions, without fear or favour as you might say, certainly without any partisanship.

Indeed, Speaker Morrison recorded in a makeshift diary (a few loose leaf pages of foolscap covering the end of 1952) that he kept on 13 November 1952, 'In the morning read up some precedents'.[148] He liked to have the facts at his fingertips and wanted to be prepared for any procedural matters that might arise whilst in the Chair. The fact that he spent time reading over the various precedents of the Commons demonstrates that he wanted to know the rules of the House so that he could always ensure that they were adhered to. Laundy has, however, criticised both Morrison and his predecessor when he wrote that, 'Both Clifton Brown and Morrison had a tendency to explain their rulings which occasionally led to difficulties'.

Alasdair Morrison has tried to set out why his father felt it necessary to explain his rulings to the House:

> I think that goes back to his lawyer's background in the sense that he was at one stage a Recorder of Walsall in the mid-1930s, and just as he made a good Speaker, I think he would have made a cracking good judge [...] and so it came as natural not to do things by impulse. It was entirely characteristic of him that in making a decision he would weigh very carefully and articulate to himself very carefully why he was making a decision in the way he would. So, having worked that out for himself, he almost felt a bounden duty to explain why he had done it to somebody else [...] my father thought that it was a good thing that Parliament had a right to know why the decision was being made because all the time you are making a decision of that kind, you are setting a precedent for the next time and he was acting almost like a judge in this kind of way.

Morrison's legal background obviously shaped the way in which he conducted himself as arbitrator of the rules and it stood him in good stead for the role he undertook.

W. S. Morrison remained Speaker for two full Parliaments and his daughter-in-law has commented upon the end of his period in the Chair:

> Later on it became much more of a struggle for him because of course, with the guns in the First World War, and he became increasingly deaf. I do know that it was a wonderful gift from

an American ambassador who gave him a little watch, as far as I remember, with a microphone in it so that it was much less evident. Obviously, there are microphones in the back of the Chair but it meant that when he was at a social gathering [...] he could just hold his hand up [...] nearer the person quite naturally. Being a big man it was quite easy to do that and he was absolutely thrilled with that.

Whilst the microphones in the back of the Chair would have helped, it would have nevertheless been very difficult for the Speaker to hear what was going on during a debate. Coupled with the deafness, Morrison's obituary in *The Times* commented that he endured a record number of all-night sittings and 'the strain began to tell on him'.[149]

Speaker Morrison decided to retire at the 1959 general election having had a medical examination from which he was advised that it would be unwise to continue for another parliament. Morrison attributed his resignation to: 'Slight deafness, greatly increased strain of being Speaker. Feared service of House might suffer if I carried on.'[150]

Indeed, Michael Ryle, who was a junior clerk in the House of Commons during the time of Speaker Morrison, has mentioned one episode relating to the deafness:

A man called George Brown [former Labour Foreign Secretary] [...] a somewhat rambunctious and powerful character with a loud voice, said something which the Speaker didn't think was quite what he should say and he called him to order. George Brown immediately challenged the Speaker and said, 'I want to have a ruling on this, a proper ruling', and the Speaker leant forward and spoke to the Clerk. Now it happened that the Speaker was getting very deaf and the Clerk spoke very loudly, so the House could hear what advice he gave. Whereupon George Brown said, 'Mr Speaker, it is your advice I want, not the advice of that *fellow* there'.[151]

The frustration of not being able to hear MPs, or indeed advisors who sat immediately in front of him, must have been a clear indicator that it was time to retire.

Morrison announced to the House on 19 February 1959 that he would not be contesting his Cirencester and Tewkesbury seat at the next election, signalling the end of his time as Speaker.

> I have decided, with regret, that I should not offer myself as a candidate at the next general election. I have recently undergone a very thorough medical examination, and my advisers, in whom I have full confidence, tell me that I would be unwise to undertake the work of another Parliament. From what they say, however, I appear to be as sound in wind and limb as a man of my age has any right to expect. I am very thankful to recall that I have not hitherto missed a day in your service through illness since I was first elected Speaker.[152]

The fact that Morrison had never missed a day in the eight years he served as Speaker shows his commitment to the office. On that occasion, Morrison admitted to the House that his deafness was the reason for quitting the Speakership:

> The infirmity of which I am personally conscious is a slight difficulty in hearing. I am aware that a certain degree of judicious deafness is not an unmixed evil in the occupant of this Chair, but I could wish that mine were sometimes more selective and less fortuitous. It adds somewhat, as hon. Members will appreciate, to the strain of performing my duties to the House.[153]

Immediately following the general election held on 8 October 1959, Morrison was invited by the Australian government to become Governor-General. Indeed, in an aide-memoire written to himself, Morrison records that the High Commissioner for Australia approached him on 27 October, nearly three weeks after ceasing to be Speaker of the House of Commons. Morrison had no idea that he was going to be offered this role and wrote: 'I had planned a very different life for myself in 1960; Had accepted many engagements for 1960, e.g. Presidency of Three Counties Agricultural Show, several school Speech Days, Openings, etc.'[154]

Alasdair Morrison outlined the background behind the Australian government inviting his father to be their country's governor-general:

It is true, and this is part of the explanation for the arrival of the invitation, that he had known Mr Menzies, who was then Prime Minister in Australia, for a long time and they were great friends. The reason for this was that they both had a strong Scottish background of which both were well aware, both were very interested in poetry, both were lawyers by background and training and they had in many respects a similar kind of temperament and respect for each other. I can see why from Menzies' point of view Dad looked like a very good candidate because, on the one hand it maintained the United Kingdom connection which Menzies was always keen on as far as Australia was concerned, on the other hand he wasn't going to get yet another 'pom' because Dad was not your typical English colonial governor by any manner of means and he didn't sound like one, he sounded like a Highland Scot. Menzies, of course, knew that Dad would do it very well because it's like being Speaker. You are supposed to act in an impartial way in the same manner and he knew that Dad could be trusted to do that and to do it very well which of course he did.

Lady Dunrossil has pointed out that her father-in-law accepting the office of Governor-General of Australia 'was controversial here [in the UK] as distinct from controversial there'. Moreover, on the second reading of Mr Speaker Morrison's Retirement Bill, Labour MPs expressed their opposition to a former Speaker taking up another position by voting against. On this, Lady Dunrossil has recalled that: 'I think he was wounded, well, she [his wife Allison] was certainly, by the kind of reaction and I think those who were close to him probably knew that financially he wasn't all that well off.'

In his aide-memoire, Morrison does take into account his financial position when considering whether he should take up the Governor-Generalship. His youngest son was still at university and he had the upkeep of the house in Gloucestershire and the flat in the Temple. He asked himself, 'Could I afford it?' and then concluded, 'Yes, with £2,000 per annum from House of Commons and provision for my widow and old age'.[155] It is clear that Morrison thought quite hard before taking up office in Australia and considered his own personal arrangements as well as any political or constitutional consequences.

It was, of course, and still is, highly unusual for a former Speaker to take on another appointment because anyone who accedes to the Chair agrees to give up politics for life. The only other Speaker in the twentieth century to take up an appointment after retiring was Whitley when he became Chairman of the Governors of the BBC in 1930. Morrison was elevated to the peerage as the Viscount Dunrossil of Vallaquie and it would have been the norm for him to see out his days on the cross-benches of the House of Lords. Morrison wrote of his reasons for accepting the appointment:

> Very great honour. Might help, and certainly not harm growth of parliamentary government in Commonwealth, that a great self-governing country should ask to submit to Her Majesty the name of the ex-Speaker of the House of Commons as their Governor-General.[156]

Lord Dunrossil, as he had become, took up the post of Governor-General of Australia on 2 February 1960 only to die suddenly one year later on 3 February 1961. Whilst Morrison wrote in late 1959 that he was 'Sound in wind and limb', clearly the strain of being Speaker and the fact that he had given up that office on medical advice meant that taking on another high-ranking appointment was his undoing.[157] Moreover, Sir Robin Chichester-Clark, believes that the strain of 'Suez could be said probably to have damaged him very seriously'. Morrison was buried with full honours at a state funeral in Canberra on 7 February 1961.

Two very different characters occupied the Chair in the years immediately following the Second World War. A wealthy English middle-class country landowner was succeeded by a less affluent Scottish barrister who had frequented the corridors of power in Whitehall for most of his parliamentary career. Clearly, Clifton Brown had a less than easy Speakership with some of his colleagues going as far as to say that he was weak and indecisive. He did, however, succeed in ensuring that the new Labour intake, who were hungry for reform, carried out their programme whilst adhering to parliamentary protocols. What he did achieve was to broaden the horizons of the Speakership by making overseas trips and adding an ambassadorial role to the office. Morrison was a much more dominant figure who enjoyed a far greater command of the House than his predecessor. This is just as well because he found himself in the Chair at the time of the Suez crisis when parliamentary niceties broke down on the floor of the House and slanging matches ensued. Morrison's force of character won the day although he did have to suspend a sitting. Clifton Brown's Speakership has received mixed reviews whereas Morrison is almost universally acclaimed as having been a very able and respected Speaker of the House of Commons. Fortunately, both Speakers came at the right time because Clifton Brown was successful in guiding the new post-war House of Commons but would have probably found it difficult to control the Suez debates. Morrison excelled in the role as Speaker and should be remembered for using his talents to tame a most unruly House of Commons and safeguard the continuance of reasoned debating.

Four

The Lawyer and the Headmaster: Sir Harry Hylton-Foster (1959–65) and Dr Horace King (1965–71)

Sir Harry Hylton-Foster QC MP, my first Speaker, was a poor Speaker, frightened of the 'bully-boys' [...] who could do more or less anything, however 'out of Order', that they wanted: and he would then try to reassert his authority by jumping on 'little people'.
– Sir Robin Maxwell-Hyslop, former Conservative MP, 2005

Like a good Headmaster, I think he [Speaker King] knew to let the naughty boys have a little bit of rope but not too much.
– Sir Richard Body, former Conservative MP, 2007

Following Harold Macmillan's general election victory in 1959, the Conservative Solicitor-General, Sir Harry Hylton-Foster, was elected to the Chair. Having been a frontbencher, Hylton-Foster faced the same criticism as his predecessor, W. S. Morrison, concerning whether or not a former minister should be elected Speaker. Hylton-Foster's sudden death in September 1965 brought about the election of the first Speaker drawn from the ranks of the Labour Party, Dr Horace King. Speaker King presided over the House during the period of the first two Wilson governments although he swiftly gave up the Chair a few months after the Conservatives' return to power in 1970.

Sir Harry Hylton-Foster was born in Ewell, Surrey on 10 April 1905 and was educated at Eton before reading law at Magdalen College, Oxford. He was called to the bar in 1928 and served as legal secretary to Viscount Finlay at the Permanent Court of International Justice. On 22 December 1931, Hylton-Foster married Audrey Pellew Clifton Brown, the daughter of one of his predecessors as Speaker, Colonel Douglas Clifton Brown. During the Second World War Hylton-Foster served in the Royal Air Force and acted as Deputy Judge Advocate in North Africa. As Conservative candidate he failed to secure the Yorkshire seat of Shipley in the 1945 general election but contested York at the 1950 general election and won by seventy-seven votes. In 1954, Hylton-Foster became Solicitor-General in Churchill's government and was knighted. The following year, he managed to retain his marginal seat at the 1955 general election but after that he decided to swap to a safer division. Hylton-Foster was fortunate enough to be selected to fight the Conservative stronghold of the Cities of London & Westminster at the 1959 general election and won by 17,188 votes.

Sir Harry Hylton-Foster was a reluctant Speaker; as a lawyer, it is said that he would have much rather have risen to the highest office of the legal profession and become Lord Chancellor. Moreover, Sir Robin Chichester-Clark, who was Ulster Unionist MP for Londonderry between 1955 and 1974, believes that Hylton-Foster was 'probably the best lawyer that was in the House of Commons at the time'. However, Macmillan insisted that Hylton-Foster became Speaker and so he gave up any chance of sitting on the Woolsack, the Lord Chancellor's (now Lord Speaker's) chair in the House of Lords. Hylton-Foster's period in the Chair started off badly and was one which was highly criticised. As seen previously, the Leader of the Opposition, Hugh Gaitskell, was not happy with

the choice of Hylton-Foster for Speaker on the grounds that the
holder of this high office should not be someone who had been
a minister immediately before being elected to the Chair. Whilst
the Labour Party did not put up an alternative candidate, the fact
that Hylton-Foster's election as Speaker was not given universal
approval was not a good start to his period in office. Despite the
controversy, Sir Harry Hylton-Foster became the 150th Speaker
of the House of Commons on 20 October 1959.

Lord Hooson, who was Liberal MP for Montgomeryshire
between 1962 and 1979, has described Sir Harry Hylton-Foster as
being 'a very nice chap and as blameless as a blancmange'; he,
therefore, did not set the world on fire during his period in the
Chair. Sir Teddy Taylor, who was elected as Conservative MP in
1964, recalls that Hylton-Foster 'didn't give the impression of great
power'. His biggest critic must be the former Conservative MP Sir
Robin Maxwell-Hyslop who thought that Hylton-Foster was very
weak in the Chair and would not rebuke more confident Members.

> Harry Hylton-Foster's greatest weakness was lack of moral cour-
> age: there were Members of whom he was afraid, who could
> break the Rules of Order with impunity. [...] That completely
> undermined his authority, and thereby, too, made it consequently
> very difficult for the Deputy Speakers to try to enforce what their
> Speaker was afraid himself to do.

This appears to be true and was all the more apparent during
Hylton-Foster's last year as Speaker when Harold Wilson's Labour
government only had a majority of four. When commenting on
the motion of censure debate on 2 August 1965, Wilson remarks
that, 'In a winding up speech in a previous debate there had
been no fewer than nineteen points of order, which had proved
almost impossible for the Speaker to control'.[158]

Labour MP Sydney Silverman did put down a motion of censure against the Speaker on 16 February 1961, following his refusal to grant him a question to the Home Secretary.[159] Silverman had wanted to ask whether a miscarriage of justice had occurred in the case of George Riley, who had been hanged for murder. Silverman debated at some length, quoting from *Erskine May*, and really mounted a challenge to the Speaker's authority but in the end the motion was defeated by 253 votes to 60. It is clear that Hylton-Foster allowed too many points of order and actually allowed his authority to be challenged. The Speaker is there to maintain order and to enforce the rules that the House has set down and so cannot afford to allow his judgements to be called into question. Hylton-Foster must have seemed very weak if he was constantly having to defend the decisions that the House had entrusted in him to make.

In terms of Hylton-Foster's Deputy Speakers, it is probably more the case that they caused him trouble rather the other way around. His chief deputy, the Chairman of Ways and Means and Conservative MP Sir Gordon Touche, was involved in two separate incidents in 1961 which caused the Labour benches to criticise him for allegedly acting in a biased manner. On 8 February 1961, whilst the House was in Committee, Touche, the Chairman, was seen having a private conversation with Martin Redmayne, the government Chief Whip. The Labour opposition put down a motion of censure because they believed that Touche's discussion with Redmayne led to him accepting a premature motion of closure which Hugh Gaitskell maintained prevented backbenchers from taking part in the debate. During the censure debate, Labour MP John Diamond said when referring to Touche that 'the government have made a mistake in appointing a man whose abilities are not appropriate to the dimensions of this task'.[160] Touche managed to survive

the motion of censure by 302 votes to 211 but nine months later
was in trouble again when he mistakenly announced an opposition victory in a division and, after numerous points of order,
had to adjourn the House because of grave disorder. Despite
all this, Speaker Hylton-Foster displayed his loyalty and backed
his deputy, but in the end Sir Gordon Touche decided to resign
from the post.

One reason why Hylton-Foster backed his deputies was
because he leant so heavily on them. One of Touche's successors,
the Labour MP and future Speaker, Dr Horace King, wrote in
his unpublished memoirs that: 'Sir Samuel Storey [Conservative
MP and Deputy Chairman of Ways and Means] and I were Mr
Speaker's slaves. We were always in the chamber long ahead of
the time that we were due to relieve him.'[161]

Hylton-Foster had been a reluctant Speaker and perhaps,
thanks to the criticism he received, he was more than happy to
let his deputies do as much of the work in the Chair as possible.

According to Laundy, it was Hylton-Foster who instituted
the Speaker's right to think over a ruling for twenty-four hours
before passing judgement, a practice that can be traced back to a
sessional order regarding complaints of privilege on 8 February
1960. Speaker Hylton-Foster interpreted the order as allowing
him to postpone his ruling for twenty-four hours to consider
whether or not a complaint of privilege should take precedence
over other business. Since then, the Speaker has been allowed to
give himself twenty-four hours to seek advice and consider what
his ruling should be.[162]

A major episode of Hylton-Foster's Speakership was the
Labour MP Tony Benn's peerage battle. On the death of
Viscount Stansgate on 17 November 1960, Tony Benn automatically succeeded to his late father's peerage. However, Benn
did not wish to leave the House of Commons and so started

a campaign to enable people to renounce hereditary titles. As soon as his father had died Tony Benn went to see the Speaker who told him that he had made an order to keep him out of the chamber. When Benn questioned this decision he was told that any man who inherits a peerage must be kept out. Benn recalls that when he asked how the Speaker knew he had inherited, Hylton-Foster replied, 'I've got your letter, saying that your father has died, and as far as I'm concerned that is *prima facie* evidence that you've succeeded'.[163]

Benn goes on to say that 'the Speaker assumed that this was just a little protest and a struggle before I was carried away'.[164] Hylton-Foster could not have been more wrong but nevertheless he was upholding the rules of the House as he had been elected to do.

When Benn won the subsequent by-election in his Bristol South East constituency, Hylton-Foster ruled him to be a 'stranger' when he was presented at the Bar of the House and so would not let him take up his seat. Benn told him that he had just been elected by a large majority and so would take his seat by force if he had to. According to Benn, the 'Speaker was shaken by this' but went on to exclude him from all the amenities of the House which were usually extended to peers who had previously been MPs.[165] Hylton-Foster gave the excuse that this was because Benn had not yet taken up his peerage which, although, technically true, seems to have been taking the letter of the law too far considering that the people of Bristol had just endorsed him.

On 31 May 1962, the Speaker relented and gave permission for Benn to use the Commons library for his research. In the end, Benn won his fight and the Peerage Act passed on 31 July 1963 changed the law to allow peers to renounce their titles thus enabling them to be Members of Parliament. Following a further by-election in Bristol South East, Hylton-Foster finally allowed Tony Benn to retake his seat on 24 October 1963. The Speaker was absolutely right to uphold the rules of Parliament and prevent Benn from taking his seat when the law still considered him to be a peer. Speakers are elected to see that the rules are adhered to and Hylton-Foster would have erred in doing anything else. However, Hylton-Foster could have allowed Benn more leeway, bearing in mind that he had won a by-election and had a mandate from Bristol. When considering Hylton-Foster's Speakership, Sir Robin Maxwell-Hyslop argued that: 'Speaker Hylton-Foster QC's lasting contribution to constitutional law was his definition of the nature of a Hybrid Bill and his (to my mind, equally important) statement on Onus of Proof when hybridity is alleged, both of which were delivered seriatim in his Ruling.'

Maxwell-Hyslop points out that 'the Clerks did not like his Ruling on Onus of Proof and sought to suppress it by omitting it from Erskine May'. Onus of Proof is the interpretation of what is a Hybrid Bill. A Public Bill is a bill that, if passed, will have general effect in some or all of the constituent parts of the United Kingdom whereas a Private Bill will have only local or personal, rather than general effect. Most bills are public bills because they affect most parts of the UK but some bills can give particular rights to individuals such as a local authority and so are deemed to be private. To this day, *Erskine May* uses Hylton-Foster's judgement and defines a Hybrid Bill as: 'a public bill which affects a particular private interest in a manner different from the private interest of other persons or bodies of the same category or class'.[166]

Criticism of Hylton-Foster's Speakership, however, came to a head in July 1965 when Conservative Members were annoyed at him for not granting the former Chancellor of the Exchequer Reginald Maudling a Private Notice Question about the work of a Foreign Office adviser. On a point of order, another

former Cabinet minister, Iain Macleod, asked the Speaker: 'If
Questions on this are disallowed, may we have an assurance
that you do not regard it as part of the function of the Chair to
protect the government from proper questioning by the House
of Commons?'[167]

This was an outright attack on the impartiality of the Speaker
and showed just how angry the Conservative benches had
become. Macleod swiftly withdrew his remarks following protests
from other MPs, which avoided a motion of no confidence in the
Chair. Such an attack from colleagues from the previous government certainly hurt the Speaker.[168] From then on certain elements
of the Conservative Party sought to remove Hylton-Foster from
the Chair and were not prepared to support his re-election next
time round.

Sir Harry Hylton-Foster died suddenly at the age of sixty when
he collapsed whilst walking along Duke Street in Westminster
on 2 September 1965. Despite a policeman attempting to give
the Speaker the 'kiss of life', Hylton-Foster was dead on arrival
at St George's Hospital at Hyde Park Corner. He was the second
Speaker to die in office during the twentieth century. His wife,
Audrey, was given the customary peerage awarded to retiring
Speakers and became the long-serving convener of the cross-
bench peers. Hylton-Foster's untimely death prevented him
from facing the possible indignity of being removed from office
because, only a few weeks before, the Chairman of the 1922
Committee and Conservative MP, Sir William Anstruther-Gray
indicated that his re-election to the Chair was unacceptable.

Dr Horace King was elected Speaker on 26 October 1965
when Parliament met again following the summer recess. King
was born on 25 May 1901 in Grangetown near Middlesbrough
and was educated at Stockton Secondary School before attending King's College, London. King stood as the Labour candidate

in the Conservative stronghold of New Forest and Christchurch at the 1945 general election but, despite Attlee's landslide victory, was unsuccessful. The following year, King was elected to Hampshire County Council on which he served until 1965. In 1950, he was elected to Parliament as MP for Southampton Test with a majority of 1,389. King held the seat at the 1951 general election but decided to swap to the safer Southampton Itchen division in 1955. Within four years of becoming a Member of Parliament he had been appointed to the Speaker's Panel of Chairmen of Committees which enabled him to eventually become Chairman of Ways and Means and Deputy Speaker in November 1964. King found his new responsibilities extremely tiring – since Speaker Hylton-Foster relied heavily on his deputies. King was sometimes in the Chair late into the night and, in his unpublished biography, he recounts:

> once during the small hours of the morning Dr King was waiting on the embankment for one of the infrequent night buses to take him to his lodgings in Kennington, when a reporter saw him there and wrote about it. As a result, the Chairman of Ways and Means, for the first time in history, was allowed by the Treasury to use a government car if the House rose after midnight.[169]

This innovation was, however, not enough to prevent King from suffering thanks to all the hours he was putting in and he recorded: 'The strain of the Deputy-Speakership had led to my physical collapse when attending the NUT [National Union of Teachers] Conference at Easter – but I had shaken that off before Parliament resumed.'[170]

Despite finding the workload of the deputy role difficult, Dr King became the first Labour Speaker on 9 September 1965 following the shock death of Hylton-Foster. The physical demands and political pressures at the time made a daunting prospect of the Speakership. Nonetheless, King did accept the office and the 151st Speaker proved to be very popular in the Chair and ensured that more questions were answered at the despatch box. King managed to do this by having an indicator on the Table of the House which showed a minus sign if question time was dragging and a red minus sign if they were not getting through nearly enough questions. If they were getting through a good number of questions then the indicator would show a plus sign. This system was employed throughout King's time in the Chair. Speaker King also initiated the practice of requesting MPs to make any points of order at the end of Question Time so that the limited time available was not unduly curtailed. King's new processes were popular in most quarters but by no means everywhere. [171]

> Although I was first in Questions I didn't leave much time for preparation. A few months ago I wouldn't have dreamt of taking the risk, but under Horace King Question Time is having the sting taken out of it. He tries to get some fifty or sixty Questions answered each day and to prevent supplementaries going on for too long. This increases the enormous advantage which the Minister always enjoys at Question Time. [172]

So, whilst Speaker King was trying his best to ensure backbenchers could ask as many questions as possible, that they were not allowed to ask long supplementaries meant that in many cases it let ministers off the hook. In his attempt to assist backbenchers, King managed to undermine them. Horace King clearly meant well but rather than standing up for the rights of backbenchers, the Speaker actually reduced their power to bring the government to account on the floor of the House.

During King's tenure, an important procedural reform enhanced the power of the Speaker. 'In my early days in the Chair there were certain procedural restrictions which barred some PNQs [Private Notice Questions]. These were later abolished by the House.'[173]

The Speaker's ability to grant Private Notice Questions (now called Urgent Questions) is crucial: it requires ministers to come to the House to answer a question on an urgent matter of public interest.

The Select Committee on Procedure examined this rule during the 1966–7 session and concluded that 'the decision on the appropriateness of a private notice question is best left to Mr Speaker'.[174] On 6 June 1967, Speaker King gave the following statement to the House:

> On occasions, that rule [on PNQs] has been considered unduly restrictive by my predecessors and by the House, particularly when Private Notice Questions of some importance have been blocked by a Question for Written Answer. Recently, the Select Committee on Procedure recommended in its Fifth Report of this Session that in future, when considering Private Notice Questions, I should be entitled to disregard any Question for Written Answer and should take account only of Questions which are liable to be answered orally within a reasonable period of time, having regard to the urgency of the subject matter. From such soundings as I have taken, I understand that it would meet with the general approval of the House if I were to adopt that recommendation and, therefore, I propose to adopt it today.[175]

The Speaker now had far greater discretion over the granting of PNQs which would enhance his role of helping backbenchers and minorities to hold the government of the day to account. King seized on the Procedure Committee's recommendation and wasted little time in implementing it although the fact that he took soundings shows that he was still very much the servant of the House and could only make changes with its support.

It is clear that Dr King did not like the isolation of Speaker's House and missed mingling with colleagues in the bars and tea rooms of the Commons – 'Perhaps the most accurate description of the Speakership is its utter remoteness'.[176] As a result of this, King did propose to take his meals occasionally in the Members' Dining Room at the table reserved for the Clerks but in the end he was persuaded not to do this by a delegation of senior MPs.[177] The impartiality of the Speakership is closely guarded and Members will not let anything call it in to question. Speaker King would, however, hold a weekly luncheon in his apartments to which he invited about seven Members from all parties. During these gatherings he would encourage MPs 'to talk about anything except politics'.[178] The ninth Duke of Buccleuch, who as Lord Dalkeith was a Conservative MP between 1960 and 1973, recalled that:

> Horace King always seemed very fair, stood for no nonsense and became quite a friend, staying with us in Scotland on one occasion at the same time as the Lebanese Ambassador who was at that time the doyen of the Diplomatic Corps.

Whilst coming from a Labour background, it would appear that Speaker King had no qualms about mingling in aristocratic circles and socialising with the grandest of MPs. The office of Speaker can quickly propel someone from the humblest of origins into the highest echelons of society.

King came to the Chair determined that he would never have to use the ultimate sanction available to him: naming a Member. On 23 May 1968 he was, however, forced to name Dame Irene Ward, the Conservative MP for Tynemouth, because she persisted in obstructing the tellers whilst they were reporting the result of a division concerning the allocation of time to the Finance Bill. Although King sympathised with Ward's point that she wanted Members to be given the right to debate the Bill for longer, he nevertheless was obliged to uphold the rules of the House. Whilst reluctant, King demonstrated that he was fully capable of controlling an unruly House because he was not afraid to use the full disciplinary powers of the Speakership if he needed to.

Despite being the first Labour Speaker, it seems that King did not openly favour his old comrades on the Labour benches. Stan Newens, who was a Labour MP from 1964 to 1970, remembers that he 'didn't find him [King] particularly helpful' when it came to being called to speak on issues such as the Vietnam War but his lack of co-operation with Newens was more a mark of his impartiality. There were, however, criticisms from the Conservative side that Speaker King did not give the opposition a fair crack of the whip when it came to debating time. [179]

The mid-1960s witnessed the advent of the Services Committee whereby control of the House of Commons section of the Palace of Westminster was assigned to the Speaker. The new Committee acted as the Speaker's advisers and assisted with various aspects of logistics and administration around the Commons.

Although this change took place in Speaker Hylton-Foster's time, his untimely demise only a few months later meant that it fell upon King to be the first holder of the office to take on this additional responsibility. Before that, control had been vested in the Lord Great Chamberlain although it was delegated to the Serjeant-at-Arms on behalf of the Speaker when the House was sitting. During recess and at weekends control reverted to the Lord Great Chamberlain. King's successor, Selwyn Lloyd, wrote that this move was resented by some Members and that the Palace became 'nationalised'. [180]

Whilst the vast bulk of the work was done by the clerks and

other members of the parliamentary staff, this change neverthe-less meant extra meetings for the Speaker. He was no longer purely responsible for what went on in the chamber, he now had the additional responsibility of managing the running of the whole building. This reform was also one which would cause the downfall of a Speaker thirty-five years later.

King undertook far more engagements abroad than any of his predecessors and enlarged the ambassadorial role for the Speakership and it has continued to develop. [181] Whilst Clifton Brown started this trend with his trips to war-torn Europe, Speaker King undoubtedly reinforced this and established an additional function for the Speakership which meant travelling to international conferences, informing foreign parliamentarians about his office and representing the House of Commons.

During his period in the Chair, King had to preside over an electoral reform conference. The conference worked through three sessions of Parliament and issued its final report on 9 February 1968. Its most significant recommendation was the lowering of the voting age to twenty but, in the end, the voting age was in fact reduced to eighteen by the Representation of the People Act 1969. King's electoral conference did, however, pave the way for this move to happen and so its work was not in vain.

On 31 May 1966, during his period as Speaker, Dr King's wife, Florence, died suddenly from a heart attack. King had been visiting the United States at the invitation of the Speaker of the House of Representatives, John McCormack, and was given the news by British Embassy staff. Mrs King had been a politician in her own right having been a Labour councillor and then alder-man on Southampton City Council for thirty-six years. She did not give up her political activism whilst her husband was Speaker and so it could be said that Speaker's House was not as impartial as it should have been. Lord Hooson recalls that 'Horace King was famous because he always used to march in front of his wife. She came up behind him.' It is doubtful whether this was the case with his first wife, Alderman Mrs Florence King, who was the mother of his only daughter and who had had a political career of her own. Lord Hooson is referring to King's second wife – his secretary Una Porter whom he married in 1967 – who did not have the same civic and political background.

King was known as being 'partial to the ladies' according to Baroness Fookes but it was another tendency that actually marred his tenure somewhat: alcohol. The strains of the office and the loss of his first wife combined to foster a fondness for the bottle.

Lord Weatherill commented that 'Dear old Horace was under the misapprehension that sherry was a non-alcoholic drink'.[182] Sir Richard Body recalls that King 'gave the impression sometimes at 10 o'clock at night he'd drunk rather more than he should have done'. Sir Robin Maxwell-Hyslop remembered going to Speaker's House and seeing how much Horace King would drink: 'He didn't say "What would you like?" He said, "I expect you drink the same as I do", hence my amazement. He poured about four fingers of brandy into a lager glass and then filled it up with the best part of half a pint of sherry!'

Sir Robin Chichester-Clark remembers an episode when Speaker King was drunk on a Commonwealth Parliamentary Association visit to Northern Ireland:

Someone gave a dinner [...] it got going and he [Horace King] tickled the ivories quite a bit and knocked back quite a few. At the end, he was left by himself, for some reason, to walk back to the hotel. When he got back to the hotel, it was all barred down for the night, it was 2 o'clock in the morning, so he batters at the door and eventually the porter appears saying, 'What the hell do you want?' sort of thing. Horace says, 'Will you please let me in?' 'Well who are you, sir?' 'I'm the Speaker of the House of Commons, London.' 'Well, if you're the Speaker of the House of Commons, I must be William of Orange!'

Fortunately, the porter let Horace King in and the Speaker, ever the good sport, did not mind recounting the joke. However, Lord Weatherill remembered what effect King's drinking had on him whilst presiding over the Commons chamber:

He was unwise enough to say, 'I will always be present for the adjournment.' Now, that didn't always take place at 10 o'clock. I mean it could be 12 o'clock, half past one, sometimes two o'clock. Poor old boy used to sit upstairs putting back the sweet sherry and was not absolutely sober when he got to the Chair. Walter Harrison and I looked after him [...] we helped the old boy out. But one day, he was in his cups [...] and faced a very difficult Point of Order and found himself saying [in a slurred way], 'Before I rule on this matter, I would like to consult the Table of clerks.' The next day, having consulted the Table, he ruled very wisely but, by that time, the boys and girls had had him and so, whenever he got up and hesitated for a moment, a buzz started round, 'Have a word with the Table, Mr Speaker', 'Why don't you talk to the Table, Mr Speaker, sir?' and he had to go.

Sir Robin Maxwell-Hyslop recalled a time when Horace King was so drunk that he could not climb the few steps to get to the Speaker's Chair:

Horace came in at twenty-five past nine and he had two goes at getting up into his Chair [...] and the second time he fell to the right across the Clerks' Table with his wig 45 degrees to the left and Bob Mellish [government Chief Whip and Labour MP]

[...] called out, 'You're a disgrace, Horace, and I'll have you out
of that Chair within three months.' Horace turned round so
abruptly that his wig was then 45 degrees out the other way and
he gave a brilliant riposte, 'How can you get me out of the Chair,
Bob, when I can't get myself in to it?'

Speaker King announced his retirement on 10 December 1970
just six months after the general election which saw Edward
Heath and the Conservatives win power. He could have retired
at the general election and allowed a new House of Commons
to select its Speaker in the same way as after the 1951 and 1959
elections. King did say in his resignation speech that:

> Some eighteen months ago I indicated to the then Leader of
> the House [Fred Peart] and the then Chief Opposition Whip
> [William Whitelaw] that if I were re-elected to a new Parliament
> I would hope to remain in the Chair for only a short time in order
> to see the new Parliament in. When the House did me the honour
> of re-electing me as Speaker, I again indicated through the usual
> channels that I would seek to retire some time during the first
> year of this Parliament. In October I reaffirmed that it was my
> intention to retire during the Christmas recess.[183]

An incident in July 1970 when a disgruntled Belfast man threw
two canisters of CS gas onto the floor of the Commons chamber
during a statement on the Common Market helped to shuffle
him towards retirement.

> Whilst the Minister Tony Barber was making his statement, a
> man stood up in the Strangers' Gallery and threw two objects on
> to the Floor of the House, close to the Front Benches. Members
> with military experience immediately scattered or ducked. I sat

tight, imagining it to be some minor nuisance. But the draught carried the fumes to the Chair and I was almost overcome [...] I heard, faintly, somebody moving that the sitting be suspended – murmured myself 'Sitting suspended', but by then was unable to move. I learned later that the Deputy Speaker and the Clerk of the House dragged me out of the Chair.[184]

For someone who suffered badly from the strains of the Speakership such an attack would have affected King badly. Sir Robin Maxwell-Hyslop said that in the end Speaker King 'was "persuaded" to retire' because of his sometimes drunken state and Stan Newens confirms this, adding that it was orchestrated by the Labour Chief Whip, Bob Mellish. King himself described the responsibilities of the role as 'unimaginable' and often stated he would retire before he became too weak for the job.[185] If this is the case, then King's assertion that he had planned to go was a face saving exercise because it was the stresses of the office causing the excessive drinking which eventually led to him having to retire slightly earlier than expected. King himself wrote: 'I had been a happy Chairman of Ways and Means. The burden I assumed on becoming Speaker took away some of that happiness.'[186]

The sudden death of Speaker Hylton-Foster had propelled King into the Chair with less than a year's experience as deputy. He had not expected to become Speaker at that time and so was totally unprepared to take up the role. The fact that he had found the Deputy Speaker role a strain should have forewarned him that the full Speakership was going to be difficult. The fact that he was unhappy in the role, had lost his wife and found the job exhausting meant that it was to his credit that he lasted more than five years in office.

On being replaced as Speaker in January 1971, Horace King was given a life peerage, taking the style Lord Maybray-King which incorporated his middle name, the maiden name of his mother. He was the first Speaker not to be given the customary hereditary viscountcy because Harold Wilson had stopped the practice and tradition of creating hereditary peers and the new Prime Minister, Edward Heath, did not see fit to re-introduce it. Only Mrs Thatcher created further hereditary peers when Harold Macmillan was granted an earldom and Willie Whitelaw and George Thomas were given viscountcies. Whilst in the House of Lords, King served as a Deputy Speaker although his obituary in *The Times* notes that it was 'a position whose duties he tended to find onerous as the years went by and he found it increasingly difficult to attend the House'.[187] King married twice more before passing away on 3 September 1986.

Whilst the 1960s might well have been an era of reform and cultural change in Britain, this mood did not reach the Speaker's Chair. The Speakerships of Sir Harry Hylton-Foster and Horace King were uninspiring because the individuals who occupied the Chair were not of the same ilk as their immediate predecessor, W. S. Morrison. There was no equivalent of the impassioned Suez debates and there were no moves to change the office of Speaker in any way. The two holders of the Speakership in this period were not as strong as some of their colleagues, but in differing ways: Sir Harry Hylton-Foster possibly too nice and a reluctant Speaker; Dr Horace King initially an effective Speaker who could command the House but whose early retirement can be traced to an alcohol dependency brought about by the loss of his wife and the strains of the Speakership. These were two fair and well-liked men who never became political heavyweights. Perhaps that is why MPs opted for the very experienced and senior parliamentarian, Selwyn Lloyd, in 1971.

Five

Weathering the Storm: Selwyn Lloyd (1971–6) and George Thomas (1976–83)

Selwyn Lloyd, I think, was one of the best Speakers because, as a former Cabinet Minister, he had the determination and the vigour to stand up to government in a polite way and he did this in a very effective way.
– Sir Teddy Taylor, former Conservative MP, 2004

He [George Thomas] had his favourites. He was particularly friendly with Mrs Thatcher, the Prime Minister. Margaret Thatcher actually said to me, 'I've nothing against you but you won't look after us like George did.' And I said, 'I hope not. That was noticed.' Dear George and dear Margaret were very thick.
– Lord Weatherill

The economic and industrial unrest of the 1970s engendered arguably the toughest political climate in post-war British history. The indecisive outcomes of the two general elections held in 1974 meant that the occupant of the Chair had to maintain order in an evenly divided House of Commons in which every vote was made on a knife edge. Speakers Selwyn Lloyd and George Thomas came to the post with a vast experience of government having both been Cabinet ministers although Lloyd had served at a much higher level and had a somewhat more chequered career than his successor. How these men coped with the challenges they faced, the way in which they were viewed by their parliamentary colleagues and what changes and reforms they instituted will form the basis of this chapter.

John Selwyn Lloyd was born on 28 July 1904 in West Kirby on the Wirral Peninsula. His father, John Wesley Lloyd, was a local doctor and devout Methodist and Selwyn (as he was known) was brought up in a very middle-class family. Lloyd was educated at Fettes College and then went on to gain a Classics scholarship to Magdalene College, Cambridge where he also read law. There he joined the Liberal Club and went on to become President of the Cambridge Union. Following university he became a lawyer at Gray's Inn but was adopted at the age of twenty-two as the Liberal candidate for Macclesfield, which he contested at the 1929 general election. It was a difficult seat for the Liberals and, despite doubling the number of votes for the party, he came third behind the Conservatives and Labour.

Lloyd quickly fell out with the Liberals over the question of free trade and, when it was known that he would not be standing again for them in Macclesfield, he was approached by the Clitheroe Conservative Association. Lloyd, however, declined because he wanted to concentrate on his legal career and had become interested in local rather than national politics. He was elected as an independent councillor on Hoylake Urban District Council in 1932 and served there until 1945. During the Second World War he reached the rank of brigadier, served as Deputy Chief of Staff of the British Second Army and was present on D-Day. In October 1944, a letter from Alan Buckley of the Wirral Conservative Association notified Lloyd that the sitting MP, Alan Graham, was not standing again and urged him to put his name forward. Having abandoned the Liberals, Lloyd applied and was unanimously selected as the Conservative candidate in January

1945. Despite the Labour landslide at the 1945 general election, Lloyd was elected with a healthy majority of 16,625 although this was a greatly reduced margin from the 25,816 majority secured by his predecessor, Captain Graham, in 1935.

When the Conservatives returned to power in 1951, Selwyn Lloyd served under Anthony Eden as a Minister of State for Foreign Affairs. In the same year, at the age of forty-seven, he married Elizabeth (known as Bae) Marshall. Together, they had a daughter, Joanna, but the marriage was not to last and Lloyd filed for divorce in early 1957. In 1954 he became Minister of Supply and went on to become Minister of Defence in 1955. Later that year Lloyd was made Foreign Secretary and so in ten years, he had managed to climb the ranks to become one of the most senior ministers in the Cabinet. Lloyd was Foreign Secretary during the Suez crisis of the autumn of 1956 and despite this leading to Eden's resignation, he remained in the role in Harold Macmillan's government and later became Chancellor of the Exchequer in the reshuffle of 1960. Lloyd was the biggest casualty and motivator behind Macmillan's 'Night of the Long Knives' in July 1962 when he sacked seven ministers in an attempt to reinvent his government following the disastrous Orpington by-election. Lloyd had been unable to tackle Britain's economic problems and the 'Pay Pause' of the early 1960s had made him extremely unpopular across the country.

Lloyd was not on the back benches for very long because he returned to the Cabinet as Leader of the House of Commons when Sir Alec Douglas-Home became Prime Minister in October 1963. When the Conservatives lost power in 1964, Lloyd continued as shadow Leader of the House and then took on Commonwealth Relations when Edward Heath became Party Leader in July 1965. However, following the 1966 general election, Heath reshuffled his shadow Cabinet and dropped Lloyd believing that: 'It was important to have experienced spokesmen, but we needed an injection of new blood. I was keen to reduce numbers.'[188]

Lloyd probably thought that his days at the forefront of national politics were over and so opted to concentrate his efforts on helping to restore the Conservative Party's organisation on the ground ready for the next general election. He did, however, remain a member of the House of Commons Services Committee, the body which advised the Speaker on his administrative responsibilities, and, in 1970, he became its chairman. Lloyd admitted that, 'This experience was of great help to me when I became Speaker'.[189] Indeed, his godson, Jonathan Aitken believes that Lloyd's membership of this committee was part of a strategy:

> I was very much aware, probably almost ahead of anybody else because, as his Private Secretary, he confided in me, that he had his eye on becoming Speaker really as early as 1963 or something like that. He made himself, which didn't take much effort because he was that anyway, a good House of Commons man as opposed to a good ministerial man. He served on various key committees [such as the Services Committee] […] he angled himself to become Speaker and of course he did.

Despite having his sights firmly set on the Speakership, Lloyd had to overcome questions surrounding the fact that he had been at the top table of government. Lloyd's involvement as Foreign Secretary in the collusion between Britain and Israel during the disastrous Suez crisis, which was exposed by Anthony Nutting in 1967, was another factor which went against him.[190] MPs were expected to support a man who had been part of a conspiracy in which the Prime Minister misled the House of Commons, and allow him to chair their proceedings and ensure impartiality.

Nevertheless, despite the attempt by Robin Maxwell-Hyslop to cause a contested election, Lloyd was elected as the 152nd Speaker on 12 January 1971.

Lloyd's greatest challenge was to overcome fears that he would favour the government because, having served as a senior Cabinet minister, he was considered to be too close to the executive. Also, Lloyd was elected shortly after a new Conservative government had come to power and so concerns from opposition MPs that he would favour his old colleagues in Heath's administration were understandable, although his Liberal background safeguarded him to a certain extent. Lord Parkinson, who was Conservative MP for Enfield West at the time, recalls that Lloyd:

> had this problem as Speaker of proving to the House that once he was Speaker he was unbiased, he was neutral and that's quite difficult when you've been a member of the Cabinet, Foreign Secretary, Chancellor of the Exchequer. So he was quite guarded in his dealings with the Conservatives and the Labour Party watched him like hawks to see if he favoured us.

Lord Hooson, who was Liberal MP for Montgomeryshire, remembers that 'Selwyn was terribly anxious to please and he didn't want to battle with the Beast of Bolsover [Labour MP and firebrand, Dennis Skinner]'. Despite being a new MP, Skinner was not afraid to cause trouble in the chamber and on 20 January 1972, following unemployment rising to more than one million, he stood directly in front of Prime Minister Edward Heath and shook his fist in his face. Lloyd had to suspend the sitting for fifteen minutes to restore order. Skinner himself does not agree with Hooson that the Speaker was afraid of him and the fact that Lloyd did suspend the sitting shows that he would take the necessary action. The Speaker, however, chose to suspend the whole

House rather than 'name' Skinner and have him suspended individually which shows that Hooson's point is most certainly the case. The former Conservative MP for Huntingdonshire, Lord Renton, argued that Lloyd 'was one of those people who tried to avoid any kind of party attitude. He didn't hold people down as much as he might have done.'

Baroness Boothroyd, who was first elected to the House of Commons in 1973 during Lloyd's time in the Chair, however, remembers that:

> Selwyn Lloyd was very stern. He used to terrify me actually. I remember once speaking in a full House late at night. I was right at the end of the list obviously. We were waiting for the division and he used to tap his [papers] like this, come on hurry it up. I never knew Selwyn Lloyd but I found him intimidating.

This might well have been the case for newer Members who were not as confident as the more well established MPs although Dennis Skinner was in the new intake and clearly Lord Hooson did not think that Lloyd had the same effect on him.

According to Sir Robin Maxwell-Hyslop, Lloyd had an 'unfortunate habit of taking several right-wing Conservative MPs off on holiday, which gave the impression at least of impaired impartiality. Lloyd's successor in the Chair, George Thomas, commented on this in his memoirs and recorded that, 'when Selwyn Lloyd had been to Spain for a holiday, he had taken among others the Tory MP Jonathan Aitken with him. Selwyn never made any bones about having the company of the Tories.'[191]

Aitken argues that, 'I had grown up with Selwyn Lloyd long before he became Speaker [...] we had a close godfather–godson relationship'. In fact, their relationship was so close that, when Lloyd first became Speaker, he acted as a character witness at

the Old Bailey for Aitken, who was acquitted for breaching the
Official Secrets Act 1911. The fact that Lloyd and Aitken were
like family was excusable but the Speaker also took on holiday
Harold Macmillan's son-in-law, the far more senior Foreign
Office minister and Conservative MP, Julian Amery.

As seen previously, impartiality is key to the Speakership
and anything that jeopardises this would bring the whole office
crashing down. Lord Parkinson supports Lloyd's decision to take
political friends on holiday saying:

> Such friends as Selwyn had were all Conservatives. He couldn't
> stop his friendships and retreat into an ivory tower, and bear in
> mind he was divorced at the time. One of the things that hit me
> when we went there that night we took him home [after a func-
> tion] was that he was really a very lonely man.

The Commons does, however, expect the Speaker to give up his
or her political friends and retreat into the ivory tower that is
Speaker's House. That might seem unfair and unkind but that
is what the Speakership entails if the holder of the office is to
be deemed impartial. Holidaying with colleagues from one side
of the political divide leaves the occupant of the Chair open
to criticism.

Even other fellow Conservatives believed that Lloyd did not
give everyone a fair crack of the whip with Sir Richard Body,
the former Conservative MP, arguing that: 'Selwyn Lloyd was
not liked. He was not a fair Speaker. I don't think he selected the
speakers for debate very fairly. I think most Speakers have tried
to make sure that minorities are heard. I don't think he made
any effort.'

Despite this criticism from his own ranks, the former Plaid
Cymru MP Lord Elis-Thomas recalls that Lloyd 'issued that

famous statement at the beginning, "We are all minorities now", of the short Parliament of 1974'; he was going to give everyone a fair crack of the whip because no one party had secured an overall majority.

Selwyn Lloyd enjoyed mixed reviews concerning his impartiality when it came to selecting speakers and some of his critics came from his own Conservative side. Lord Weatherill, who was a senior whip at the time, recalled that: 'He [Lloyd] was a former Chancellor of the Exchequer, former Foreign Secretary, didn't know anybody in the House of Commons. They had to give him another deputy because he didn't know who to call.'

The fact that, according to Lord Parkinson, Lloyd was a very lonely man could be because he was shy and felt awkward among colleagues and so he failed to get to know other MPs well. Lord Naseby, who as Michael Morris was Conservative MP for Northampton South, agrees with Weatherill and remembers that:

Selwyn never learned any of the names of the new Members in 1974. In fact, Geoffrey Pattie [Conservative MP for Chertsey and Walton] and I went to see him. We complained because we used to stand up regularly and were never called. We learned somewhere or another that he hadn't really learned the names of any of us. So, he said that he'd noticed we'd been getting up but we'd have to bide our time.

For a Speaker to ensure fairness it is absolutely essential that he or she learns the names of each and every one of the more than 600 MPs. This is not an easy job but a Speaker must be seen to be giving everyone an equal chance and should not preclude someone from speaking just because he does not know their name. This is a weakness that none of the other post-war Speakers have been criticised for and lends weight to

the argument that a Speaker should have served an apprenticeship as a Deputy Speaker because at least this role enables
someone to learn all the names and gain greater knowledge
of procedure.

Members of the Labour Parliamentary Party tested Lloyd's
mettle on 25 January 1971, only a few days after he was elected
to the Chair. The incident arose when a group of thirty or so
Labour MPs demonstrated in front of the Table of the House
against the guillotining of the Industrial Relations Bill. Lloyd
had no choice but to suspend the sitting and Tony Benn, then
Labour MP for Bristol South East, wrote in his diary that a
group of MPs agreed to talk to the demonstrators in the tearoom
'but they were determined to go on'. [192] In the end, Francis
Pym, the government Chief Whip, got up and moved that
the question be put. This was agreed upon and when the
Speaker declined to hear points of order it brought the matter
to an end.

Fortunately, Pym came to the Speaker's aid because otherwise this would have been even more difficult for Lloyd to have
managed and could have been an early embarrassment resulting
in irrevocable damage. Lloyd did not have the benefit of having
already had experience in the Chair and so he certainly enjoyed
a baptism of fire into the role.

Lloyd himself wrote in some 'Impressions of the 1971/72
session' that 'Northern Ireland was a constant irritant' and
indeed it was an incident early on in his Speakership concerning
an Ulster MP which caused him great criticism. [193] The incident,
which took place on 31 January 1972, involved Bernadette Devlin,
the Independent Unity MP for Mid Ulster. Reginald Maudling,
the Home Secretary, gave a statement to the House on the
Bogside Massacre (Bloody Sunday) in which thirteen Catholics
had been killed by British troops in Londonderry following the

illegal march undertaken against the parade ban. When the
Speaker failed to allow Devlin to speak, she had to raise points
of order and got more and more angry about the fact she was
not being allowed to participate. Tony Benn described what
happened next in his diary entry: 'At one point, she stamped
down the gangway and went over and attacked Maudling physically, an extraordinary sight. She smacked him and pulled his
hair.'[194] She was dragged off the Home Secretary and removed
from the chamber.

Devlin, who had been present at the shootings in Londonderry,
had already accused Maudling of being a liar and a 'murdering hypocrite' but had not been disciplined by Lloyd for using
this unparliamentary language.[195] Benn believes, however, that
the 'Speaker, very wisely, didn't do anything about it' probably
because any action from the Chair could have made matters
worse.[196] However, not all Members shared Benn's view and
Lloyd's biographer, D. R. Thorpe states that, 'All Speakers have
their bad moments. 31 January 1972 was Selwyn's'.[197] The government Chief Whip, Francis Pym, warned Selwyn that sections
of the government took a dim view of his deliberate inaction.
Unsurprisingly, Selwyn felt the criticism deeply, suspecting he
had undermined the authority of the Speakership and jeopard-
ised his personal standing.[198]

Lloyd, realising the precarious position he was in, decided that
he had no choice but to make a statement to the House which he
did the next day:

I have considered what happened yesterday. When strong feelings exist or are aroused, there are times when the Chair can
appropriately be deaf or indeed blind. In my view, I went to
the absolute limits of tolerance, perhaps beyond them. What
I now want to make clear is that if an hon. Member uses

unparliamentary language or acts in an unparliamentary manner and when ordered to, refuses to withdraw or desist, I will not hesitate to act in accordance with the Standing Orders.

The reputation of the House and the position of the Chair are now at risk. That is something which I, so long as I am Speaker, cannot tolerate.[199]

Some MPs were still upset and Lloyd notes that there was an attempt at tabling a motion of criticism but this only attracted the signatures of Conservative MPs Sir Gerald Nabarro, Anthony Fell and Ivor Stanbrook. Interestingly, this indication of no confidence came from colleagues on his own side which showed that the Conservatives were not all prepared to rally to save a criticised Speaker who had come from their own ranks. Lloyd knew that his lack of action would be criticised but he firmly believed that any attempt at intervention from the Chair would have been futile. He felt that if he had used his disciplinary powers against Devlin, 'she would at once have become a martyr'. There might have been further riots in Northern Ireland, and the loss of more innocent lives.[200]

This could have been true but what no one has commented on is the fact that Lloyd himself could well have brought on the physical attack on the Home Secretary by consistently failing to call Devlin to speak in the main debate. At the time, there were only twelve MPs representing Northern Ireland in the Commons and, as this debate was about an incident in the Province, Devlin would have expected to have been called. The fact that the Speaker did not call her could well have frustrated her even more and made her angrier than she was already. The Speaker has a duty to ensure that minority and specialist views are heard and, as an Ulster MP and a member of a minority party, she should have been called. Indeed, only two Northern

Ireland representatives, Robin Chichester-Clark and Gerry
Fitt, were actually called to speak during the debate. Devlin's
colleague, Frank McManus, complained, in a point of order,
that, despite being present at the march, she was not being
called to speak. Lloyd did not heed this comment and Devlin
even protested to the chamber saying that, 'I have a right, as
the only representative in this House who was an eye witness,
to ask a question'.[201]

This was absolutely true and perhaps, if Devlin had not
finished off the sentence with 'of that murdering hypocrite' then
Lloyd would have been compelled to have allowed her to put a
question.[202] Lloyd's caution and reluctance to call someone who
he knew would cause trouble could have actually made matters
worse. In his private notes on the period, Lloyd wrote, 'Bernadette
Devlin had her outburst. I was much criticised for ignoring it, but
judging by her behaviour since, I was right (touch wood).'[203]

Lord Parkinson, who was present during the debate, agreed
with Lloyd's handling of the matter commenting:

Poor old Selwyn. What do you do when you have this extraordinary little Irish woman – brilliant, brilliant orator? It had all
happened in a jiff and it was a very difficult one for him to handle
but people felt he should have been firmer. But in a funny way
she was wanting to be martyred. She wanted this to be worldwide publicity and the more he imposed the penalty on her, the
bigger the penalty the bigger the story. So, I think in a lot of
ways, I was never a critic of his about that because I always felt
he showed rather a grown up attitude in not getting her more
publicity than she'd already got.[204]

Lloyd's inaction over Devlin's performance could well have
forced his resignation which in turn would have caused great

damage to the office. Fortunately for Lloyd he survived because many Members, like Parkinson, could see that any discipline from the Chair could have made matters worse and too few MPs were prepared to put their head up above the parapet and remove the Speaker. Once again, the Commons tolerated perceived weakness from the Chair in order to preserve the dignity of the office rather than protect the holder of it.

Speaker Lloyd took the unusual step of departing from a ruling made by his immediate predecessor. This arose from what became the Lord Lambton case which occurred at the end of Speaker King's period in the Chair. Lambton, the Conservative Member for Berwick-upon-Tweed, disclaimed the earldom of Durham which he inherited from his father on 23 February 1970 so that he could remain an MP. He requested, however, the right to be able to continue to use his courtesy title of Lord Lambton. King sought the advice of the Garter King of Arms who replied that when a peer renounces a title, he also renounces all titles and rights associated with that peerage and so the Speaker rejected Lambton's request. According to Philip Laundy, Lambton was warned by the Speaker and the Clerk of the House that he risked disqualification if he continued to style himself as a lord and used it on his nomination papers.[205]

Lambton was, however, re-elected to Parliament at the 1970 general election using the words 'commonly called Lord Lambton'. As soon as Lloyd was elected Speaker, Lambton renewed his request and this is where the volte-face from the Chair arose. Lloyd, having made his own enquiries, announced on 7 February 1972 that: 'In my view the practice of the House is that hon. Members should be called and described as they wish, and as they are known in their constituencies. I have therefore decided to accede to this request.'[206] The Labour MP Charles Pannell immediately tabled a motion seeking to reverse

Lloyd's new ruling. On 9 March, the question was referred to
the Committee of Privileges which later backed the stance Lloyd
had taken on the matter. In this sense, a Speaker is virtually all
powerful because he or she can make a new ruling which can
countermand anything that has gone before. The only way in
which a Speaker can be reined in is if MPs put down a motion to
overturn a ruling. The Lambton case, whilst in the grand scheme
of things is very trivial, shows quite clearly that a new Speaker
can reverse any decisions made by his predecessors so long as
the Commons does not summon up the courage to restrain him.

D. R. Thorpe believes there were two important reforms
introduced during Lloyd's period in the Chair: one was his
usage of the 'Blue Book' and the other was the introduction
of a third Deputy Speaker.[207] When Lloyd was elected Speaker
he soon realised the difficulty of ensuring fairness when calling
MPs to speak in the chamber. Although officials prepared a list
of those who had written in asking to speak and recorded next
to the name how often that MP had spoken during the session,
it gave no indication as to how long that Member had spoken for
or the topics on which they had debated.[208]

Lloyd therefore introduced the Blue Book which allowed him
to keep track of which MPs had spoken and for how long. Lloyd
described how he compiled the Blue Book: 'Every Member's
name was in it. I kept it up to date myself, entering the date,
subject and length of each backbench speech.'[209] This information was then used by Lloyd and his deputies to decide on who
should be called to speak in a debate.

Despite the Blue Book, Lloyd still found it difficult to remember
the names of MPs. Nevertheless, this was an amazing amount of
additional work for the Speaker to take on although it did show
just how much Lloyd was determined to be fair.

The introduction of the third Deputy Speaker was a major

reform for the overall execution of the office. During the post-war period, the House of Commons had seen fit to appoint additional Deputy Chairmen of Ways and Means on three occasions (Sir Robert Young in 1948, Sir William Anstruther-Gray in 1957 and Sir Harry Legge-Bourke in 1964) and they assisted in chairing proceedings in the chamber. However, during Lloyd's time this ad hoc arrangement was formalised with the office of the third deputy. On 13 February 1972, Lloyd expanded on notes that he had recorded which gave his impressions of the Speakership three months after he had taken office: '*Sleep*. This was a real problem, as the Committee Stage of the Industrial Relations Bill was going through [...] With only 2 Deputies it was not possible for me to be off completely any night.'[210]

Lloyd wrote this after the appointment of the third Deputy in 1971 but it gives a flavour as to why he wanted an extra pair of hands. Lloyd had seen that the Speakership had killed off Sir Harry Hylton-Foster and had driven Horace King to drink and ill health and so, at the age of sixty-seven, he did not want to follow suit. On 22 November 1971, Lance Mallalieu, the Labour MP for Brigg, was appointed as Deputy Speaker and Second Deputy Chairman of Ways and Means. This gave Lloyd the additional body he needed to ensure that he did not have to chair debates after 10 p.m. and so conserve his energies for the more important periods of the day during parliamentary questions. But Lloyd kept close control of his deputies and did not allow them any discretion when it came to choosing who to call. This was pointed out by his senior deputy and successor, George Thomas, who commented: 'Selwyn used to keep a pretty tight rein on his deputies [...] Selwyn made his promises [on who he was going to call to speak in debate] and it was up to us to keep them.'[211]

The creation of the third deputy also meant that there were

amendments to the Standing Orders in order to allow the Deputy Speakers to be able to 'name' unruly Members and to be able to accept the closure of debates. This meant that the Speaker did not have to return to the Chair at the end of the day's sitting nor if an incident occurred where an MP needed to be disciplined. The creation of the third deputy, plus the additional powers conferred on the Deputy Speakers, must have eased the burden on Lloyd. However, during the short, hung Parliament of March to October 1974, no third Deputy Speaker was appointed because of the closeness of the arithmetic in the House of Commons. This was probably the time when Lloyd could have really done with the extra deputy and shows that, in these instances, the office of Speaker can be completely beholden to the will of the two front benches.

On 2 August 1972, Lloyd announced that the Prime Minister (Edward Heath) had asked him to preside over a Speaker's Conference on Electoral Reform and that he had agreed so to do. Lloyd described that the Conference had twenty-nine Members although the average attendance was about half. It met once a week and Lloyd proposed that the Deputy Speaker be allowed to stand in for him from time to time but this was narrowly defeated.[212]

It seems Lloyd was also willing to delegate the chairmanship of a Speaker's Conference to one of his lieutenants. Whilst Lloyd undoubtedly enjoyed the grandeur of the office of Speaker, it would appear that he was not happy with all the work that it entailed and would do his best to reduce his responsibilities.

Lloyd believed that the only real achievement that the Conference managed was the change to election expenses. With the February 1974 general election imminent, the rules governing candidates' election expenses had to be altered because inflation had meant that the current regulations would prevent even a modest campaign being conducted. Fortunately, Lloyd managed to get the conference to agree and so the Heath government accepted its recommendations to increase the amount candidates could spend. This was included in the Representation of the People Act 1974.

When the February 1974 general election did not produce a clear outcome, Heath tried to put together a coalition government with the Liberals. D. R. Thorpe explains that 'some felt that the Speaker might have a significant role to play in any constitutional crisis that might arise in the course of the year'.[213] In previous years, such as during the 1931 financial crisis, it had been the monarch who had filled this role but by 1974 it was considered that the Queen could not play such an active part in the way that her grandfather had.

Lloyd felt that the Speaker engaging in any kind of horse-trading could seriously compromise his impartiality although his office and experience did make him an obvious choice for the role. In the end, the October 1974 general election quickly resolved the problem although the episode did show that the Speaker could well be called upon to sort out a constitutional crisis.

On 16 December 1974, Willie Whitelaw went to Speaker's House to discuss the current political position. Whitelaw told Lloyd that the only two people he could consult were the former Prime Minister, Sir Alec Douglas-Home, and himself because clearly there was now a big question mark over Heath's leadership of the Conservative Party following his two defeats at the polls that year. It therefore came as no surprise to Lloyd that there was a leadership contest and Margaret Thatcher became leader. Despite the fact that Lloyd was Speaker and therefore removed from party politics, this did not stop old colleagues from asking for advice. It is very doubtful however that leading Labour politicians would have approached Lloyd on similar grounds; Speakers never really discard their roots no matter how hard they try.

On 3 November 1975 Lloyd issued a statement saying that he did not intend to seek re-election at the next general election and later that month he wrote to the Prime Minister, Harold Wilson, indicating that he would be retiring in the very near future. Lloyd was clearly of the view that he should go mid-parliament so that MPs could choose someone who they had all seen in action. Waiting until an election would mean that new MPs would be part of the selection but would not have worked with any of the potential candidates. Jonathan Aitken also believes that his godfather 'had an intimation or two of bad health' and that he 'was suddenly realising that he wasn't as fast on his feet'. Lloyd retired on 3 February 1976 after being Speaker for five years and having achieved one last hurrah in his political life. He took the unusual step of staying on as an MP so that he could conduct the election of his successor and declared:

> To mark the fact that I am an ordinary Member I have decided, as is my right, to stay on as a Member of this House. [HON. MEMBERS: 'Hear, hear.'] I am grateful for that response. I have also noticed the uneasiness on the surfaces of the usual channels at the prospect of having yet another floating voter. Although I shall stay on, it will be only for a few days. This time next week, or thereabouts, I hope to be unprofitably employed either in the Chiltern Hundreds of Stoke, Desborough and Burnham or perhaps in the Manor of Northstead.[214]

Although within the rules, this decision was unprecedented in the post-war period because sitting Speakers normally resign from both the Chair and as an MP at the same time. Even though Lloyd only stayed on as an MP for a few days, it does show that a retired Speaker does not have to automatically resign his seat and could return to the back benches if he so wanted. Lloyd's action could well be used as a precedent for the future if a former Speaker did not want to give up his or her job as an MP and indeed this was mooted at the time of Michael Martin's departure from the Chair.

Whilst Lloyd had never become Prime Minister, he managed to finish his political career with one of the highest parliamentary offices. He was most definitely the 'comeback kid' who showed that politicians can survive career setbacks if opportunities present themselves. Having retired from the Speakership and from the Commons, Lloyd was elevated to the House of Lords although the policy of only giving a life peerage and not the usual viscountcy was continued. Having changed his name by deed poll so that he could incorporate both his names in his title, he became Lord Selwyn-Lloyd of the Wirral. Lloyd's period in the House of Lords was short-lived. He soon became ill and underwent surgery in London for a brain tumour that was discovered to be incurable. Lloyd died on 17 May 1978 thus ending a most remarkable political career that saw high ministerial office culminating in presiding over a Parliament in which he had served for so long.

Lloyd's successor, George Thomas, had served as his senior Deputy Speaker and Chairman of Ways and Means and so was the natural choice to take over in the Chair. Thomas was born on 29 January 1909 in Port Talbot, Wales and was the son of a Welsh speaking miner and the daughter of a founder of the English Methodist Church in Wales. Thomas's father, Zachariah, went off to fight during the First World War. It was discovered that he had been paying his soldier's allowance to a woman in Kent and so Thomas's mother had to go to court with her marriage certificate to prove that she was Zachariah's wife. Thomas's father never returned to South Wales and died of tuberculosis in 1925.

Unlike, his brothers and sisters, Thomas was allowed to continue with his schooling rather than become a miner or go into domestic service. He passed the scholarship examination and went on to what became the Tonypandy Grammar School. On leaving school, he became a pupil teacher firstly in Wales and then in Essex. Thomas completed his teacher training in Southampton and then taught in London and Cardiff. During the Second World War, Thomas volunteered for the armed forces but was found to be medically unfit for duty (although he was never told why) and so became a member of the reservist police force in South Glamorgan instead.

In 1944, Elizabeth Andrews, who was the women's organiser of the Welsh Labour Party and a friend of Thomas's mother, suggested that he put his name forward as a parliamentary candidate. Thomas was initially selected to contest the dual member seat of Blackburn with Barbara Castle but was worried that he would not be able to spend enough time there as it was so far away from South Wales. The Cardiff selections came up and, whilst he lost out by one vote to future Prime Minister, James Callaghan, in Cardiff South, he was later selected for the Cardiff Central seat. Thomas was elected as MP for Cardiff Central at the 1945 general election with a majority of 4,524. This seat was, however, abolished during the first Attlee government and so Thomas was selected for the newly created Cardiff West constituency which he won at the 1950 general election and then continued to represent until he retired from the House of Commons in 1983.

Early in 1951, just before the general election, Sir Charles MacAndrew, the Chairman of Ways and Means and Deputy Speaker, invited Thomas to join the Panel of Chairmen who

preside over the standing committees that examine bills. As
Thomas was the only Welsh MP on the Speaker's Panel of
Chairman, he was virtually automatically appointed as the first
chairman of the Welsh Grand Committee. This work undoubtedly gave Thomas the experience he needed to later go on to be
Deputy Speaker and then Speaker and so his future was mapped
out at an early stage of his parliamentary career.

When it seemed that Labour would regain power in 1964,
the Party's Chief Whip, Bert Bowden, called Thomas into his
office at the House of Commons and told him that if they won
the general election then he would be made Chairman of Ways
and Means. Thomas was delighted at this prospect but Bowden
added the caveat, 'Of course, if we have a majority of only about
half a dozen, we will have to give the job to a Tory, for we will
need the vote'.[215] Labour were returned with a majority of just
four and so the new Prime Minister, Harold Wilson, appointed
Thomas as a junior Home Office minister believing that the
Conservatives wanted the incumbent Chairman of Ways and
Means, Sir William Anstruther-Gray to remain in post. Within
a week of becoming a Home Office minister, Thomas learned
that Anstruther-Gray no longer wanted to remain Deputy
Speaker. Wilson quite graciously gave Thomas the option of
swapping and becoming Deputy Speaker as originally intended
but he chose to pursue a ministerial career and remain in the
Home Office. In the end, Dr Horace King was Labour's choice
as Deputy Speaker and Chairman of Ways and Means and, as
we have seen, later became the first Speaker from the Labour
benches. On his decision to pursue a ministerial career, Thomas
wrote: 'If it were not for the genuine misunderstanding about
Anstruther-Gray, I would have missed six years' ministerial experience, but I might well have become Speaker ten years before
I did.'[216]

Becoming Speaker much earlier would have meant that
Thomas would have probably retired from the House of
Commons a decade earlier than he actually did and he would
not have been able to give the service to his native Wales that this
postponement permitted.

Following the 1966 general election there was the usual ministerial reshuffle and Thomas became Minister of State at the
Welsh Office. The major event for Thomas in this period was
the Aberfan mining disaster on 21 October 1966 when a coal tip
slid down the mountain and buried the primary school below.
Of the 144 people killed, 116 were primary-school-aged children.
Thomas was at the scene within an hour of being telephoned
and he visited all the families affected by the tragedy. Later he
was criticised for allowing part of the disaster fund to be used to
pay for the removal of the coal tip.

In June 1967, Thomas left the Welsh Office to become a minister in the Commonwealth Office which meant that he spent most
of his time touring the newly independent African countries.
This appointment was short-lived because in April 1968, Harold
Wilson invited George Thomas to join the Cabinet as Secretary
of State for Wales. The highlight of being Secretary of State was
that he was responsible for the investiture of Prince Charles as
Prince of Wales which took place in Caernarvon on 1 July 1969.
All this experience surely made him a better Speaker when he
eventually gained the office than he would have been had he
been elected to the Chair a decade earlier.

When Labour lost power in 1970, Thomas continued on the
front bench as shadow Welsh Secretary and when they finally
regained power in 1974 he expected to get his old job back.
Thomas was shocked when, having been invited to Downing
Street to see the Prime Minister, Wilson offered him Deputy
Speaker and Chairman of Ways and Means rather than a

return to the Cabinet. Thomas was a firm believer in the United Kingdom and his anti-devolution beliefs meant that he was the only former Cabinet minister still sitting in the Commons not to be reappointed to Harold Wilson's Cabinet. He had to make-do with the vague promise that Selwyn Lloyd was getting old and that he would soon become Speaker. At this stage, however, the Prime Minister of the day still did exercise a lot of influence when it came to selecting who would become Speaker. The fact that Thomas did eventually become Speaker, as Wilson virtually promised he would, demonstrates this.

Thomas was Deputy Speaker and Chairman of Ways and Means for just under two years and during that time he took the office very seriously indeed. One of Thomas's biographers, Ramon Hunston, believes that: 'When George first became Deputy Speaker, he found it difficult to get used to.'[217] This is because he had been a loyal Labour member for such a long time and now he had to be apolitical.

Thomas had, after all, been a Cabinet minister and a very vocal campaigner but, despite this, he wrote in his memoirs: 'I resolved from the first day in my new role that party politics were ended so far as I was concerned.'[218] Despite this, he of course stood as a Labour candidate at the October 1974 general election because otherwise he would not have been re-elected to the House of Commons.

The impartiality which Thomas imposed on himself undoubtedly stood him in good stead when Speaker Lloyd did eventually retire in February 1976. Had Thomas made glaring mistakes and openly shown favouritism to his colleagues in the government then it is quite possible that the backbenchers could have asserted their right to choose their own Speaker seven years earlier. In the end, George Thomas was the obvious choice to succeed Lloyd and it established the pattern that anyone who

is chosen as Speaker should have had experience chairing the
House beforehand.

George Thomas was elected the 153rd Speaker on 3 February
1976. Bernard Donoughue, who was senior policy adviser to
Harold Wilson, recorded in his diary entry for that day how
Thomas had longed to be Speaker and was so grateful to the
Prime Minister for securing it for him. Donoughue also mentions
that it was rather sad that the new Speaker's mother was not
there to see her son elected because Thomas was 'a bachelor'
and a 'complete mother's boy, worshipping "Mam" as everybody
in South Wales called her. When she died the light went out of
his life.'[219]

Thomas soon realised that it was a huge leap from being an
experienced MP and Deputy Speaker to actual Speaker: 'There
was a side of the Commons that had remained hidden to me
throughout my thirty-one years there. It was as dark as the other
side of the moon, and it was unattractive.'[220]

The dark side was the pressure that was put on the Speaker by
the more forthright MPs who had no qualms about undermining the Speakership to get their own way. One episode when
this was apparent was when Speaker Thomas took the view that
supplementary questions after a ministerial statement were going
on too long and Members who had no knowledge of the topic
in hand were asking questions for the sake of it. He therefore
resolved to take no more than three questions on each side of
the House so that he could avoid the terrible tension that built
up with people waiting to be called and the trouble that would
follow if they were not. Thomas had witnessed this under Selwyn
Lloyd and he was determined not to make the same mistake.

Indeed, Lord Hooson recalls that 'He [George Thomas] would
say to me before he became Speaker, "If I were Speaker I'd
put that so-and-so [Dennis Skinner] down".' Clearly, Thomas,

as senior Deputy Speaker, knew the problems that Lloyd had encountered and wanted to attempt to overcome them by employing this method of working. However, Thomas wrote that 'the bully-boys were trying it on' and continued that 'many members were genuinely appalled that people were trying to force me into calling them and there was general approval when I told the House that such action was counter-productive'.[221] Thomas had to stamp his authority on the House at the outset; he intended to be completely impartial and could not be bullied into favouring those who shouted the loudest. Hooson remembers how Speaker Thomas managed this:

> I remember one marvellous day when I was with George in his office in the House of Commons and the Beast of Bolsover [Dennis Skinner] came in and said, 'George,' he said, 'You didn't call me today!' And George, wagging his finger, 'I didn't see you', he said. 'Oh you did!' 'Have you come to interview George Thomas, the Member of Parliament, or Mr Speaker?' 'Oh, does it make a difference?' 'Yes, it does,' he said. That was a typical George way of dealing with it and he said, 'If you are speaking to Mr Speaker, I did not see you today and I only call speakers that I see and I look around and I often must fail to see many and obviously I failed to see you.' The Beast of Bolsover is a hell of a nice chap but he nearly burst a blood vessel.

George Thomas was also under pressure from government and opposition whips when it came to making rulings. He wrote that key Members from both sides would come to sound out what his rulings would be on certain matters. They would then tell him that a poor view would be taken if the ruling did not go in their favour. Thomas felt that these MPs were trying to control him.[222]

When Thomas's memoirs were published, it was the first time

that any Speaker had indicated publicly that there was a power struggle between the Chair and the whips of the major parties. It is not, however, surprising that the party managers would want to be able to control the Speaker so that they could enjoy an easier ride in the chamber. Despite this pressure, Thomas was having none of it and he revealed how he threatened to resign the Speakership and then publicly announce the reason for his resignation from the back benches. This threat led to assurances that he would not be pushed around.[223]

Whether Thomas would have resigned the Speakership only a short time after having acceded to the office is unclear but what he did have to do was to show his strength of character and prove that he was his own man and not the creature of the whips.

Like his predecessor, Thomas had to deal with a House of Commons that was evenly divided and on 6 April 1976, when the Labour MP for Rotherham, Brian O'Malley, died, the government lost its overall majority. This meant that the House was even more prone to becoming extremely unruly. 'Whereas Selwyn Lloyd had boasted that he had not named or suspended anyone throughout his Speakership,' wrote Thomas, 'that policy was no good for me.'[224] It was not long before he was forced to suspend the sitting.

The Aircraft and Shipbuilding Industries Bill, which has previously been mentioned, had been reintroduced whilst Selwyn Lloyd was still Speaker and was in committee stage by the time George Thomas was elected to the Chair. The Conservatives opposed this bill and Robin Maxwell-Hyslop, who had become an authority on Commons procedure, set about proving that the bill was hybrid because some shipbuilders had been excluded from the legislation. If it were found that the bill was hybrid, meaning that it did not deal equally and fairly with every shipyard concerned, then it would not be allowed to proceed. Maxwell-Hyslop asked the Speaker to give a considered ruling over the next few days and he agreed to do so.[225]

Thomas admitted, however, that his 'advisers wobbled and changed the advice they gave' showing that the buck does stop with the Speaker because, in the end, he has to put his head above the parapet and make the crucial ruling.[226] The former Deputy Prime Minister Michael Heseltine recalls: 'The clerks, in advising him [the Speaker] had not given him the full quotation in the precedent they had put before him, a ruling by Mr Speaker Hylton-Foster in 1962.'[227] Fortunately, Maxwell-Hyslop remembered the ruling almost word for word and presented it to the Speaker.

So, Thomas ruled that the bill was hybrid. Maxwell-Hyslop believed that this was an important moment, not only when considering George Thomas's Speakership but also in defining the independence of the Chair.

When he [Speaker Thomas] had ruled in my favour, in 1976, that the Aircraft & Shipbuilding Industries Bill was 'prima facie hybrid', I moved down the Opposition benches to thank him (on his left side, of course). I was just beaten to it by the Leader of the House, Michael Foot, whom I heard say angrily: 'I never thought that you would do to an old colleague what you have done to me!'

George Thomas looked at him glacially, and said, 'Michael: Mr Speaker has NO OLD COLLEAGUES!', and turned away dismissively, to me, on his other side. I then thanked him warmly for his decision.

Maxwell-Hyslop believed that this was 'as historic a statement of the independence of the Chair, as Speaker Lenthall's famous response to King Charles I ('May it please your Majesty, I have neither eyes to see, nor tongue to speak, save as this House is pleased to direct me')'.

But despite Thomas's ruling, Michael Foot announced a procedural motion designed to overrule it. The motion proposed that 'any Standing Orders relating to Private Business, and consideration of the application of any such Standing Orders, are dispensed with'.[228] Thomas was annoyed and upset at the action taken by the government and later wrote: 'For any government to overrule the Speaker, as the Callaghan government did, is really so offensive that the Speaker ought to resign once the motion is carried.'[229]

Foot's motion certainly demonstrated that the government of the day can ride roughshod over the Speakership if it so chooses. Despite all the prestige and trappings of the office of Speaker, in the end it can be overruled by a simple majority in the Commons.

On the first vote, which was the Conservative amendment seeking to overturn Foot's motion, there was a tie of 303 to 303. In such circumstances the Speaker has to exercise the casting vote. The future Labour leader and MP for Bedwellty, Neil Kinnock, shouted, 'Vote Labour, George', but the Speaker followed a precedent set by one of his predecessors, Denison, who had refused to cast a deciding vote in favour of a motion with such potential power. He felt that a question of such significance should not be decided by the vote of the presiding officer but by the whole House. 'For these reasons, my vote has to go with the Noes and I declare the Noes have it,' announced Thomas [230]

The Conservative amendment was therefore lost and the House had to move on to the government's motion to approve the bill. According to precedent, if there was another tied vote then the Speaker would vote against and the bill would fall.

When it came to the vote, however, the government managed to win by one vote (304 to 303) to everyone's surprise. However, their victory was because Labour had broken their pairing agreement with the Conservatives and allowed Tom Pendry, the Labour MP for Stalybridge and Hyde, to cast his vote. Heseltine recounts: 'The symbol of the authority of the Commons is the mace and it was the authority of the Commons that had been abused. I picked it up with both hands and offered it to the jeering, ranting rows of Labour MPs.'[231]

At that point, Thomas had no choice but to suspend the sitting of the House for twenty minutes because of 'gross disorder'. A note came up to the Speaker's apartments from Margaret Thatcher, who was then Leader of the Opposition, saying that Heseltine would apologise immediately to the House.

Thomas was not, however, prepared to resolve the matter that night. He dealt with this potentially explosive episode when he returned to the chamber by standing his ground, which meant (according to House custom) that no one else could speak. He explained that the sitting was suspended until the following morning because of disorder in the house and promptly left the chair. 'There was a great roar of laughter because members had expected more of the earlier antics.'[232] Thomas's bold and decisive action at this moment established an air of authority and showed that he was the man to resolve such a crisis.

Thomas's biographer, E. H. Robertson, commented that his 'skills at maintaining order in the classroom when he was a teacher came in useful!'[233] It would appear that Speakers who had formerly been school teachers (such as George Thomas and Horace King) were good at keeping order in the chamber because maintaining discipline in a classroom is not dissimilar to maintaining discipline in the Commons chamber. The future Speaker Betty Boothroyd recalls how Thomas considered ways of maintaining order in the House: 'He [Thomas] used to say, "I think of little lines sometimes that I can use when there is a bad atmosphere. Just a line to make people laugh and to reduce the tension".'

Like his predecessor, he also ensured that he was fair when it came to calling MPs to participate in a debate. Whilst he did not have Speaker Lloyd's Blue Book, he did keep records of who had spoken in order to guarantee that everyone was given a fair chance. On one occasion, the Labour MP David Winnick questioned the Speaker on the basis on which he called MPs to ask questions of the Prime Minister. Thomas thought that this was an impertinent question and told Winnick, 'Everyone who has been called this afternoon has not been called more than once before. The honourable member himself has been called four times. I keep a register.'[234]

Thomas was good at maintaining order in the Commons chamber thanks to his good humour and his experience in the classroom. This skill was crucial in the late 1970s when the Commons could have easily had more unruly episodes and more occasions when debates could have been suspended.

When Mrs Thatcher tabled a motion of no confidence in the government in March 1979, George Thomas knew that the voting would be tight. Both sides of the House wanted to know how Thomas would vote in the event of a tie; he told them, 'once again', that he would be reliant on Speaker Denison's ruling and would vote with the government.[235]

As it was, the vote on 28 March 1979 resulted in the opposition winning by 311 to 310 and the Callaghan government resigning. Speaker Thomas was not required to use his casting vote. Had the Labour Party managed to find one more vote then Thomas would have had to have saved the government.

Despite his good command of the House, George Thomas has been accused of bias. It appears, however, that this depended very much on who was Prime Minister of the day. During the period 1976–9, Thomas was accused of being too friendly towards the Labour side and then, as seen at the beginning of this chapter, during 1979–83, it was argued that he was too close to Mrs Thatcher. Baroness Fookes, who was Conservative MP for Plymouth Drake at that time, has said that, 'There was a view, which I don't share, but there was a view of him that he enjoyed being popular'. Thomas very much wanted to be liked and sometimes this could be used against him. At the beginning of his Speakership, Thomas records that the Conservative Chief Whip, Humphrey Atkins, came to see him and 'then went on to say that several of his senior colleagues had told him that they thought I was too friendly with Cledwyn Hughes [former Labour Cabinet minister] and the Prime Minister'.[236] When Thomas challenged Atkins of accusing him of bias, the Conservative whip soon backed down which shows that, at that time, MPs did not want to openly criticise the Speaker in case it harmed the overall office.

It must be extremely difficult for a Speaker to relinquish all contact with long-standing political friends and, after all, George Thomas and Jim Callaghan had both served together as Cardiff MPs for more than thirty years. Despite this friendship, relations between the two men were often cold. The Prime Minister's adviser, Bernard Donoughue, recorded that on one occasion, when George Thomas had agreed to grant an emergency debate on British Leyland, Callaghan stormed back to his office and wrote a letter of protest to the Speaker.[237]

If Thomas had been overtly favourable to his old Labour friends then he would not have granted emergency debates, such as the one on British Leyland, which were difficult for the government.

It was during the period of Mrs Thatcher's premiership,
however, that George Thomas was seen to have favoured the
governing party as Lord Weatherill's comment at the beginning of the chapter depicts. Lord Elis-Thomas, who was a Plaid
Cymru MP from 1974 to 1992, has said that:

> I wouldn't like to point out the specific instances that he was, as
> it were, out and out biased towards the government because he
> would never get away with that as a Speaker because the officials
> would never allow that to happen but I did have a feeling that he
> had a care for the Prime Minister then that was beyond the call
> of duty.

There is correspondence between George Thomas and
Margaret Thatcher which supports this argument and displays
the Speaker's admiration for and friendliness towards her. On 18
December 1980, Thomas wrote to the Prime Minister indicating that he was considering retiring as Speaker in February or
March the next year. He ended this letter with: 'I content myself
for the present with saying that I shall *always* be grateful to
you for your friendship. Every blessing to you in your heroic
efforts to put our country back on its feet. You *deserve* to succeed
& I hope and pray that you will.'[238]

Whilst this was a very private note, it nevertheless shows just
how friendly George Thomas was with the Prime Minister and
how his personal political sympathies had shifted. Lord Parkinson
puts the closeness between Thatcher and Thomas down to their
shared Christian values: 'They were both Methodists and she was
quite a staunch Methodist, she was brought up as a Methodist
and George was too. They had quite a lot in common in a
way and she liked him.'

Mrs Thatcher herself confirms that their shared values were

the reason why they got on so well and enjoyed mutual respect and admiration: 'My respect for George Thomas, already great, was to grow over the years. He was a deeply committed Christian with a shining integrity that gave him as Speaker a special kind of authority.'[239]

Thomas's Christianity coupled with his traditionalism and patriotism aligned him with many of Mrs Thatcher's views. They were so friendly that he used to buy birthday and Christmas presents for her children Mark and Carol Thatcher. Thomas had a strong personal regard for Mrs Thatcher and probably felt that he had to show that, despite coming from a Labour background, he was not against the Conservatives. Nevertheless, Thomas went over the top and this is why fellow parliamentarians and commentators have noted a warmness to the Prime Minister that could be considered as an impairment to the impartiality that the Speaker is supposed to exude.

The one area where it can most definitely be argued that Thomas was biased towards Mrs Thatcher's government was his decision to drastically reduce the number of Private Notice Questions that he allowed. However, whilst he allowed forty-five PNQs to be asked during the first year of the Thatcher government, this was quickly reduced to just eight in 1980–81, nine in 1981–2 and a mere seven in 1982–3.[240] This is compared to the twenty-one he allowed in 1977–8 and the twenty-nine in 1978–9 during the final years of the Labour government.[241] These statistics certainly point to Speaker Thomas being guilty of giving Mrs Thatcher and her ministers an easier time than their Labour predecessors. In this Thomas was quite different from Speaker Lloyd who averaged about sixty PNQs per year and who was quite keen to be seen as a servant of the House rather than of his old friends in government. Interestingly enough, the journalist Edward Pearce later wrote that 'nobody complained' that Thomas allowed very few PNQs and this is really the only evidence that demonstrates favour being shown to the Conservative government.[242] Once again, MPs chose not to take on the authority of the Speaker for fear of bringing the office into disrepute. The lack of PNQs was clearly not considered important enough for Members to question the impartiality of the Speaker. The fact that Thomas decided to grant fewer PNQs during the first Thatcher administration, however, shows that he was prepared to take risks with the office in order to satisfy his own prejudices.

One of the reasons why Thomas decided not to retire from the Speakership in early 1981, as he had indicated in his letter to Margaret Thatcher, was because he was invited to read the lesson at the wedding of Prince Charles and Lady Diana Spencer on 29 July 1981. A letter from the Archbishop of Canterbury, Robert Runcie, set out the reasons why the Prince of Wales wanted Speaker Thomas to play a role in the Royal Wedding: as a Methodist he could represent the Free Churches, as Speaker he would represent Parliament and as a Welshman he could represent Wales.[243]

He also had one of the most famous and, thanks to his Welsh accent, distinctive voices in the country. And so, Thomas read Corinthians 19 to the 750 million people across the world who were either watching the Royal Wedding on television or listening to it on the radio. Never before had a Speaker of the House of Commons received such global recognition. Thomas's participation in the proceedings of the Royal Wedding served to put a face to the voice that had become famous thanks to the sound broadcasting of the Commons which began early on in his Speakership. Thomas himself wrote that: 'Nothing did more to open up the proceedings in Parliament and coincidentally focus attention on the role of the Speaker than the broadcasting of Parliament, which began on 3 April 1978.'[244]

Thomas's successor, Lord Weatherill, has commented that 'It's a great advantage to have an accent' and indeed it was this that helped George to become a household name. On the first morning of permanent BBC broadcasting of House proceedings, Speaker Thomas was asked to speak a little louder into the microphones to make sure his voice could be heard. As a result, the first 'Order! Order!' of the session boomed out in his broad Welsh accent – and a public profile synonymous with that 'Order! Order!' soon followed.[245]

Thomas's 'Order! Order!' became the opening to the BBC's *Today in Parliament* programme and so was heard by everyone tuning in. In the same way that Speaker Morrison's Scottish accent has received recognition, Thomas's Welsh one resonated with his audience. Unlike Morrison, Speaker Thomas was heard by millions who were listening to the programme on their radios. George Thomas became the most well-known person to hold the rank of Speaker up until that point thanks to sound broadcasting and because of the part he played in the Royal Wedding. These two factors meant that the ordinary man or woman on the street now knew who the Speaker was whereas previously such knowledge would have been the preserve of an elite interested in politics. Only fellow parliamentarians, journalists and those who had visited the House of Commons gallery would have seen and heard the Speaker in action prior to George Thomas.

The broadcasting of the proceedings of the House of Commons had another impact for the Speaker and changed the way that the occupant of the Chair had to handle the chamber. Thomas recorded that the character of the House changed because MPs who never usually spoke suddenly started

contributing in debates. Both sides of the House were determined to use broadcasting for their own advantage and so party
political differences became more angrily expressed.[246]

Thomas had to adapt to these new circumstances and ensure
that he maintained control over MPs who were determined to
participate in debates so that their constituents could hear them
on the radio.

Towards the end of Thomas's Speakership he was
called upon to preside over a House of Commons when
the country was in a state of armed conflict. The invasion
of the Falkland Islands on 2 April 1982 led to the unusual
step of recalling Parliament for a Saturday debate. Thomas
recalled that, 'From the moment I entered the Chamber
it was obvious that the debate was going to be one of the
most dramatic in recent times'.[247] It did not, however, turn
out to be anything like the Suez debates of 1956, the last
time that there had to be a special Saturday debate. Unlike
Speaker Morrison, George Thomas did not have to put up
with exceptionally unruly behaviour and was not forced to
suspend the sitting. Fortunately, this was because there was no
great division between the parties unlike in 1956. Thomas's
admiration and affection for Mrs Thatcher is once again
highlighted in the way that he summed up the actions of the
government during the Falklands War: 'The Prime Minister
showed remarkable courage and determination throughout
the whole of the tragedy, and she knew tragedy was inevitable
once the islands had been invaded by Argentina. But by her
action she saved the good name of Britain.'[248]

Whilst Thomas did have to suspend Labour MP Andrew
Faulds during the debate for questioning the Chair and unruly
behaviour, he nevertheless ensured a broad cross-section of
opinion was heard in the Commons chamber. His clear personal

bias towards Margaret Thatcher was not allowed to manifest itself when he was in the Chair.

Like his predecessor, George Thomas had to chair a Speaker's Conference on Electoral Reform. This time it was to consider and make recommendations on the number of parliamentary constituencies in Northern Ireland and it sat between July 1977 and February 1978. The Prime Minister, James Callaghan, had asked the Speaker to preside over this committee and Tony Benn explains in his diaries that the motivation behind this was to 'give more seats to the Unionists just to buy a bit of extra support for the Labour government'.[249] The Prime Minister can, perhaps, manipulate the Speakership to fulfil his own political ends; by setting up this conference, Callaghan was attempting to persuade the Ulster Unionists to prop up his minority government. As a result of this Speaker's Conference, the number of parliamentary constituencies in Northern Ireland increased from twelve to seventeen although this was too late to come into force for the 1979 general election.

George Thomas certainly opened up Speaker's House and he loved to entertain fellow MPs, members of the Royal Family and local and foreign dignitaries. A year after Thomas became Speaker he took the unprecedented step of inviting the Queen to dinner. Richard Barlas, the Clerk of the House at the time, wrote to the Speaker saying:

> It was an honour to dine with Her Majesty [...] I have since spoken to some of my fellow guests who were full of admiration for the success of the dinner and in particular for the part which you played in it yourself. Their only surprise was that none of your predecessors had thought of such an occasion.[250]

Thomas was clearly a pro when it came to promoting the office of Speaker and indeed himself. By inviting the Queen to dine in the Speaker's apartments he added a veneer of prestige not previously associated with the Speakership.

Whilst he adored Mrs Thatcher probably in the same matriarchal way that he adored his 'Mam', such comments flesh out accusations from the veteran Labour MP, Leo Abse, that George Thomas was a closet homosexual who was scared his secret would come out. Abse maintained that he had had to lend Thomas money to pay off blackmailers.[251] Whatever the case, his fondness for Mrs Thatcher and penchant for lavish dinner parties indicate Thomas's insecurity and an anxiety to please and receive praise. This is why he was so close to Mrs Thatcher and why he held such grand dinner parties. Lord Parkinson remarks: 'You know, if you're a single person, his mother died, he was very close to his mother, then adulation and public approval is really the substitute for family warmth.'

This sums up how George Thomas tackled the Speakership. He enhanced the role in order to fill the void in his life that was the lack of a family around him. With the Speakership often being called the 'loneliest job in Westminster', Thomas ensured his schedule was filled with parties and dinners to ward off loneliness, something that also manifested itself in his 'adoption' of Mark and Carol Thatcher, showering them with gifts.

In the end, Thomas decided to retire when the 1983 general election was called which happened to be two years later than he had indicated when he wrote to the Prime Minister in late 1980. Mrs Thatcher took the unusual step of reviving hereditary peerages and George Thomas was created the 1st Viscount Tonypandy which perhaps proves that there was an unduly strong relationship between him and the Prime Minister. However, the former Conservative MP Lord Naseby believes that, 'the reason he [Thomas] was given a hereditary title was more to do with the fact that Willie [Whitelaw] was given one, to maintain balance'. The fact that neither Thomas nor Whitelaw had heirs meant that the nature of their titles did not in practice matter that much. Like his predecessors, Lord Tonypandy took his seat on the cross-benches of the House of Lords to maintain the fact that once elected to the Chair all association with party politics had ended. When Thomas published his memoirs in 1985 they were immediately criticised for their indiscretion. 'Lord Tonypandy has […] now written his memoirs and it cannot be said that in so doing he has been as well governed by wisdom as he was when he was Speaker.'[252] The following day, a letter from James Callaghan was published which ended by saying:

> When the House of Commons honoured Mr Speaker's retirement nearly two years ago I then spoke as 'one old friend to another'. That was my genuine feeling and until Lord Tonypandy's memoirs appeared last week I had every reason to believe that the feeling was mutual. I am deeply sorry to find it is not.[253]

However, Callaghan's sense of betrayal did not outweigh his affection for Thomas sufficiently to prevent him from visiting the former Speaker on his deathbed.

Six

The Television Stars: Bernard (Jack) Weatherill (1983–92) and Betty Boothroyd (1992–2000)

Jack's great strength [...] was that everybody knew that Margaret Thatcher didn't want him.

– Lord Parkinson, former Conservative Cabinet minister, 2009

She [Betty Boothroyd] was the absolutely superb public face of Westminster. She had enormous presence and charm and she kept order better than any Speaker I've known.

– Tam Dalyell, former Father of the House, 2009

The close of the twentieth century saw the backbenchers exert their right to elect a Speaker of their own choosing. Both Speakers Weatherill and Boothroyd were most definitely the choice of the backbenchers rather than the Prime Minister. The televising of the proceedings of the House of Commons, which was introduced in 1989, meant that both Weatherill and Boothroyd gained household recognition which, apart from George Thomas, none of their predecessors had ever enjoyed.

Bruce Bernard Weatherill was born on 25 November 1920 in Guildford, Surrey. He was a twin and he and his sister were always known as Jack and Jill. His father, Bernard Weatherill, was a tailor by trade and was a Fabian Socialist who had once led a tailors' strike. Weatherill sent his son to Malvern College but did not allow him to go to university because he wanted him to become an apprentice tailor and go into the family business. On 3 September 1939, Weatherill enlisted in the Oxfordshire and Buckinghamshire Light Infantry but was then 'sent home to grow up'.[254] In 1940 he was commissioned into the 4/7th Dragoon Guards but he soon transferred to the Indian Army because he felt that he was the only officer without a title. Weatherill's days in India left a lasting impression on him; he became a vegetarian after seeing the Bengal famine in 1942 and he also learned to speak Urdu. It was also during his time that he saw a grave of an East India Company administrator which read: 'He was trusted absolutely.' This was the memorial that Weatherill himself wanted.[255]

After the Second World War, Weatherill returned to the family business and also became an enthusiastic Young Conservative later becoming Chairman of Guildford Conservative Association, Vice Chairman of South East Area Conservatives and a member of the executive committee of the National Union. In an interview with the BBC just before he died, Weatherill described how he became a parliamentary candidate and then an MP:

> It never occurred to me that I would be elected. I think they had some difficulty in finding a candidate in [North] East Croydon. We've got that strong link with the Indian sub-continent. I spoke, in those days, quite good Hindustani because I'd been in an Indian cavalry regiment. I was persuaded by Quintin Hogg [future Lord Chancellor, Lord Hailsham] to go down and stand as a candidate who more or less said to me, 'Don't get too excited about it, you haven't a hope in hell.' But we clambered in with a tiny majority.[256]

His majority was in fact 3,831 which was not that tiny considering the Conservatives lost the 1964 general election. Croydon North East was traditionally a Conservative seat and so Weatherill should have been more confident about his chances. He was so shocked at becoming an MP that he was really apprehensive about taking on this role at first.

> When I was elected in 1964, I spent the whole of the first day [in Parliament] locked up in the loo and around about 7 o'clock I was hoping to escape to see if I could find a canteen and get something to eat and slink off home. I heard two of my customers, one saying to the other, 'I don't know what this place is coming to Tom, they've got our tailor in here now.'[257]

Despite having a successful business, he was not from the landed gentry like a large section of the parliamentary party and Lord Parkinson remarks that:

> Jack had a slight problem with his background which he had no need to have but he did have [...] The Conservative Party he joined was not a particularly democratic party [...] office was essentially the province of the privileged and, going in when Jack did, that was very much the prevailing attitude [...] That would have given him a slight touch of paranoia about his background and the party's attitude to him.

The appointment of Sir Alec Douglas-Home as Conservative leader and Prime Minister in October 1963 was the last time that the party allowed their leader to emerge after consultation with the grandees. The election of Edward Heath was not only a move away from the privileged few choosing the leader but also a move towards allowing ambitious people from more humble beginnings to lead the party. Under Heath's leadership, Weatherill became an opposition whip in 1967 and a government whip when the Conservatives returned to power in 1970.

In 1973, Weatherill became Deputy Chief Whip, a position he continued to hold when the Conservatives lost power in 1974. Weatherill retained this post when Margaret Thatcher became party leader in 1975. Mrs Thatcher's secretary, Caroline Stephens, used to greet him with a hot, sweet tea when he had to deliver bad news.[258]

Weatherill conducted himself as a whip in a gentlemanly manner. He was prepared to honour the agreement that the two major parties would pair sick with sick on the night of the no confidence motion on 28 March 1979 which forced James Callaghan to call a general election. Had Walter Harrison, the government Deputy Chief Whip, not declined Weatherill's offer to abstain then the vote would have been a tie and Speaker Thomas would have saved the Callaghan administration in accordance with precedent. The fact that Weatherill was already seen as the bringer of bad news meant that his offer to pair on that crucial vote would not go down well with Mrs Thatcher. This is undoubtedly one of the reasons Weatherill was not offered a post in the new Conservative government formed following the 1979 general election.

By tradition, whips do not take part in debates in the chamber and so are not allowed to shine in front of their colleagues. Junior whips therefore rely on the Chief Whip to advance their careers. Humphrey Atkins's failure to give favourable reports about Weatherill meant that he never went any further in government. The whole weekend after the election went by and Weatherill did not receive a telephone call inviting him to continue as a whip or become a minister. Instead, as somewhat of an afterthought, he was offered the Deputy Speakership as Chairman of Ways of Means because the previous incumbent, Oscar Murton, had retired from Parliament.

Weatherill served as George Thomas's deputy for four years and during this time he did not get on with the Speaker. Despite this dislike, and a threat of resignation, Weatherill stuck it out and proved himself to be a competent Deputy Speaker who gained the respect of the House. In his memoirs, the former Chancellor of the Exchequer, Foreign Secretary and Deputy Prime Minister, Geoffrey Howe, recalls Weatherill's kindness when he was still Chairman of Ways and Means. During Howe's budget speech on 15 March 1983, he started by saying that: 'The longest Budget speech that I have been able to trace was given by Mr Gladstone on 18 April 1953.' The wrong century caused slight uproar in the House until Weatherill stepped in and gave Howe the chance to correct his mistake.[259]

A coup from the back benches, led by the Conservative MP Robin Maxwell-Hyslop, meant that Mrs Thatcher was not able to offer up the Speakership as a consolation prize to one of the ministers she wanted to retire. Indeed, the irony is that Mrs Thatcher had wanted Humphrey Atkins to be Speaker, the very man who Parkinson believes prevented Weatherill from gaining ministerial office. Maxwell-Hyslop argued that:

> What Margaret Thatcher, and her government, wanted was NOT an independent Speaker but a Speaker *beholden* to her for his appointment, whose disposition would, therefore, be favourable to the government which had secured his appointment.

This meant that throughout his period as Speaker, Weatherill had to be wary of some members of the government because he knew that the Prime Minister did not really want him to be there.

I think without a doubt they were trying to get me out because, after I'd been Speaker for about six weeks, quite late one night, Mr Dobson, who was the accountant in the House of Commons, infiltrated himself quite late at night roundabout six o'clock. He said, 'A word, sir?' So, I said, 'Come in Mr Dobson. What do you want?' He said, 'I don't know whether you're interested, sir, in any way but the Speaker gets a full pension whenever he retires. If you retire tomorrow you'll get a full pension.' I said, 'But Mr Dobson, I've only just started!' He said, 'I know. I just thought you'd like to know, sir.' So, I have a sort of idea that they might have put up Mr Dobson to tempt me.

In a term he would have learned from his time in the Whips' Office, Weatherill described the tactics used to undermine him as 'Black Glove': a perpetrator of negative campaigning would not leave a trace as to their identity like a burglar wearing gloves in order not to leave finger prints. Weatherill described how it manifested itself during his period in the Chair:

Black glove is a political phrase not known to too many people [...] rather nasty things are said and written about you and the great art is finding whose fingers are in it. Well, I did discover this. Margaret Thatcher had her spin doctors too notably in the person of Bernard Ingham [No. 10 Press Secretary] and some pretty unflattering articles appeared [...] and I must say that George Thomas wasn't all that helpful because he was up there in the House of Lords and he was frequently criticising what I'd done which is a disgraceful thing to do really.

Weatherill was determined to ensure that backbenchers had their say and were allowed to scrutinise the government. According to the journalist Edward Pearce, Weatherill believed that Private

Notice Questions, which were in the gift of the Speaker and
required ministers to come to the House to answer questions,
were the way in which the power of the backbencher could be
strengthened. Weatherill wanted to increase the number of PNQs
granted, and return them to the levels allowed by Selwyn Lloyd,
who had averaged about sixty per session. In his first session as
Speaker, Weatherill allowed forty-eight PNQs which were double
the number granted by Thomas for the previous three years.
Weatherill went on to grant twenty-six PNQs in the 1984–5 session
and then forty-three in the 1985–6 session which meant that ministers had to come to the House and defend their actions.[260]

  Such a stance, whilst popular with the opposition and backbenchers, was not greeted with the same enthusiasm by the
government. Lord Howe recalls that Mrs Thatcher 'was irritated
with Weatherill for appearing to be hostile'. Edward Pearce
described how this eventually came to a head in 1988: 'We should
adjust ourselves to a new kind of blood sport. It is called Jack
bashing. It will be practised by journalists close to the government
and by official spokesmen giving off-the-record briefings.'[261]

  However, Andrew Alexander, an independent-minded journalist, wrote an article in the *Daily Mail* entitled 'Sorry, there's a
fault in the Speaker', in which he said that 'Weatherill, though
a very nice chap – and perhaps why people are so reluctant to
admit that there is a problem – is not up to the job'.[262] The article
goes on to accuse Weatherill of allowing unruly behaviour in the
House and criticises him for not disciplining the Labour MP Ron
Brown, when he argued with him on 19 April 1988.[263] Alexander
compared Weatherill with his predecessor and argued:

  In some ways the House was spoilt by George [Thomas]. He
  was super – witty – and calming when passions were getting
  out of hand, firm and determined when sheer bad behaviour

threatened [...] Instead of that we had the absurd spectacle of a Whip doing the Speaker's job.[264]

In the *Sunday Telegraph*, Donald Macintyre wrote describing a private meeting between the Speaker and Norman Tebbit, the former Cabinet minister. Tebbit had gone to Weatherill to complain about the fact that he had granted the opposition a one-day emergency debate on a matter which was causing the government some problems (social security reform). Macintyre claimed that: 'The Speaker inferred, whether rightly or wrongly, that Mr Tebbit was threatening that if he continued to make life uneasy for the government he would find it increasingly difficult to hang on to his job.'[265]

Macintyre reported that Weatherill 'ended the meeting [...] by bluntly asking Mr Tebbit to leave' after a 'particularly bruising exchange'.[266] Weatherill's archives, however, contain an exchange of friendly letters between himself and Tebbit in which they both agree that what was written in the *Sunday Telegraph* was 'a travesty of the truth'.[267] According to the letters, the information was gleaned from a reporter overhearing a remark made by Weatherill at a private gathering.[268] However, the article itself explains that Tebbit's visit to the Speaker was the most high profile example of the 'grumbling campaign' by certain Conservative MPs against the Speaker. Macintyre's article states that these MPs sought to bring about Weatherill's resignation and were being encouraged by 'elements in the government itself'.[269]

Campaigns to remove a sitting Speaker are not unique to Michael Martin although unlike in that case, the moves to get rid of Weatherill were unsuccessful. Weatherill explained how he managed to survive:

One day Jonathan Aitken came to me and said, 'You realise Mr Speaker this is a put up job and they're trying to make you resign

[...] You've got to go and see the editors.' I said, 'I don't know any editors.' And he said, 'Well, we do!' And the result of that was that I began seeing the editors in the evening time. They used to come and talk to me and leading articles began to appear in the newspapers, particularly the heavy newspapers, saying how important it was to have a Speaker who would stand up to a powerful Prime Minister.

Aitken remembers advising the Speaker that he 'could see a journalist or two completely off the record' and he set about arranging the interviews. As a result of this, Edward Pearce recalls that Weatherill 'rung me up wanting friends in the press and I set about being that'. Another ally was Matthew Parris, the former Conservative MP who had resigned his seat in 1986 to become a full-time journalist and presenter of the weekly political television programme, *Weekend World*. Parris remembers how he helped the Speaker:

> I knew that Jack was really hurting and I said to him, 'Why don't you be our guest on *Weekend World*?' No Speaker had ever done such a thing [...] and Jack thought long and hard about it and he came on the programme and then I've no doubt, in fact Jack told me privately, that he was really trying to save himself and his Speakership from what was beginning to look like a media conspiracy inspired by his enemies mostly in government and I think he succeeded.

In the interview, Weatherill declared that, 'What may have been alleged is not going to put me off in any way from doing what I believe to be my undoubted duty'.[270] As a result of this action, Weatherill recalled that: 'After about three weeks or so of this, a very, very powerful emissary came from No. 10 late one night and said to me, "Mr Speaker, the Prime Minister asks if we may have a truce?"'

The television interview was a clever move by Weatherill and his supporters because positive newspaper articles which reinforced the message that the Speaker should not be bullied by an over-powerful executive followed. The truce must have been honoured and the negative press died away. What did follow was speculation about who would succeed Weatherill and this was undoubtedly a hint from his critics that they still wanted him to retire.[271]

Weatherill also had his critics on the Labour benches. At the Parliamentary Labour Party meeting on 30 November 1988, it was recorded that:

[Labour MPs] Dennis Skinner and Bob Hughes urged the Chair to make representations to the Speaker on the organised disruption perpetrated by Tory backbenchers during the speech of Gordon Brown, the shadow Chief Secretary, whose integrity had been impugned by an allegation that he had sought to alter the Hansard report of his speech. James Lamond [Labour MP for Oldham Central and Royton] said that the Speaker had been quite wrong not to defend Gordon Brown and to permit the disruption.[272]

This discussion allowed other gripes to be aired with it being recorded that 'The Speaker was also criticised by [Labour MPs] Ann Clwyd and Joan Walley for the unfair hearing which Labour women Members were receiving in the Chamber'.[273] At the subsequent meeting on 7 December 1988, it was noted that: 'The Chair reported on his highly successful meeting with the Speaker on the issues highlighted by the Party meeting the previous week which had resulted in the Speaker making a statement to the House and the integrity of the shadow Chief Secretary upheld.'[274]

Weatherill could not afford to upset the Labour Party and fight a war on two fronts if he were to survive in the job and so he offered them an olive branch in the form of a statement to the House.

It was not only the two major parties which had had cause to criticise Weatherill. At the beginning of his Speakership, he had faced a backlash from the Liberal Party. The creation of the Social Democratic Party in 1981 meant that there was a competition between SDP and Liberal MPs over who got the traditional amount of debating time allocated to the third party. On 27 October 1983, Weatherill announced that: 'I am sure that the House would consider it extremely unfair if in every debate, and given that we have 650 hon. Members, the Chair had to call a Member of the Social Democratic party and one for the Liberal party.'[275]

This ruling sparked criticism from Liberal MP Russell Johnston, who argued in *The Times* that Liberal MPs were not being given enough time to speak during debates.[276] The Liberal Party had had its nose put out of joint by the creation of the SDP because it had to share its debating time with them. Following the 1983 general election, the SDP had two Privy Counsellors (Roy Jenkins and David Owen) compared to the solitary David Steel for the Liberals. Privy Counsellors are given precedence when seeking to be called and this meant that the SDP was more likely to speak in a debate despite having eleven fewer MPs. David [now Lord] Steel, who was Liberal leader at the time, recalls that:

He [Weatherill] wasn't as kind to the Liberal minority as he should have been given the strength that we had and he wasn't as good as George Thomas had been in that regard so he wasn't as mindful of minorities. I think his old days of the two party system were still very much engrained.

Steel is referring to Weatherill's previous role as Deputy Chief Whip and believes that this experience made him wedded to the two-party system. Weatherill responded to this by saying: 'Well, he [Steel] would [say that] wouldn't he? That's not true. My predecessors never saw the Liberal whips. I made a point of seeing the Liberal whips.'

David (now Lord) Alton, who was Liberal Chief Whip between 1985 and 1987, disagrees with his former party leader and recalls how he used to meet with the Speaker:

> Each week we had a private meeting to discuss the management of business and to iron out any difficulties. Having been a Whip himself he fully understood the realities of political life and I not only found him to be immensely fair but on a personal level he gave me a great deal of encouragement and helpful advice [...] He believed passionately in the rights of backbenchers and he was also insistent that opposition voices should be heard. This won him no credit with Mrs Thatcher – but from my vantage point he had an undistinguished admirer.

Being a whip had meant that he had enjoyed a much closer association with the House of Commons than he might otherwise had done if he had become a departmental minister and this probably made him the skilled operator he undoubtedly became at overcoming all the various threats to his Speakership. When countering the criticism of him from elements of the Liberal Party, Weatherill argued:

> It was well known that I was the choice of the backbenchers and that I gave them all a fair run but, of course, the bigger [the party], the more Members of Parliament there are, the greater their chance of catching the Speaker's eye.

This is a view supported by many politicians who served with him. Dafydd (now Lord) Elis-Thomas, who was a Plaid Cymru MP, believes that Weatherill always ensured that minority parties were properly listened to. This is contrary to the view put forward by Steel. Of course, 'minorities' does not just mean the smaller parties because it also relates to special interest groups and differing opinions within political parties. The former long-serving and often rebellious Labour MP, Tam Dalyell, argues that:

> I think Jack Weatherill was one of the great Speakers of the House of Commons [...] He always had time for the awkward squad of which he called me the troop sergeant and, as such, I realised he was being entirely fair. He believed that the dissenters should give their opinion.

In many cases, the minorities within the two main parties were more numerous than the combined forces of the SDP and Liberals and so evidently Weatherill thought it fair to go on parliamentary strength rather than votes cast at the ballot box when calling Members to speak.

Weatherill worked with his team of Deputy Speakers in order to ensure that Members got a fair chance of putting down questions and raising matters affecting their constituencies.

> The truth is [...] that if I had studied the Labour Party for a thousand years I wouldn't have known as much about it as Betty [Boothroyd] and Harold Walker [his 2 Labour deputies] and I relied very heavily on them and Paul Dean [Deputy Speaker] [...] the list of those who were to speak was arranged by us all together, it wasn't just me, because they knew much more about the opposition than I did. So I think the Deputies are the great unsung heroes.[277]

Weatherill had no qualms about taking on the Thatcher government if it meant preserving the rights of the House of Commons. In mid-1987, the Thatcher government was adamant that MPs could not debate the efforts of ministers to prevent the publication of *Spycatcher*, the memoirs of the former MI5 officer Peter Wright, under the *sub judice* rule. Weatherill ruled against *sub judice* on the basis that the matter was being determined by the Australian courts rather than in the UK.[278] Weatherill recalled that:

> She [Margaret Thatcher] sent Michael Havers, the Attorney General, to the High Court to get an injunction [...] Michael Havers came to see me and said he'd got this injunction from the High Court and he'd assume that I'd be upholding it in Parliament and I said, 'Well, I'm not going to be able to do that.' He said, 'What do you mean? I've got this injunction.' I said, 'When did you last read Article 9 of the Bill of Rights?' He said, 'What's that say?' I said, 'You're supposed to know Michael. It says, "No court in the land can overrule the high court of Parliament".' I said, 'I don't intend to be the first Speaker since 1688 curtailing speech in Parliament'.[279]

The 1688–9 Bill of Rights lays down the limits of the Sovereign's power and sets out the rights of Parliament including the rules for freedom of speech in Parliament. Article 9 confers on 'proceedings in Parliament' protection from being 'impeached or questioned' in any 'court or place out of Parliament'.[280] It therefore has a very significant place in British parliamentary history in terms of relations between the Crown (the executive) and Parliament. What this episode does show is that Weatherill was clearly very conscious of his history and procedure which rather contradicts Tony Benn's point that Speakers are not interested in these matters. Weatherill was also standing up to the executive in a manner that compares well with the tradition started by Speaker Lenthall in 1642.

Weatherill was not, however, as strong on the *Spycatcher* issue as his obituaries and his recollection would make out because he did not allow a full debate on the topic when it was put to him by two Labour MPs. On both occasions Weatherill declined and on the second occasion he ruled:

> As the House knows, I have consistently ruled that there can be no question of proceedings in the Australian courts being treated as falling within the ambit of the sub judice rule of this House. The same would apply to any proceedings in the United States courts, although I have no knowledge of any such proceedings. With regard to the publication of Mr. Wright's book in this country, I have to rule that that subject cannot be raised in the House at this juncture. There are four relevant groups of cases pending in the United Kingdom courts, and all are inter-related.[281]

The legal wranglings had clearly moved on between the two requests and the fact that there were now cases being heard in British courts meant that Weatherill had no choice but to declare the matter *sub judice* when John Morris asked for an emergency debate. This was not, however, the case when Tony Benn made the same request three months earlier when Weatherill made it clear that there was nothing preventing MPs from debating the topic. Despite this fact, the Speaker still ruled that *Spycatcher* did not merit an emergency debate and so even though he ruled that it was permissible to talk about the topic, he did not grant MPs the occasion when they could make use of his ruling. On this matter, Weatherill clearly struck a balance. He ruled that the topic could be discussed, which infuriated the government, but he did not take the extra step of allowing a full blown debate on the subject because that would have been going too far. A Speaker has to be fair but he or she must also be aware of the politics which keep him or her in the Chair. Any Speaker who makes a complete enemy of the government side would not last very long and so he or she has to be very mindful of this intrigue. Weatherill clearly played the system well, probably thanks to his days as a whip, and so whilst he was prepared to challenge the government when he felt they were trying to prevent debate in the House, he knew that he could not go overboard for fear of losing the complete confidence of that side of the chamber. *Spycatcher* is a really good example of just how limited the Speaker's powers can be in reality because unless the Speaker is prepared to be forced out of office or resign over a matter then he or she has to know when to stop pushing the government. Weatherill made his point but was clearly not prepared to go any further.

Only a few months earlier, in January 1987, Weatherill had had another security issue to deal with in the form of controversy surrounding the BBC documentary on the Zircon spy satellite. The government had demanded that the programme, which was part of the *Secret Society* series, not be shown on the grounds of national security and the BBC complied. When Duncan Campbell, the journalist who had put together the documentary, published its contents in an article in the *New Statesman* instead, the police raided the BBC offices in Glasgow in order to ascertain from where his information came. Labour MP Robin Cook managed to get hold of a video of the shelved documentary and wanted to show the film within the confines of the House of Commons; the government applied to the High Court for an injunction. Although this injunction was dismissed on the basis of parliamentary privilege, Weatherill decided to ban the showing of the film in the House of Commons. This was because he had received a personal briefing on Privy Council terms from the Attorney-General (they were both Privy Counsellors and so able to discuss sensitive matters in confidence) dealing with the implications for national security.[282] James Callaghan raised a point of order with the Speaker enquiring about his ruling on the Zircon film and this was supported by Tony Benn and Michael Foot. The Speaker was clearly uneasy about this and so Benn decided to put together an amendment calling on the matter to be referred to the Committee of Privileges.[283]

MPs were clearly concerned that their rights were being restricted by having this information banned and so a debate ensued. Weatherill sympathised with this view and allowed Benn to move his manuscript amendment over and above ten other amendments on the order paper. The amendment was passed unanimously.[284]

Whilst Weatherill had obviously felt compelled to ban the showing of the film in the first instance, once he had the support of the opposition and a growing number of backbenchers, he knew that he had to use his powers to defend the rights of MPs. Afterwards, Weatherill wrote to Tony Benn saying: 'I am keeping a list of those who in my time as Speaker have, by powerful argument, changed the course of a debate. Your *admirable* speech yesterday will always be an example to be quoted.'[285]

Despite yet again annoying the government, who had after all applied for the High Court injunction, Weatherill gauged the mood of the House and knew that he had little choice but to backpedal from his previous ruling and allow it to be considered by the Committee of Privileges. Any other course would have led to fierce arguments on the floor of the House and criticism of his decision from all sides of the chamber. As also seen with the *Spycatcher* affair, Weatherill was determined to protect the rights of MPs. The constitutional lawyer, A. W. Bradley claims that Speaker Weatherill's delivery of a lecture on Article 9 of the Bill of Rights to the Commonwealth Speakers' Conference in Kuala Lumpur only ten days before helped form his decision.[286]

Whilst Weatherill was determined to defend parliamentary privilege, this was because he wanted to uphold the rights of backbenchers and of minority groupings. He freely admitted:

> I was a backbench Speaker [...] I gave the backbenchers precedence. Margaret Thatcher and certainly probably David Steel and others took the view that perhaps I was over-generous to the backbenchers but they were my constituency, they put me here.

As he lacked the support of Mrs Thatcher, he could hardly upset those who had put him in the Speaker's Chair if he had wanted to continue holding the office. In the end, the Committee of Privileges upheld his original ruling to ban the showing of the film decreeing that it did not infringe on the privileges of MPs.[287] The Speaker is, however, the servant of the House and by allowing disgruntled Members to refer the decision, Weatherill was able to deflect any criticism and still make a show of defending their rights. Weatherill was excellent at seizing the chance to get out of a difficult situation.

Throughout his time as Speaker, Weatherill was determined to guarantee the supremacy of Parliament and he did not want anything to detract from it as the great forum of the nation. At the very end of his Speakership, during Prime Minister's Questions on 12 March 1992, the Leader of the Opposition, Neil Kinnock, challenged the Prime Minister, John Major, to take part in a televised 'presidential' debate in the forthcoming general election. However, whilst restoring order, Weatherill threw in the comment, 'This is the public debate'.[288] It was his last Prime Minister's Questions as Speaker and so he was probably not concerned about breaking with tradition and making his view known on the subject. What is clear is that Weatherill did not want televised debates to replace or become more important than the debates which take place in the House of Commons. It took another eighteen years before such debates would take place during a general election campaign.

As well as the role chairing the debates, Tam Dalyell remembers how Jack Weatherill was superb at receiving guests from all over the world. In his obituary in *The Independent*, Dalyell explores this further:

> With his knowledge of Asian languages and Indian Army experience, Weatherill was a huge success with visitors from the Subcontinent. My abiding memory, however, is the way he greeted my guests Kayapan Ruini and Megaron (who had a ring attached to his lip), chiefs of the Amazonian tribes.[289]

As seen in the chapter on the Speaker's role, Weatherill was also used in an ambassadorial capacity. The former Labour Cabinet minister, founding member of the Social Democratic Party and now Liberal Democrat peer, Shirley Williams, recalls that when the Soviet leader Mikhail Gorbachev visited London in 1989 it was at the invitation of Speaker Weatherill and not of the government. Despite this fact there were opportunities for Gorbachev to meet with the party leaders.[290]

The Speakership had undoubtedly become a diplomatic tool with which informal and less threatening meetings could be arranged with foreign leaders. Weatherill's style, however, contrasted quite starkly with that of his predecessor in this respect because Speaker Thomas had revelled in receiving the great and the good from across the world. The fact that, on his mother's advice, Weatherill always carried with him his tailor's thimble 'to keep me humble' demonstrates that he was determined to keep his feet well and truly on the ground despite having risen to high office.

Of course, Weatherill was the first Speaker to chair televised House of Commons debates and television enabled viewers to gain a greater understanding of his role. Weatherill had always been in favour of Commons proceedings being televised because he believed that radio broadcasting alone, which only really covered rowdy Question Times, distorted the work of the House.[291] In the end, Weatherill was not successful in his wish to see the televising of the Commons until towards the end of his Speakership on 21 November 1989. Whilst his predecessor had been a household name thanks to being broadcast over the radio, television made the Speaker of the House of Commons a much more recognisable figure in British politics. Weatherill himself commented that:

> When I paid an official visit to America, you know that Question Time is broadcast regularly in America, when I paid an official visit the headlines in the *Washington Post* said, 'If the Speaker of the House of Commons was to walk down Broadway today wearing his regalia he would be instantly recognised. If he'd done that a year ago we would have probably arrested him.'[292]

Whilst Weatherill became nowhere near as famous as his predecessor, he did make the role of Speaker even more understood and recognisable thanks to television. Weatherill argued that: 'I took my role as being […] not a star role. I took the view that the Speaker was the conductor of the national orchestra: that the stars were on the floor.'[293]

Weatherill has been described by many as a truly 'House of Commons man' and this is thanks in part to his parliamentary career as a whip, Deputy Speaker and then Speaker, all of which focused on the internal matters of the Commons rather than what was going on in the country. He retired as Speaker at the 1992 general election and was awarded the customary peerage. Weatherill took full part in the work of the House of Lords and in 1993 he was elected alternate Convenor of the crossbench peers (a position whose duty it is to keep the non-aligned peers up to date with the business of the House) and following the death of Baroness Hylton-Foster in 1995, he became Convenor. When Tony Blair's Labour government proposed abolishing the right of hereditary peers to vote in the House of Lords, Weatherill was instrumental in helping Lord Cranborne, the Conservative leader in the Lords, secure an agreement to retain ninety-two of them in the House of Lords Act 1999. Like his predecessor, Weatherill was a eurosceptic and in 2006 he became patron of the 'Better Off Out' campaign which calls on Britain to leave the European Union. Unlike Thomas, he decided against writing his own memoirs saying, 'I'm not going to: too many confidences'.[294] Having been diagnosed with prostate cancer, Lord Weatherill died after a short illness at a hospice near his home in Surrey on 6 May 2007.

Weatherill's successor was one of his deputies, Betty Boothroyd, who was elected on 27 April 1992, the first day of the new Parliament following John Major's surprise general election victory. Boothroyd was not only the first female Speaker, she was also the first to be chosen from the opposition benches. Like her predecessor, she was also the backbenchers' choice.

Boothroyd was born into a working-class Labour background in Dewsbury, West Yorkshire on 8 October 1929. Her father, Archibald Boothroyd, and her mother, Mary, were both members of the local Textile Workers' Union and the Labour Party. Boothroyd herself commented:

I felt I came out of the womb into the Labour Movement. Throughout my life it's been like coal dust, I can't scrub it out from under my finger nails. I came into a family that was Labour inclined. I was brought up in that atmosphere where our house would be, even when I was a tiny tot, the committee room on local election polling day.[295]

Boothroyd was their only child and, because her father had thought that he would never have children, she was idolised. Her father was often out of work and it fell on her mother to support the family and, because of this hardship, they both pushed Betty to do well at school. They were both delighted when their daughter won a scholarship to the Dewsbury Technical College because they thought it would mean that she would not follow them into the mill.

When she was eight years old, Boothroyd was enrolled in the Vivienne School of Dancing in Dewsbury which was run by Vivien Meakin. As well as learning to dance, Boothroyd took part in shows and pantomimes. The actress Dame Thora Hird believed that this background helped Boothroyd enormously in her future role as Speaker: 'She's theatrical so there must be a touch of it goes into her work which means she will present something verbally just that little bit better than some of your MPs.'[296]

It is this stage background which led Boothroyd to leave Dewsbury just after the Second World War and go to London to become a Tiller Girl, the famous line of high kicking chorus dancers. Boothroyd herself admits that 'It was an adventure that was blown out of all proportion by the press in later years'.[297] Indeed, both Michael Cockerell in his television documentary and Paul Routledge in his biography both question whether Boothroyd was in fact ever a Tiller Girl on the West End Stage.[298]

Boothroyd herself admits that she 'never made it to the Tiller line at London's Victoria Palace or their second line at Blackpool's Winter Gardens'.[299] She was packed off to appear at a panto-mime in Luton and used a foot infection as an excuse to return to Dewsbury and so, as Boothroyd puts it in her autobiography, her 'Tiller days ended in disappointment'.[300] This connection with the Tiller Girls, whether it be exaggerated or not, nevertheless helped Betty Boothroyd in later years with her political career. It gave her that something special which others did not have and made her far more interesting to the media which helped to give her a much bigger profile than she otherwise might have enjoyed.

Archibald Boothroyd died shortly after Boothroyd's return to Dewsbury in May 1948 and this meant that mother and daugh-ter built up an even closer bond. Boothroyd set about becoming active in the local Labour Party and joined the League of Labour Youth. Her involvement steadily increased so that she acted as an assistant agent in the 1950 general election and unsuccessfully stood for Dewsbury Town Council in 1952. Following the local elections she quit her job with the British Road Services in Batley in order to work full-time for the Labour Party at Transport House in London. It was not long before Boothroyd managed to find work in the House of Commons when Barbara Castle, the future Cabinet minister and Labour MP for Blackburn, and Geoffrey de Freitas, the Labour MP for Lincoln, agreed to share her as their secretary. Castle was surprised when Boothroyd set about becoming an MP because she felt that 'she was more a backroom girl'.[301] However, Boothroyd felt that, 'I wouldn't mind doing this job. I could do it as well as anyone else could' and so she managed to get herself selected as the Labour candidate in the Leicester South East by-election of November 1957.[302] The Conservatives had, however, enjoyed a majority of 11,541 at the 1955 general election and so it was no surprise when

Boothroyd did not gain the seat. At the 1959 general election she contested the more marginal Peterborough constituency but the Conservatives managed to increase their majority by over 1,000 votes.

Having lost two parliamentary elections, Boothroyd decided to travel to the United States in 1960 to help out on John F. Kennedy's presidential campaign. Despite working on the Democratic campaign, Boothroyd ended up working for a Republican Congressman from Massachusetts, Silvio O. Conte, a man who was admired by the new President Kennedy and who had friends on both sides of the political divide. With all this experience behind her, Boothroyd returned to England in time for Christmas 1961 with renewed vigour to achieve her goal of becoming a Member of Parliament.

Geoffrey de Freitas had become High Commissioner to Ghana so Boothroyd could not return to her old job at the House of Commons. She was, however, fortunate enough to secure employment with the newly created Labour life peer, the farmer, Harry Walston. When she failed to be selected as a candidate for the 1964 general election, Boothroyd continued to work for Lord Walston who became a junior Foreign Office minister in Harold Wilson's government. In 1965, Boothroyd was elected as a councillor in the London Borough of Hammersmith although, with her sights still firmly set on Westminster, she only served one term. Again, Boothroyd was unsuccessful at securing a candidacy when she was beaten by David Owen (future Labour Foreign Secretary and leader of the Social Democrats) at the Plymouth Sutton selection meeting. In 1968, the veteran Labour MP, Sydney Silverman, died and so a vacancy existed in his marginal Nelson & Colne seat. Boothroyd managed to win the nomination to fight the by-election but the unpopularity of Wilson's government meant that she lost by 3,522 votes to the future Conservative Cabinet minister,

David Waddington. The Nelson & Colne Labour Party decided not to re-select Boothroyd for the general election although she managed to secure the candidacy in the nearby Rossendale seat. However, she fared no better there and lost this marginal Labour constituency to the Conservatives in 1970. All this rejection could not have been easy and the fact that Boothroyd carried on with her quest to enter Parliament displays her strength of character and sheer determination.

Boothroyd was finally elected to the House of Commons at the West Bromwich by-election on 24 May 1973. Her constituency was redrawn under the boundary review and so Boothroyd was selected for the new seat of West Bromwich West for the February 1974 general election in which she won by a massive 13,431. She increased her majority in October to 14,799 and was appointed as an Assistant Government Whip in Wilson's administration becoming the first female Labour whip appointed whilst the party was in government. Having experience in the whips' office meant that Boothroyd's preparation for the Speakership was very similar to her predecessor's. The similarities were to continue as she continued her parliamentary career.

Between 1975 and 1977, Boothroyd was one of the MPs who also became Members of the European Parliament before direct elections were introduced. She chose to remain at Westminster and when Labour lost power in 1979, Boothroyd joined the Speaker's Panel of Chairmen and chaired standing committees to examine legislation. This experience was good training for the Speakership because these committees are mini versions of the House of Commons. Coupled with the fact that she had served on the House of Commons Commission, the body which oversees the administration of the House, between 1983 and 1987, this background made Boothroyd an obvious choice to fill one of the vacant Deputy Speaker positions following the 1987 general election. On 7 July 1987, Boothroyd took her place as Second Deputy Chairman of Ways of Means, the most junior of the three Deputy Speakers. She was only the second woman in history to hold the post of a Deputy Speaker in the House of Commons, the first being the Conservative MP Betty Harvie Anderson. Anderson only held the post between 1970 and 1973 and felt compelled to stand down when her local Conservative Association kept complaining that she was neglecting her constituency.

Boothroyd immediately resigned from Labour's National Executive Committee, on which she had been a member since 1981 and where she had spent a long time battling the hard left of the party, because, as she puts it, they were 'no longer a threat' and Weatherill 'made my appointment conditional on my quitting frontline party politics'.[303] Despite the fact that the Speaker has no formal power over the selection of his or her deputies (in those days the party managers chose and then the House ratified the appointments), the occupant of the Chair nevertheless had a say over who was put forward to join the team before the introduction of Deputy Speaker elections in 2010.

Despite having had a female Deputy Speaker in the 1970s, it was still a bit of a novelty because Boothroyd recalls:

The Member who was talking at the time, who was making a speech at the time, looked up in astonishment and he said, 'What do we call you?' And I stood up and I said, 'Call me Madam!' They did! It stuck because although there had been a female Deputy Speaker before me, in Hansard it had always been recorded as 'Mr Deputy Speaker' and I wasn't going to have that. For about a week it was printed that I was Mr Deputy Speaker and, anyway, I took them on and I felt that I should assert my gender and I did.[304]

Boothroyd worked long hours but loved her new role and threw herself into it. She sat in the Chair from 4.30 to 6 p.m. and then from 8.30 to 9.30 p.m. When the House sat late into the night, Boothroyd also chaired from 4.30 to 7 a.m. She was fortunate enough to have a tiny bedroom in her office which she used during all-night sittings but she records in her memoirs: 'Whatever the hour when we finished, I attended the Speaker's noon conference, but it was an undeniable ordeal.'[305]

As the most junior of the Speakership team, Boothroyd clearly got the worst deal when it came to the allocation of who chaired which debates. However, it was undoubtedly this hard work and dedication to duty which made her a contender for the Speakership itself and so she was quickly tipped for the top job. Boothroyd knew she was in with a good chance and so, after a few years as Deputy Speaker, she was confident enough to commission the designer Hardy Amies to create a navy gown with Tudor roses embroidered on the sleeves for her to wear in the chamber. In her memoirs, Boothroyd comments, 'If Members thought I would look even better in the Speaker's robes, I was already prepared.'[306] That was clearly her agenda.

When Jack Weatherill announced his intention not to stand at the 1992 general election and, therefore, to retire as Speaker, Neil Kinnock, the leader of the Labour Party, was determined to ensure that Boothroyd would get the job. Even though Labour did not win the election, they were convinced that it was their turn to have the Speakership and at the meeting of the Parliamentary Labour Party on the morning of the vote, the suggestion that they should all support Betty Boothroyd 'was greeted with enthusiastic acclaim'.[307] So, with the support of Conservatives such as the former Cabinet minister John Biffen, Boothroyd was elected as the first female Speaker, and the first Speaker elected from the opposition benches, on 27 April 1992.

Unlike her two immediate predecessors, Boothroyd had been chosen by a contested election for the office. With the names of those who voted recorded in Hansard, one could give rise to claims that the Speaker would favour those who voted for her. In order to ensure total impartiality, however, Boothroyd maintains that: 'I never looked at that division list, that is the list to see who voted for me and who voted against. I never looked at that for well over a year so it didn't colour my thinking at all'.[308]

Boothroyd's first major decision was to dispense with the traditional wig that had been the trademark of the uniform associated with the office of Speaker. In her memoirs, she recalls:

Before I decided not to wear the Speaker's traditional full-bottomed wig, I took Clifford's [Clifford Boulton, the Clerk of the House] advice and sought the agreement of both front benches. 'Never forget that you are a servant of the House,' he advised. I would have been uneasy in a full-bottomed wig. Besides I had sufficient thatch of my own.[309]

The fact that Boothroyd was a woman undoubtedly allowed her to get away with dispensing with the wig because, unlike most of her male predecessors, she had a fine head of hair of her own. Her decision not to wear the wig, however, has meant that her successors have followed suit and the most famous part of the Speaker's uniform has now been consigned to the history books.

Boothroyd showed straight away that she was not afraid of disciplining unruly Members. On 2 July 1992, Labour MP Dennis Skinner described the Minister for Agriculture, Fisheries and Food, John Gummer, as a 'little squirt'.[310] Boothroyd required Skinner to withdraw his remark but he refused stating that the term was not listed in *Erskine May*. The Speaker ruled, however, that the term was unparliamentary and so when Skinner refused to withdraw the remark once again she ordered him to leave the chamber. Boothroyd had taken on the 'Beast of Bolsover', the man who had scared Selwyn Lloyd, and won.

Boothroyd's confident start was not enough to prevent a group of Scottish Labour MPs from disrupting a health debate in December 1992. The group rushed forward and stood in front of the Mace whilst Boothroyd's most senior deputy, the Conservative MP Michael Morris, was in the Chair. Morris had no choice but to suspend the sitting and he recalls that:

> I absolutely made the right decision to suspend. My error was not suspending for long enough because five minutes doesn't give any time to cool down. So, we had a debriefing afterwards, Betty, I and the other two [Deputy Speakers] and we agreed that the norm would be half an hour unless we felt that shorter would be better. From then onwards the sort of norm became half an hour. That would enable both sets of Chief Whips to get hold of their troops.

This came about because even when Boothroyd came into the chamber and took charge, the Scottish Labour MPs would not come to order. Madam Speaker demonstrated that she was not going to tolerate such bad behaviour because, when she returned to the chamber after having suspended the House for a second time, she adjourned the House for the Christmas break.[311] Boothroyd showed that she was not going to allow such blatant acts of defiance in the chamber.

Boothroyd overruled her deputy, Michael Morris, in April 1993 when he decided not to allow a vote on the Social Chapter during the debates on the Maastricht Treaty. Morris's ruling was too much for Tony Benn and he tabled a motion regretting the decision and asking for it to be reconsidered. Boothroyd comments in her memoirs: 'It was the first time the chair had been criticised in this way for twenty years.'[312]

Boothroyd was lobbied heavily from both sides of the chamber. It was paramount that she distance herself from Members in order to remain neutral and aloof whilst she took this important decision; she could not allow colleagues to have reason for accusing her of favouritism towards her old Labour comrades. In the end, however, she gave them what they wanted and reversed Morris's decision by allowing a vote. She believed that what she had done was right because she 'felt it in the mood of the House and the country'.[313] When reflecting on Boothroyd's decision, Morris has said, 'You have to accept it. She's the Speaker. But I did feel aggrieved, yes, but she was wrong. I personally think she knew in her heart she was wrong.' Boothroyd clearly felt that Benn's challenge to the authority of the Chair could have had greater repercussions and so she gave in to the pressure to hold a vote. The combined strength of all the opposition parties and the Conservative rebels meant that a vote could have been forced through against the wishes of the Chair. This would have totally undermined the Speakership and Boothroyd was not prepared to risk that.

Boothroyd's honeymoon period finally came to an end just over a year after her election as Speaker in June 1993 when the Conservative MP Michael Mates resigned as Minister of State for Northern Ireland, owing to his involvement with the financier Asil Nadir who was facing thirteen charges of fraud and false accounting involving £30 million. By tradition, outgoing ministers are allowed to make an uninterrupted statement to the Commons covering the reasons causing their resignation. Boothroyd, who had been assured by Mates on the telephone that he would not discuss the trial, however, felt it necessary to take the unusual step of halting the outgoing minister's

speech because she felt he was moving into *sub judice*. Despite
several warnings from the Chair, Mates continued with his
statement until at one point Boothroyd went as far to say, 'I
am now requiring the hon. Gentleman to resume his seat'.[314]
This serious sanction from the Speaker should have been the
end of it but the argument between Mates and the Speaker
continued and in the end he was allowed to finish his statement
to the House. Boothroyd recalls that: 'It was a full House and
they were all baying to hear what he [Mates] had to say and I
think that was the most difficult time I really had as Speaker
keeping that in order.'

The problem was that Boothroyd failed to maintain order
because she allowed herself to enter into an exchange with an
MP, which enabled him to defy her. The writer and broadcaster,
Gyles Brandreth, who was Conservative MP for Chester, wrote
in his diary that the Clerk kept urging the Speaker to get Mates to
stop. She tried and tried but he would not be stopped. Brandreth
concludes: 'On he went. It was agony.'[315]

The Mates affair undoubtedly undermined Boothroyd's
authority as Speaker and she thought that she 'would never
recover from it'.[316] In her memoirs she wrote, 'I was not wrong
in trying to prevent Mates from breaching an important rule; my
error was in fluffing it'.[317] Whilst Boothroyd had been temporarily damaged, MPs were not going to ditch their Speaker so soon
after her election and she soon recovered. Boothroyd would learn
from this early mistake and ensure that she never got drawn into
such a row again.

A month later, on 22 July 1993, Boothroyd was forced to use
the Speaker's casting vote when Labour put forward a wrecking amendment restoring the Social Chapter to the Maastricht
Treaty. Boothroyd stated in a lecture she gave in November 1997
that 'Every day I had in my pocket a piece of paper setting out

the way in which I would use that vote and an explanation to give the House for it'.[318] She therefore followed the rules observed by her predecessors and so, with the result being 317 to 317, she voted with the Noes because it was not her place to create a majority when one did not exist. Boothroyd writes, 'We learned later that my vote was unnecessary, because the tellers had under-counted the government's vote by one'.[319] She had demonstrated, however, that she was completely fair and was not about to break with the long-established conventions of the Speakership; Sir John Major has no complaints with the way she handled the debates. Major had only secured a twenty-one seat majority at the 1992 general election and this quickly whittled away to noth-ing following disastrous by-election defeats, defections and nine eurosceptic Conservative rebels defying the whip. Boothroyd always had to be prepared to use the Speaker's casting vote.

Any damage inflicted on Boothroyd by the Mates affair and the difficult time she had had with the Maastricht Treaty was soon overcome by her show of authority in the Commons chamber on 29 November 1993. On that occasion she was obliged to order Dr Ian Paisley, the veteran Democratic Unionist MP for North Antrim, to leave the chamber after he accused the Secretary of State for Northern Ireland, Sir Patrick Mayhew, of using 'false-hoods'.[320] Boothroyd recalls what happened afterwards:

About a couple of weeks later, one of the badge messengers came to me in the Chair, I was in the Chair at midnight, and he said, 'Mr Paisley would like to see you.' I was a bit scared. I said, 'I'm leaving the Chair. Ask him to come into my downstairs study.' Of course, he was a big man in those days [...] and I sat there at the end of my desk with all the chandeliers on and the Pugin sliver gleaming to give me a bit of confidence because all sensible people had gone to bed of course. And Ian Paisley came round the door and he said, 'I want to thank you. I want to thank you for the gracious way you threw me out the other day.' He said, 'I got front page of the *Belfast Times* [sic] and you got page 3!' I said, 'Come and sit down.' First and last time I've been a Page 3 Girl. All ended happily ever after.[321]

Speaker Boothroyd was not frightened to take on even the most fiercest and powerful parliamentarians. She had demonstrated that over a year earlier with Dennis Skinner and now she had proved once again that she was in command of the chamber. As one of her deputies, Lord Lofthouse, put it, 'She was the boss. Make no mistake about that.'

Boothroyd even had to take on the Prime Minister on 14 April 1994 when John Major claimed that Margaret Beckett, the deputy leader of the Labour Party, had 'peddled an untruth' when she asked him a question about elderly people being denied the right to hospital treatment on the grounds of their age.[322] Members immediately cried 'Withdraw' because, as with Ian Paisley, MPs cannot call each other liars. This prompted Boothroyd to stop proceedings and say: 'Order. I am sure that the Prime Minister will reflect and I hope that he will withdraw his remark.'[323]

Madam Speaker was not afraid to pull up the Prime Minister if she felt he was out of order. Major did not withdraw what he said, however, instead he altered his phrasing by saying, 'Despite the fact that what the right hon. Lady says is inaccurate'.[324] MPs were not satisfied with this and so Boothroyd had to step in again: 'Order. I do wish that the House would listen to the comments that are being made and not make such a row. I have asked the Prime Minister politely to reflect and I hope that he will withdraw what he said.'[325]

Major had no intention of withdrawing an accusation he believed to be correct and so he carried on. At that point

Boothroyd gave up trying which was a clear demonstration of the weakness of the Chair to reprimand the Prime Minister. Madam Speaker could have insisted and attempted to use her disciplinary powers but there was no way she would have won a vote which sought to suspend the Prime Minister from the House. In the end, Boothroyd justified her actions later that day when Labour MP Nick Brown made a point of order: 'Of course, I heard clearly the Prime Minister's remarks which, I have to say, I felt were unparliamentary. However, it is for me to decide whether the rephrasing that he offered was acceptable and I deemed that it was acceptable.'[326]

Madam Speaker managed to cover herself and explain away Major's defiance of her authority. Her options were limited; she could have stopped Prime Minister's Question Time and caused a massive row. Boothroyd chose, however, not to fight a battle she could not win whilst also making her feelings clear. This episode is nevertheless a good example of the impotency of the Chair when it comes to reprimanding a very senior government minister.

During her time as Speaker during the Major government, Boothroyd enjoyed excellent relations with the then Leader of the House, the Conservative MP Tony Newton. The same cannot be said, however, for the government Chief Whip at the time, the Conservative MP Richard Ryder. Boothroyd admits that she never got on with Richard Ryder because of her habit of calling 'time's up' at the end of Prime Minister's Question Time. This phrase came about because towards the end of Question Time Boothroyd's secretary, Sir Peter Kitcatt, used to whisper to her 'minute to go' and then 'time's up'. The Speaker simply repeated what Kitcatt had whispered in her ear. Boothroyd recalls:

Richard Ryder came to see me, after a while, and he was very concerned because he believed that I was saying 'time's up!' to

John Major, who was Prime Minister, who's back was to the wall
then, his majorities, sleaze, losing by-elections and all that. Nothing
was further from the truth. It was 'time's up', we move on.

Ryder himself refutes this allegation and believes that his relationship with Boothroyd was 'courteous and business-like' going
on to state that, 'As for her "time's up" phrase – it never, ever
bothered me. Nor do I ever recall expressing a view on it then
or later.' Boothroyd maintains, however, that she never got on
with Ryder believing that he 'was an establishment Tory [...]
and having a woman and having Labour with a Tory government was something that someone like Ryder could not accept
somehow'. As Chief Whip he had tried and failed to deliver the
former Conservative Northern Ireland Secretary, Peter Brooke,
as Speaker and so he probably resented Boothroyd for getting so
many of his troops to vote for her.

Boothroyd's Speakership also coincided with the 'Cash-for-
Questions' saga which saw two government ministers, Neil
Hamilton and Tim Smith eventually found guilty of accepting
money from the owner of Harrods, Mohamed Al-Fayed, for
putting down parliamentary questions. This episode of what
also became known as 'Tory sleaze' brought about the creation
of the independent Parliamentary Commissioner for Standards
whose job it was to investigate and report to a Committee of the
House which then determined the outcome. This new post came
under the remit of the House of Commons Commission chaired
by the Speaker. Boothroyd has stated that: 'Members who fall
short of our standards must be judged by Parliament – though I
would be quite relaxed if a review of the law of privilege that is
currently in hand determined that, where appropriate, Members
should be subject to prosecution in the courts on charges of
criminal corruption.'[327]

Unlike her predecessors, Boothroyd had a much larger job to do in ensuring that the misdemeanours of a few Members did not discredit the whole House.

Boothroyd was safely re-elected in West Bromwich West at the 1997 general election and was quickly re-appointed as Speaker in the new Labour dominated House of Commons. One of the first things that the new Prime Minister, Tony Blair, did was to change Prime Minister's Questions from two fifteen-minute sessions to one thirty-minute session each week. Boothroyd recalls that she 'was neither forewarned nor consulted about this – merely informed'.[328] Although she goes on to say she 'understood the thinking behind it and did not object' this was nevertheless an act of gross discourtesy to the Chair because it had large scale repercussions to the parliamentary week.[329] It also showed just how powerless even a well-respected and popular Speaker can be in the face of a mighty executive.

When John Major, who was now the Leader of the Opposition, came to see the Speaker, she made it clear that, as the opposition leader had had three questions for each of the fifteen-minute sessions, he would now have six questions at each of the longer thirty-minute sessions.[330] Although Boothroyd had been totally ignored, she did manage to make a point which demonstrated that the Chair was not going to completely kowtow to the new government.

The fact that the Labour Party had a massive Commons majority of 179 also presented other challenges to Boothroyd's Speakership. Boothroyd recalls that in 1997, apart from a few minor exceptions, none of the new Labour ministers had ever held government office. They did not understand that they should announce policy in the House before they announced it in the media and this was unacceptable to Boothroyd.[331]

Madam Speaker's frustration over this matter came to a

head on 5 April 2000, when the Minister for Sport Kate Hoey announced a new sports strategy on the radio. In response to a point of order from Conservative MP Peter Ainsworth, Boothroyd remarked:

> It seems to me that there is a situation developing in some departments in which the interest of Parliament is regarded as secondary to media presentation, or is overlooked altogether. I hope that Ministers will set in hand a review of procedures right across Whitehall to ensure that the events that took place this morning are never allowed to happen again.[332]

Despite this clear condemnation from the Chair, one of her critics as Speaker is Tam Dalyell who, even though his praise for Boothroyd is quoted at the beginning of this chapter, believes that: 'What I think she ought to have done was to be far, far tougher on the government making statements outside the House of Commons. I mean she would wring her hands and say it was awful. She could have done far more about it.'

Boothroyd defends herself by saying that, 'I've let it be known to individual ministers. I've certainly let it be known to the Prime Minister' about being annoyed at the government's failure to report important policies to Parliament before announcing them on the media.[333] She has also said that, 'Eventually, I called in the Cabinet Secretary and had a word with him about it. That improved matters.'[334]

Although Boothroyd enjoyed fame and popularity as Speaker, she is most certainly not without her critics. Dalyell argues that:

> If you asked me, now this is a very small minority opinion, 'Do you think she was a good Speaker?' then the answer is, 'No.' [...]
> She was very reluctant, in a way that Jack Weatherill had not

been, to give Private Notice Questions when I thought that the situation absolutely called for PNQs. She tended to be a bit weak in the face of government.

The statistics certainly bear out this argument because in many of the parliamentary sessions whilst Boothroyd was Speaker the number of PNQs allowed runs into only single figures. In the sessions following general elections, however, she allowed twenty-six (1992–3) and twenty-nine (1997–8) although this was still below the sort of numbers granted by Weatherill.[335] In response to this criticism, Boothroyd argues that: 'I think I was tough actually [...] but Tam [Dalyell] always wanted his own way and Tam came up with all sorts of ideas about Private Notice Questions so he thought he should always get them. They didn't always fit into the category.'

One noteworthy PNQ granted by Boothroyd was in July 1997 when she allowed Peter Lilley, the then shadow Chancellor of the Exchequer, to delay the new Labour government's first budget by fifteen minutes and ask about an alleged leak into what the Chancellor was about to announce.[336] Boothroyd argues that: 'The opposition believed there'd been a leak on the budget and it was right that I held it up in order to have an exchange across the floor of the House as to whether there had been a leak or not.'

Despite the Labour government's huge majority, Boothroyd had put down a marker clearly demonstrating the authority of the Chair and how it could be used to ensure that the opposition, however weak and small, could still have a say and put down questions.

Tam Dalyell is not Boothroyd's only critic. Sir Teddy Taylor, who was a Conservative MP for forty years, believes that:

I think you'll find a lot of people will say she was a wonderful Speaker. I must say I can't agree with that [...] She's the only

Speaker [...] whom I've gained the impression from her [...] the only one who appeared to have her personal opinions influencing the selection of speakers.

In his diary entry for 21 March 1994, Giles Radice, the former Labour MP and friend of Boothroyd, records that he had a meeting with the Speaker in her drawing room. She explained that she was having problems with the Labour leader, John Smith, because the Conservatives had been trying to embarrass him over council troubles in his Monklands constituency. The Speaker asked Radice if he would be her unofficial Parliamentary Private Secretary but he declined: he was too old but would, of course, still be her friend and adviser.[337]

The Speaker is, of course, not supposed to have any political friends and his or her advisers should be drawn from the House of Commons staff and not from the ranks of his or her former political party. Boothroyd recalls that:

The real story (so far as I was concerned) had nothing to do with Monklands. John Smith was leader of the Opposition. During Questions or in debate he was being severely criticized (perhaps about Monklands) by government benches. John's PPS was Hilary Armstrong but Hilary was [...] shouting and bawling and barracking as she was attempting to protect John. I reprimanded Hilary across the floor of the House, much to her embarrassment and John's also. Indeed she left the chamber shedding tears. John came to see me in my private apartments to tear a strip off me for the manner in which I had dealt with Hilary. Tough! So this is why I must have spoken to Giles about keeping an eye open about my popularity, or lack of it in the House.

Radice's next diary entry demonstrates just how close he was to the Speaker and how keen she was to rebuild some support with the Labour side. He recalls that Boothroyd telephoned him at 8.15 a.m. to ask him, as there was an opportunity for the Labour side, to put down a supplementary question on the European Union to the Prime Minister.[338]

This does, to a certain extent support what Sir Teddy Taylor has argued because Boothroyd was clearly giving one of her old friends the opportunity to put down a question and therefore giving him preference over other Members. Radice himself believes that the reason she asked him to put down the question was not because she was favouring the Labour Party but because 'She was pro-European. That was her bias.' Boothroyd herself believes that it was her duty as Speaker to ensure that both sides of any argument were discussed on the floor of the House:

> They [John Major's government] were not very good Europeans at all and I think there had to be a balance there [...] and the voice of those who felt about the European Union had to be heard and it wasn't being heard because the party in power was not very sympathetic to the European Union.

Part of the Speaker's role is undoubtedly to make sure that minority opinion is heard but this does prove Teddy Taylor's point that Boothroyd did not bury her views or her old allegiances when she became Speaker.

When John Major's government refused to allow the opposition a preview of the Scott Report, which under the direction of Lord Justice Scott had investigated the alleged arms sales to Iraq during the 1980s, Boothroyd supported the opposition. Whilst admitting that she could not force the government to release the report early, Boothroyd nevertheless stated to the House that:

> In my experience the questioning on any statement is much better
> focused when some steps have been taken to enable Opposition
> spokesmen and minority-party spokesmen to have access some
> time in advance to the text of complicated reports, provided steps
> are taken to maintain confidentiality.[339]

The reaction to this, as Boothroyd wrote in her memoirs was that the 'government's embarrassment led to my being accused, in the usual unattributable way, of being unfair'.[340] Whilst to some on the government benches this could have been seen as Boothroyd helping her old Labour comrades, she was in fact fulfilling the Speaker's duty of allowing MPs to effectively scrutinise and challenge the executive. Speakers can always be accused of bias but on this occasion Boothroyd was merely sticking up for the rights of the Commons.

In his television documentary on the life of Betty Boothroyd, Michael Cockerell argues that: 'Although reform can only come from MPs themselves, Betty Boothroyd's critics felt that she personally represented a major obstacle to modernisation. They argued that she supported unsocial working hours because she was so wedded to Westminster.'[341]

Boothroyd has said that, 'One mustn't run away with the idea that it is the Speaker who brings in reform. That is not the case. The Speaker is first and foremost the servant of the House.'[342] However, in response to calls from the so-called 'Blair Babes', the influx of women Labour MPs elected in 1997, to make Parliament more female friendly, she has also stated quite clearly that, 'I wouldn't dream of having babies in committees or in the chamber. It was either babies or me!' Just because the House of Commons had its first female Speaker, it did not mean that 'women's lib' would take hold in Westminster. Former Labour MP Peter Bradley believes that:

I don't think Betty really was always terribly sympathetic to women Members of Parliament, particularly the younger ones, and I know several who were almost reduced to tears and certainly felt utterly humiliated when they were trying to get a question out or to make a speech and weren't given the protection and sometimes felt the impatience of Betty in the Chair.[343]

When Boothroyd entered Parliament in 1973, there were only twenty-six other female MPs and so she had to have the strength and conviction to make her way in what was a totally male-dominated arena. In 1997, a record 119 female MPs were elected and according to former Labour MP Oona King,

There is also that syndrome of, you know, I had to walk six miles through the snow to work when I was a lad, sort of thing, or I was a lass as it may be with Betty and the fact that people have had to do that in the past does not mean that that is a sound basis for a future democracy to build itself on.[344]

Boothroyd was, however, determined to defend the traditions of the Parliament she loved. She was not prepared, in her view, to see its powers and rights diminished in any way by reforms such as shorter working hours because, as she herself has put it:

It took me so long to get into the House of Commons, so many years, so many campaigns and once I got there I was so dedicated and committed and, if you like, married to the House that it just absorbed me. It took over my life.[345]

This certainly explains why she never married and it also explains why achieving the highest office the House of Commons can bestow on one of its Members was so fitting for Boothroyd.

Despite some of the internal criticism at Westminster, Boothroyd nevertheless became the most well-known and most popular Speaker in history. Cockerell believes that, 'She helped to make Parliament sexy. She always had a keen eye for publicity and would always make her entrance like the star of a big production number.'[346] Whilst being one of her critics, Tam Dalyell argues that, 'as a public persona she did Westminster a huge amount of good'. The dignity and strength with which she executed her duties as Speaker undoubtedly commanded respect. Indeed, the way in which she carried off big state occasions such as the visit of South African President Nelson Mandela in 1996 and the fact that she undertook more foreign visits to other Parliaments than any of her predecessors meant, as Cockerell puts it, she became 'a political superstar'.[347] Radio had made Speaker Thomas a household name but the medium of television had made Betty Boothroyd just as famous a political figure as any senior government minister. The result of Boothroyd's personal fame would be that in future the role of the Speaker would come under the spotlight far more than it had ever done before.

Even though Boothroyd was undoubtedly the star on the Westminster stage, Sir Alan Haselhurst, who became Deputy Speaker and Chairman of Ways and Means in 1997, believes that she 'was a very collegiate speaker'.[348] Haselhurst has described how:

> After the formal meeting, the Speaker's conference, which takes place each day, where the clerks are present, the three senior clerks, the Speaker's Secretary, the Serjeant-at-Arms, we would retire upstairs to the private study where she [Boothroyd] would then tell us what she wished us to know, ask us about things perhaps as well.

Janet Fookes, who was a Deputy Speaker to Boothroyd during the 1992–7 session, agrees with Haselhurst:

She [Boothroyd] was very keen we should work as a team and she believed in taking us into her confidence as it were about problems that were facing the Speaker and the way we set about dealing with anything.

Boothroyd herself claims that 'I always backed my deputies. Whatever they did, I backed them [...] as far as I was concerned they were the team and they were right.' Geoffrey Lofthouse, another one of Boothroyd's deputies, agreed saying that, 'on every occasion she would support you openly', although she would tell you off in private if she felt you had made a mistake.

Sir Alan Haselhurst also remembers how Boothroyd wanted to look after her deputies when it came to the increased work-load created by the introduction of debates in Westminster Hall in late 1999. Haselhurst recalls:

I said to Betty that we would do an hour, the Deputy Speakers would do an hour [presiding over Westminster Hall] and that we would then use members of the Panel for the rest of it and she said, 'As much as that, love?' And I said, 'Well...' She said, 'I'd only do half an hour if I were you.' And so we did half an hour and we expected someone to relieve us.

Boothroyd undoubtedly included her deputies in the day to day decision-making and engendered a strong sense of team work thanks to the support and respect she gave to those who assisted her in chairing the Commons. Despite her great public standing and importance, Boothroyd clearly never got too high and mighty whereby she would not take the help and advice of colleagues in her team.

Boothroyd announced her retirement as Speaker on 12 July 2000 choosing to stand down during the course of a Parliament rather that at the end of one. Boothroyd gave her justification for this decision:

> As recommended by the Procedure Committee in 1972, I believe that there is clear advantage in a new Speaker being elected during the course of a Parliament. In particular, it ensures that all Members are familiar with the qualities of potential successors. My decision will give my successor a run-in before the general election.[349]

The reaction from MPs was a sorrowful 'Oh' and then spontaneous applause demonstrating just how popular she was with her colleagues. Cockerell observed that, 'The first Madam Speaker was that rare phenomenon in public life: a star who left the stage with the audience wanting more'.[350] Boothroyd retired at a time of her own choosing when she was at the height of her popularity. She did not have to suffer the indignity of being pushed out because she had gone on for too long and become tired. In this way, Boothroyd undoubtedly secured her reputation as one of the great Speakers of the House of Commons. Lord Lofthouse stated that, 'I felt sorry for some of the incoming Speakers who had to follow on from such a formidable lady'.

Like her predecessors, Boothroyd was elevated to the House of Lords and became the Baroness Boothroyd of Sandwell, the borough of her West Bromwich constituency. Unlike Weatherill, she chose to publish her memoirs shortly after her retirement although they did not provoke the sort of backlash that George Thomas's had received because she did not give away behind the scenes confidences in the same way he had. She has also commented on the Speakership since her retirement unlike her predecessor. Following the resignation of Michael Martin in May 2009, Boothroyd sent out a press release:

Speaker Martin has taken the initial brunt of the criticism levelled against the Commons for its failure to observe the high standards of ethical conduct expected of it. His apology on behalf of all Members for the scandals that have been uncovered merit our thanks.[351]

Privately, she was appalled at Martin for bringing the office of Speaker into such disrepute, although she stopped short of making this known publicly.[352] The importance and majesty her time as Speaker had brought to the office had been rocked to its very foundations by Boothroyd's successor in the Chair and her success surely contributed to his failure. Boothroyd has also criticised Martin's successor, John Bercow, for dispensing with the Speaker's ceremonial dress in favour of a simple black academic gown, telling him that he was 'letting the side down a little bit'.[353] In the interview with journalist and broadcaster Andrew Neil she made it clear she had invited herself to Speaker's House to tell Bercow how she expected him to carry out his duties.[354]

Boothroyd set extremely high standards and is clearly still determined to defend the office she did so much to promote. Moreover, her more recent speeches against the coalition government's unsuccessful proposals for reform of the House of Lords demonstrate her ongoing defence of and passion for Parliament's traditions and institutions.[355]

Jack Weatherill and Betty Boothroyd battled with governments which enjoyed massive majorities in order to ensure that backbenchers were able to have their say, although Weatherill faced far more criticism from all sides of the House than his successor ever did. Boothroyd managed to raise the profile of the Speakership and, thanks to her own personality and *modus operandi*, she became a worldwide celebrity. Weatherill's tenure coincided with televised coverage of the Commons and this helped public recognition of the office. By dispensing with the wig, Boothroyd made the individual Speaker more famous because she emerged from behind the shield of regalia. She became a star through the force of her own personality rather than because she held an office which came with a historic costume. They were both outstanding ambassadors to Parliament and models of what good MPs should be. Weatherill and Boothroyd's periods in the Chair were the glory days of the Speakership when it reached even greater pre-eminence. The strong image and reputation they had built up, however, would be damaged by the end of the first decade of the new millennium.

Seven

A Shop Steward in the Chair: Michael Martin (2000–2009)

Anyone will have a hard job after Betty Boothroyd, who has been a real star.
– Former Labour MP and shadow Cabinet minister, Lord Radice, 2000[356]

Michael Martin was the first Catholic to become Speaker since Sir Thomas More was elected to the Chair prior to the Reformation in 1523. He was also the first Speaker to represent a Scottish constituency for over 150 years and had risen through the ranks from the most humblest of origins. This background, coupled with the work done by his predecessors to improve the status of the office in the public eye could have made Martin one of the most renowned Speakers of all time. It will, however, undoubtedly be the controversy which surrounded his period in office and his ultimate downfall for which he is remembered.

Michael Martin was born in Glasgow in 1945, the son of a merchant seaman and a cleaner, and lived in a tenement in the Anderston part of the city with four brothers and a sister. As a Catholic, Martin attended the St Patrick's Boys' School in Anderston but, having moved up to Springburn, left on his fifteenth birthday in order to take up employment as an apprentice sheet metal worker with a local engineering company. He soon became involved in the trade union movement and was a shop steward for the Amalgamated Union of Engineering Workers, later becoming a full-time officer of the National Union of Public Employees in the late 1970s.

Martin's trade union affiliations propelled him into politics and he joined the Labour Party at the age of twenty-one. In 1973, he was elected as a Labour councillor to the Glasgow Corporation which later became Glasgow District Council. The Liberal Democrat MP, Vince Cable, who was also a Labour councillor in Glasgow in the 1970s, recalls that Martin 'was quiet and uncontroversial, and he stuck very closely to the line of his union and of his mentor, the MP for Springburn, Dick Buchanan'.[357] It was, therefore, no surprise that when Buchanan decided to retire as MP Martin was selected to take his place. Despite the Conservative victory at the 1979 general election, Labour did reasonably well in Scotland and particularly in Glasgow, where they managed to gain Glasgow Cathcart from the Conservatives and increase their share of the vote across the city. Martin himself was elected with a majority of 12,771 and secured a massive 67.8 per cent share of the votes cast in Springburn.

In his first term as an MP, Martin chaired the Parliamentary Labour Party's Industry and Economic Group sub-committee and he also served as Parliamentary Private Secretary to Denis Healey, who was at that time deputy leader of the Labour Party. Even though the Conservatives won a landslide victory in 1983, Labour remained the dominant force in Scottish politics with Martin holding Glasgow Springburn with an increased majority of 17,599.

In the 1983–7 parliament, Martin's experience as a worker in Glasgow was again put to good use and he was appointed to serve on the Trade and Industry Select Committee. He was committed to ensuring that workers' rights were preserved and that young people received the training they needed to become skilled workers. Martin was by now becoming a well-established local MP in Glasgow who fought hard for his working-class constituents and so when the election came he was returned with a 22,063 majority. Martin had managed to turn what was already a reasonably safe seat for Labour into an impregnable bastion.

It was the 1987–92 parliament that first gave Michael Martin his first taste of chairing committees of MPs when he became a member of the Speaker's Panel of Chairmen. In that role he became Chairman of the Scottish Grand Committee and gained experience of what it was like to preside over a large group of MPs. Sir Robin Maxwell-Hyslop, who had served with Martin on the Trade and Industry Select Committee, wrote that 'he was never a "Labour Whips' tool": he was always his own man' and clearly this independence had made him acceptable for chairing such a large parliamentary body.

During the 1992–7 parliament, Martin gained further experience when he became Chairman of the Commons Administrative Committee. Geoffrey Lofthouse, who was a Labour MP and a Deputy Speaker, decided to retire at the 1997 general election which meant that there was a vacancy on Betty Boothroyd's team. As this was a Labour nomination (Boothroyd had been Labour and the other two deputies were Conservatives) Martin's experience chairing various different Commons committees made him the obvious choice for the role. On 14 May 1997, Michael Martin became First Deputy Chairman of Ways and Means and Deputy Speaker and so was third in the pecking order behind Boothroyd as Speaker and Sir Alan Haselhurst as Chairman of Ways and Means.

Up until that point, five out of the eight post-war Speakers had served as a Deputy Speaker before being elected to the main job and so, when Boothroyd announced her retirement in July

2000, Martin was one of those considered to replace her. The parliamentary sketch writer for the *Daily Mail*, Quentin Letts, argues that he 'had seen Martin in operation as Deputy Speaker for some time and was not impressed by his grasp of detail or his projection of character'. Nevertheless, Michael Martin was one of the twelve candidates who put their names forward for the Speakership along with the other deputies, Sir Alan Haselhurst and the Conservative MP Sir Michael Lord. When asked, Baroness Boothroyd, has said that, 'It never entered my head that he would be a candidate [...] I could never believe that he even wanted it.'

Michael Martin won the election held on 23 October 2000 and became the 156th Speaker of the House of Commons. The manner in which he was elected, however, was not a good start to his period in the Chair because, as the former Labour MP Chris Mullin wrote in his diary, Members voted according to their tribe: most of Labour supported Michael Martin and most of the Tories went for George Young.[358]

Martin did not even manage to find someone from the opposition benches to second his nomination in order to demonstrate that he enjoyed cross-party support – vital for a successful Speakership. Moreover, the former Labour MP Giles Radice recorded that, 'It is noticeable that, contrary to custom, many Tories do not vote for Michael and eight actually vote against him.'[359]

Mullin also noted that that the Tories rather thought that, by convention, it was their turn to take the Speakership.[360] Although, as already discussed, this convention of alternating the Speakership between the two main political parties was a very recent phenomenon, the Conservatives had put up a very credible candidate (who had the support of the Labour government front bench) but had been blocked by the massive Labour majority on the back benches. Mullin recorded that there was unease in the Labour ranks: many were of the opinion that Martin was not up to the job, and the clerks agreed.[361] Knowing this, Labour backbenchers were still prepared to vote for Martin because, as Mullin goes on to admit, 'I should have voted for George [Young], but faced with a choice between an Etonian baronet and a lad from the slums of Glasgow, my heart over-ruled my head'.[362] Labour had voted for one of their own for ideological reasons rather than considering who would best serve the House.

Criticism of Michael Martin began from the outset. The former political commentator for *The Times*, Peter Riddell, wrote on the day after Martin's election that: 'The worst candidate for Speaker was last night elected in the worst possible way. Michael Martin is a mediocrity who has never shown the potential to fulfil the demands of the Speakership.'[363]

Worse still was the onslaught that Martin was going to receive from the *Daily Mail*'s Quentin Letts, who dubbed him 'Gorbals Mick'.[364] Letts explains how he came by the nickname:

I came up with it on the day of his election and included it in my *Daily Mail* sketch that day. Martin's campaign for the Speakership [...] made much of his Glaswegian background. They really played that part of the thing hard. On the morning of the Speakership election, Michael White of *The Guardian* was refer-ring to him in matey fashion as 'Mick Martin'. I had not heard him called 'Mick' before and it struck me that we had, here, an element of him being hyped as an ordinary Joe [...] Another thing I should point out is that *Private Eye* for many years referred to Charlie Wilson, former editor of *The Times*, as 'Gorbals Wilson', so there was a precedent for 'Gorbals' being used as a nickname for cartoon shorthand for someone from Glasgow.

This catchy nickname stuck with Michael Martin throughout
his nearly nine years as Speaker, often used by other journalists
in their columns. Martin's supporters believed that he was the
victim of 'overt class prejudice' and speculated that the nickname contained 'anti-Catholic overtones'.[365] Martin put it down
to ignorance because he did not even come from the Gorbals
part of Glasgow. The Speaker was nevertheless so incensed by
the 'Gorbals Mick' branding that he attempted to get his own
back on its creator. Letts recalls:

> It was made known to me that if I persisted with my criticisms of
> Martin, my Commons pass would be withdrawn. This would, in
> effect, prevent me doing my job – though I thought it through,
> and reckoned it would have been possible to sketch from the
> public gallery (the Strangers' Gallery) [...] the managing director
> of the *Mail*, Robin Esser, took the Serjeant (at Arms) out for a
> drink at the Garrick to calm down officialdom.

This was an extremely drastic stance from a Speaker clearly
ruffled by the 'Gorbals Mick' moniker given to him. As a politician, Martin should have been used to being criticised and
this move was an abuse of his power and a total over-reaction.
During his Speakership, Martin became increasingly concerned
about the criticism levelled against him by journalists and in 2007
it emerged that he had spent more than £20,000 of taxpayers'
money on the services of the libel firm Carter-Ruck who sent
off warning letters to newspapers which had published negative
stories.[366] In contrast, Speaker Weatherill had worked with the
press when criticised in the late 1980s; all Martin did was to fuel
even more bad publicity.

Martin was, however, the first Speaker to court the media in a
very direct manner, something which had been growing indirectly

over the years since George Thomas became the first Speaker to become a household name. One of Martin's first acts as Speaker was to hold a press conference at Speaker's House. No previous Speaker had ever done such a thing. It was expected that Martin would outline his proposals for parliamentary reform but instead Letts branded him 'a cautious old pussycat'.[367]

The so-called 'Blair Babes', the new large intake of female Labour MPs first elected in 1997, thought that Martin was going to be much more family friendly than Betty Boothroyd had been and so they had backed him over the preferred candidate of the leadership. This press conference, however, gave the first signal that Martin was actually a reversion to the old type of Speaker who did not see it as his job to take a leading role in effecting procedural reform, although it did show Martin seeking a public profile, wanting everyone to know what he was doing. Martin's employment of Mike Granatt, a former director of the Government Information Service, as his senior media adviser also demonstrated the growing need for the Speaker to project himself beyond the confines of the Commons, in particular from the media. Speaker Martin decided not to reinstate the traditional full-bottomed wig that Betty Boothroyd had chosen not to wear. Martin gave his reason for this during his only television interview whilst Speaker: 'The tradition I did get rid of was the wig because I didn't think the wig would have sat well on me as an individual.'[368]

Martin also chose to alter the customary Speaker's uniform by dispensing with traditional stockings in favour of black, flannel trousers and wearing a normal pair of black Oxfords rather than shoes with a buckle and Tudor heel. Unlike his predecessor, Martin did not seek the permission of the two front benches to change his uniform. Perhaps he felt that this was unnecessary because the wig had already been discarded but it was also an assertion of his newfound authority. In April 2002, the Speaker's advisers put pressure on Martin to wear the wig when the Queen addressed Parliament on the occasion of her Golden Jubilee. When Martin told them that he did not have a wig to wear, they went and found one – but Martin still insisted that he would not wear it.[369] Martin overcame this attempt to bring back the wig; he was not prepared to be coerced into doing something he did not want to do. He was in charge and that was that.

Speaker Martin did not experience as close a relationship with his deputies as Betty Boothroyd had enjoyed. Unlike his predecessor, he had beaten two of his Deputy Speakers in the election for the Chair. Sir Alan Haselhurst, who was the most senior deputy and one of those Martin had beaten to become Speaker, has said how much Boothroyd would take the team into her confidence, often retiring upstairs after formal meetings for a chat. Haselhurst has said of Michael Martin that: 'In the nine years that he was Speaker, I never once went upstairs. He didn't talk to us very much, and increasingly he left the work of compiling the lists and so on to the deputies. In that sense there was a detachment about him.'[370]

Furthermore, Haselhurst recalls that even the formal meetings in the Speaker's Study 'were relatively short and he rarely, put it this way, unbended to us about things'. With such a lack of a collegiate approach to the Speakership, Martin was not a team player. This placed a greater burden on Martin himself.

The class struggle was a recurring theme throughout Martin's Speakership. A year after he was chosen Speaker, Martin sacked the Diary Secretary, Charlotte Every, for allegedly being too posh and a 'typical Sloane Ranger'.[371] The final straw was apparently when she addressed him as 'Mr Martin' rather than as 'Mr Speaker'.[372] Next to go, in May 2003, was the veteran Speaker's Secretary, Sir Nicolas Bevan, who had served since 1993, allegedly because Martin found him to be 'too pompous'.[373] In June 2007, the upper class Serjeant-at-Arms, Major-General Peter Grant Peterkin, also fell victim to Speaker Martin's class war because, according to Greg Hurst, Political Correspondent for *The Times*, of 'his poor relationship with [...] the Speaker, who is notoriously prickly about his own working-class background in Glasgow'.[374]

These were not the only staffing problems during the Martin Speakership. Bevan's replacement as Speaker's Secretary, the former Crown Prosecution Service lawyer, Roger Daw, only lasted eighteen months in the job before he felt compelled to resign. Simon Walters, the Political Editor of the *Mail on Sunday* wrote that Daw resigned in December 2004 following a series of rows with the Speaker which 'included Mr Martin accusing Mr Daw, his principal adviser, of entering his study without permission and claiming his aide did not know enough about his ceremonial role, including which outfits to wear'.[375] Peter Riddell believes that Martin 'found it difficult to deal with people from different, more middle and particularly upper class backgrounds' and this explains why he fell out with so many of his key office staff. He, of course, had to employ people with whom he felt he could work effectively but at the same time he needed those who knew the history of the office in order to continue its traditions, regardless of their background.

Martin did, however, use his working-class background as a force for good whilst he was Speaker. In the only television interview he gave during his time in office, Martin stated:

When I came in here to the House, I discovered that we have excellent craftsmen with this lovely work – furniture restorers, upholsterers, then your traditional construction crafts, electricians and plumbers but no one serving an apprenticeship. The

Clerk of the House said, 'You can do anything you want Mr Speaker.' I said, 'Right, I want the construction people in here. There are schools across the river. Get the pupils from that school to get day release and we're getting an apprenticeship scheme going.' I've been able to do, as Speaker, what I wanted someone to do for me – give me a skill. I got a skill as a metal worker and I was pleased at that and I've been able to do it here and I'm proud of that.[376]

This scheme demonstrated that the Speakership could have a role which extended beyond the House of Commons.

The way in which Martin was elected, with an obvious reliance on the support of the overwhelming numbers on the Labour back benches, meant that any indication of bias was looked for very closely. Martin caused concern in October 2001 following a statement by the then Home Secretary, David Blunkett, when he announced that he welcomed the abolition of asylum seeker vouchers.[377] The former Conservative MP turned political journalist, Matthew Parris, wrote: 'Speakers do not comment on the merits of government policies. They just don't. Ever. Some Tories will think Mr Martin was bending the rules, but I expect this may have been a genuine mistake.'[378]

Parris was most probably right about it being a mistake but, nevertheless, Martin had overstepped the mark and he was quick to apologise to the House the next day.[379]

Doubts over Martin's impartiality reached new heights in November 2006 when he stopped the then Leader of the Opposition, David Cameron, in mid question and ruled that he could not ask the Prime Minister, Tony Blair, whether he would be happy for the Chancellor of the Exchequer, Gordon Brown, to succeed him.[380] Martin explained why he had stopped Cameron and ruled that: 'Questions should be about the business of the government. The issue of who will be the next leader of the Labour Party is for the Labour Party to talk about and decide.'[381]

Greg Hurst and Anthony Brown wrote in *The Times* that 'Mr Cameron, looking perplexed and flushed with anger, rose and tried to challenge the Speaker's ruling'.[382] In the end, Cameron got away with asking Blair whether he would be happy for Brown to succeed him as Prime Minister.[383] Conservative MPs were clearly furious that their leader had been rebuked by the Speaker and there was uproar in the chamber. Whilst Martin had technically been right with his ruling, his timing meant that it looked as though he was shielding his old Labour colleagues from difficult questions. A Speaker has to be careful not to look biased and on this occasion that's how Martin made himself appear.

Martin can also be accused of helping his old comrades on the Labour front bench by his reluctance to grant Private Notice Questions (which became known as Urgent Questions in 2002). Betty Boothroyd had been nowhere near as generous with PNQs as her predecessor, Jack Weatherill, had been but Martin granted even fewer. In most years the number of Urgent Questions granted by Martin ran only into single figures and the most he ever allowed was fourteen during the 2005–2006 session. Matthew Parris has said that: 'Ministers absolutely hate being dragged to the despatch box because the Speaker has said that they should debate something that ministers don't find convenient to debate. They hate it. Always will.'

With this in mind, it is no wonder that his refusal to allow many Urgent Questions was seen as Martin protecting ministers from answering awkward questions. Despite this, Martin did require the Prime Minister, Tony Blair, to answer an Urgent Question on the fire-fighters' dispute in November 2002. Indeed, Robin Cook wrote in his diary that this was the first time that he knew that the Prime Minister had been obliged to come to the

House and answer an Urgent Question. Cook wrote that this 'is a twenty-two carat innovation by Michael, who is probably now having pins stuck in a wax effigy of him in the Whips' Office'.[384]

This was not quite an innovation because Speaker Weatherill had required Mrs Thatcher to answer a Private Notice Question during his period in the Chair.[385] Martin's new stance was, however, not set to continue and this occasion certainly did not mark the beginning of a renaissance in the granting of Urgent Questions. Martin showed that he had the makings of a good Speaker who was willing to ensure unwelcome scrutiny of the government of the day but, in the end, he failed to build on this early success. Sir Alan Haselhurst believes that: 'I don't think that you could argue really that there was a serious bias at all. I don't think that he was that kind of person but, I mean, he was understandably more friendly with more people in the Labour Party.'

Despite his friendliness with old Labour colleagues, Martin was not afraid to rebuke them if the need arose. On 10 February 2003, the then Father of the House Tam Dalyell raised a point of order with the Speaker concerning his outrage that the government had given the House a dossier on Iraq which had been compiled from an out-of-date Californian PhD.[386] Dalyell was upset that Martin had not granted him an Urgent Question on the topic so that it could be debated on the floor of the House. Martin was unsurprisingly true to form and not prepared to grant the Urgent Question. A row ensued. Dalyell would not resume his seat even when instructed to do so by Martin and finally he walked out. Martin had shown that he would not tolerate having one of his rulings openly questioned in the chamber even by someone as worthy as the Father of the House and a fellow Scottish MP at that.

Indeed, Martin was not always helpful to his former colleagues on the Labour benches. During the debate on Iraq on 25 October

2002, the Speaker decided to ignore the pointless and supportive amendment put down by the Conservatives and went instead for the more critical one from the Liberal Democrats. Robin Cook argued that this was 'another assertion of the independence of the Speaker, as by convention the Chair always selects the amendment of the Official Opposition'.[387]

This move by Martin once again did not signal the start of things to come. It did, however, demonstrate that the Speaker was more than capable of using his position to ensure that minority parties were heard and that the government was brought to account. What he failed to do was to continue on this course. If he had done then the accusations of bias would perhaps have been far fewer.

Two years into his Speakership, on 29 October 2002, Michael Martin succeeded in changing the rules so that he could be given the right to miss a Friday sitting of the Commons whenever he wanted without seeking the permission of the House.[388] Martin clearly felt that he needed to miss Friday sittings when they arose even though the House of Commons does not meet on every Friday it is in session. From March 2003, Speaker Martin never presided over a Friday sitting and instead left it to one of his deputies to take it in turns to be in charge. Although previous Speakers had leant on their deputies, none had done so in such an obvious way and Martin appeared to be abdicating his important responsibilities. Unlike his recent predecessors, however, Martin represented a Scottish constituency and so he had to travel back and forth at the weekend and needed extra time.

In February 2006, Speaker Martin was admitted to hospital following chest pains which resulted in an angioplasty procedure to clear blockages in his heart. Martin was absent from the House for nearly two months which meant that, under the rules, the Chairman of Ways and Means assumed the duties of the Speaker.[389] Sir Alan Haselhurst has said that Martin did not like it when he was doing the Speaker's job in his absence. Every day, according to Standing Orders, the Clerk had to read out a statement explaining why the Deputy Speaker was taking the Chair. In the end Roger Sands found this tiresome and spoke to Geoff Hoon, the Leader of the House. Haselhurst recalls that 'Geoff told me that the Speaker blew a fuse, but Roger ignored it and did it on a weekly basis anyway.'[390]

Martin was bound to be defensive about his position following all the criticism in the press. Nevertheless, this reaction demonstrated that he was insecure and did not want the House coming to the conclusion that it was better off without him.

In 2008, Martin became the first Speaker in twenty years to preside over a Speaker's Conference. The idea of a conference to consider electoral matters was put forward by the Prime Minister, Gordon Brown, and on 22 July 2008, Michael Martin announced the terms of reference for the committee as being: 'To consider and make recommendations for rectifying the disparity between the representation of women and ethnic minorities in the House of Commons and their representation in the UK population at large; and to consider such other matters as might, by agreement, be referred to for consideration.'[391]

Although Martin was the chairman of the conference, in practice he left it up to his vice chairman, the Labour MP Anne Begg. Martin did not see the Speaker's Conference to its conclusion because it had only really started to gather evidence by the time he left office in June 2009.

Throughout most of his time as Speaker, controversy surrounded the amount of money claimed by Michael Martin and his wife as expenses for travel, entertainment and other official duties. Question marks over Martin's expenses were first highlighted by the *Mail on Sunday* in July 2004, naming this saga

'Gorbalsgate'.[392] The article claimed that the Speaker's wife was being paid £20,000 for secretarial duties despite the fact it could not be ascertained what she actually did.[393] After some further investigation, Simon Walters, the Political Editor of the *Mail on Sunday*, wrote an article the following week stating that Martin had claimed up to £70,000 in housing grants from the Commons meant to help MPs who need second homes to carry out their parliamentary duties, even though he lived in Speaker's House.[394]

Martin's predecessors had worked extremely hard to build up the image and prestige of the Speakership and this behaviour did nothing to further that cause. These articles should have made Martin more careful about what he claimed; from then on his expenses were under the microscope. The Speaker's expenses, however, were discussed again in late 2007 when *The Times* pointed out that Mrs Martin had claimed more than £4,000 for taxis since May 2004 in order to shop for food for official functions.[395] In response to these allegations, Mark Wallace, the Campaign Director of the Taxpayers' Alliance, wrote to the Parliamentary Commissioner for Standards, John Lyon, on 24 February 2008 inviting him to investigate reports that the Speaker had abused the allowance system given to him for his household expenditure.[396] Following a full investigation by Lyon, his report concluded that:

> The use by the Speaker's wife to take taxi journeys funded from public funds in support of the normal official duties of Mr Speaker was reasonable in all the circumstances and was within the arrangements for Mr Speaker's expenditure established in 2002.[397]

Despite being cleared of any wrongdoing, one result of this whole saga was the resignation of the Speaker's media adviser, Mike

Granatt, who relinquished his post because he had unknowingly misinformed journalists about the circumstances of Mrs Martin's taxi journeys. Granatt was clearly uncomfortable with the entire affair and was not prepared to do a job in which he was not given all the facts. The columnist Matthew Parris has pointed out that, such episodes 'looked none too good on the front pages of newspapers'. Although the taxi claims were within the rules, such large expenses claims appeared extravagant and it seemed strange that the Speaker's wife would have to shop for food when there was an entire staff to do such things for them. The fact that a member of the public had reported the Speaker to the Parliamentary Commissioner was a clear indication that the office had moved away from simply being responsible to the House of Commons. The world beyond Westminster had expectations of the Speaker and Michael Martin was not meeting them.

At the same time as the taxi journey controversy was going on, in early 2008 it emerged that Martin had been using the Air Miles that he had accrued from official visits to pay for members of his family to fly to London from Glasgow.[398] It was also revealed that Mary Martin had claimed £50,000 to pay for flights to support her husband.[399] Again, all this was within the rules but it appeared that the Speaker and his wife were making excessive claims.

Michael Martin also faced breaches of security in the House of Commons during his time as Speaker. During 2004, purple powder was thrown down from the gallery and fox hunting supporters stormed the chamber. Peter Hain, who was Leader of the House at the time, recalls in his memoirs that 'the shock of the hunting invasion had left him [Speaker Martin] almost paralysed'.[400] Hain goes on to say that he was dismayed to find out that Martin was not going to allow a discussion on security matters during Business Questions. He concludes that: 'It reflected both his [Martin's] own lack of self-confidence and his determination to keep hold of security matters, not to allow them to be seen as the responsibility of anyone else.'[401]

In the end, Hain took it upon himself to outline a series of reforms which gave the police and the Security Service greater operational authority. Martin's lack of action when it came to addressing serious matters would of course later be his undoing.

Michael Martin's Speakership suffered yet another blow following his handling of the events surrounding the arrest of the then shadow Immigration Minister Damian Green. On 27 November 2008, Green was arrested at his home in Kent because a Home Office official, Christopher Galley, had leaked some restricted papers to the shadow minister, who had passed the documents to the *Daily Mail* and other newspapers. The police had decided to arrest Green for 'aiding, abetting, counselling or procuring misconduct in public office' with Galley and a judge granted a search warrant for the MP's home and constituency office.[402] The judge did not, however, grant a search warrant for Green's parliamentary office and it is here where Martin's role in the affair came into question. On the afternoon of Thursday 27 November 2008, officers from SO15, the Counter Terrorism Command of the Metropolitan Police Service, began a search of Green's offices in Portcullis House on the Parliamentary Estate. The veteran columnist, William Rees-Mogg, branded this action as 'an historic attack on liberty and democracy' because it constituted 'the most serious breach of the privilege of Parliament in modern times'.[403] The Professor of Constitutional Law at King's College, London, Robert Blackburn, and the Deputy Principal Clerk of the House of Commons, Andrew Kennon, describe parliamentary privileges as 'freedom of speech in debate, freedom from arrest, and freedom of access to the Queen "whenever occasion shall require"'.[404]

In 1642, Speaker William Lenthall had refused to help Charles I in his attempt to arrest five MPs thus establishing the fact that the Chair was the servant of the House and not of the Crown. Nearly 400 years later, it appeared that Speaker Martin was not living up to this illustrious history and pressure mounted for Martin to make a statement to the House. Martin waited until the State Opening of Parliament and made his statement on 3 December 2008.[405] In that statement, Martin made it clear that privilege did not make the parliamentary estate 'a haven from the law' and claimed that: 'I must make it clear to the House that I was not asked the question of whether consent should be given, or whether a warrant should have been insisted on. I did not personally authorise the search.'[406]

Martin appeared to be shirking his responsibilities and was pushing the blame onto his staff. In his diaries, Chris Mullin records that the Speaker's statement only made matters worse and that all he did was to dump on the Serjeant-at-Arms, Jill Pay. Mullin concludes that 'the bottom line is that Mr Speaker Martin has let us all down. If we'd had someone like George Young, this would never have happened.'[407]

Martin's statement had indeed placed the blame on the Serjeant-at-Arms despite the fact that his predecessor, Betty Boothroyd, made it clear that the 'buck stops' with the Speaker. The entire episode was a mess and the Speaker was at the centre of it. For someone like Mullin to suggest that George Young would have made a better Speaker shows that Martin was losing the confidence of those who had reluctantly voted for him on the Labour benches. Matthew Parris is of the opinion that Martin 'was already in trouble before the Damian Green affair and so people found in that affair further ammunition'. Peter Riddell believes that these events were important because the Damian Green affair 'meant that when he [Martin] wanted friends he didn't have them and that was crucial in spring 2009'.[408]

In the end, the Crown Prosecution Service decided that it was not going to bring charges against Damian Green. The result of this affair was that the Speaker issued a new protocol on 8 December 2008 which stated that, 'In future a warrant will always be required for a search of a Member's office'.[409] Following on from the Speaker's instruction, the Commons set up a Committee on Issues of Privilege just after Martin resigned to investigate the matter and complete a report entitled 'Police Searches on the Parliamentary Estate'. After taking evidence from all the key players, the Committee concluded that:

> While the House and its Speaker could and should no doubt have been better served by their officials, the Speaker himself should have been asking the right questions and he should have taken more responsibility for exercising the authority of his high office.[410]

This was a damning indictment of Michael Martin's handling of the whole affair and served to confirm what many had already known. This case was undoubtedly the beginning of the end for Martin; his poor handling of the events lost him some support that would have been crucial in the months ahead. He had failed to act to defend the rights of a Member of Parliament and his mistake was common knowledge beyond Westminster.

Already wounded by the Damian Green affair, it was to be the revelations on MPs' expenses exposed by the *Daily Telegraph* in early May 2009 that cemented the end of Martin's Speakership. As Chairman of the House of Commons Commission, the body which runs the administration of the House, Martin was ultimately responsible for the Fees Office and the expenses regime. Since 2005, Martin had been working to ensure that the precise

details of MPs' expense claims were not revealed to the general
public. Journalist and Freedom of Information campaigner,
Heather Brooke, claimed that he was 'the man who did the most
to stymie my campaign to open up Parliament to the people'.[411]
Indeed, in 2006, when Brooke was pursuing her investigation
with another Freedom of Information request on MPs' expenses,
Martin signed a certificate stating that the disclosure of the
names of people working for MPs would be 'likely to prejudice
the effective conduct of public affairs' and would also endan-
ger their 'health and safety'.[412] Over the next two years further
information about MPs' allowances and staffing was extracted
and in May 2007 the *Sunday Times* disclosed that Conservative
MP Derek Conway had used public money to employ his son
as a parliamentary researcher even though he was a full-time
student at Newcastle University at the time.[413] A month later,
Martin appealed against the Information Commissioner's decision to publish the details of fourteen named MPs' expenses.[414]
The subsequent tribunal upheld the decision of the Information
Commissioner and Martin's attempt to shield colleagues from
embarrassing revelations was defeated. The journalists Robert
Winnett and Gordon Rayner have pointed out that the Speaker's
own legal team advised him not to go ahead with any further
appeals but he was not going to allow them to 'poke their noses
into what he regarded as the sacred world of MPs' finances'.[415]

On 25 March 2008, Martin announced that he would be taking
legal action and lodging an appeal to stop the release of the full
details. The journalist, Andrew Rawnsley, has commented that:
'Behaving like the shop steward he once was, Martin was at the
fore of the futile court battle to try to shield MPs from exposure
of the corrupted expenses system over which he had presided.'[416]

On 7 May 2008, the appeal was heard at London's High Court
with Nigel Griffin QC appearing for the Commons. He argued

that the publication of receipts would be a 'substantial intrusion' into the lives of MPs.[417] On 16 May the High Court judges ruled that details of MPs' expenses should be published thus dealing a final blow to Martin's campaign to keep such information private.[418] Martin had been trying to protect the interests of colleagues just as he had done when he was a trade unionist in Glasgow. He was also trying to protect himself from the embarrassment that revelations about MPs' expenses would cause. With the failure of the court appeal, the Speaker would now have to reap the whirlwind that he had personally whipped up.

Michael Martin's position could have been saved if the raft of expenses reforms put forward by the Members Estimate Committee, which he chaired, had been accepted by MPs. However, in July 2008, MPs voted against reforms, which would have required them to submit receipts with every claim and be subjected to spot checks, by 172 to 144.[419] One of Martin's closest allies, the Labour peer and former Minister of State for Scotland, George Foulkes, claimed that 'reforms suggested by him [Martin] have been sabotaged by those now seeking to smear him'.[420] Perhaps the Speaker was trying to turn things around but this was too little, too late. In early 2009, MPs plotted to exempt their expenses from the Freedom of Information law which would have nullified the High Court ruling.[421] After some confusion, the Leader of the Opposition, David Cameron, made it clear that he would be urging his fellow Conservative MPs to vote against such a move thus stopping it dead in its tracks.[422] The *Daily Telegraph* managed to obtain a leaked disc containing some details of MPs' expenses and so on 8 May 2009 the newspaper began publishing these files on a daily basis.[423] Martin was now pushed to the fore because, as the figurehead of the House of Commons and the man responsible for the allowance system, he was expected to remedy this state of affairs. What he did not grasp was that, as a modern Speaker, this expectation did not just lie with fellow MPs; the wider British public also looked to him to take action. As Peter Riddell wrote, 'Mr Martin seemed an apologist for MPs rather than a champion of voters'.[424]

On 11 May 2009, Speaker Martin publicly displayed just how rattled he had become over the expenses scandal when he rebuked the Labour MP Kate Hoey for raising a point of order suggesting that calling in the police to investigate the leaked disc was a waste of money. Martin snapped back saying: 'I listen to her often when I turn on the television at midnight, and I hear her public utterances and pearls of wisdom on Sky News – it is easy to talk then.'[425]

Martin then went on to admonish Liberal Democrat MP Norman Baker, branding him 'another individual Member who is keen to say to the press whatever the press want to hear'.[426] Such a personal attack on other MPs from the Chair was totally unprecedented in the post-war period. Chris Mullin, who was present in the chamber at the time, wrote of the Speaker: 'I've never seen him so worked up. Actually it was way over the top. Gave the impression that he is rattled, which I imagine he is.'[427]

The following day, the Labour MP David Winnick asked Martin to apologise to Hoey ending with 'Should not the Speaker always refrain from personal comments?'[428] When Martin refused to apologise, Winnick remarked, 'That is not adequate', to which the Speaker responded, 'If that is not adequate, the hon. Gentleman knows what he must do'.[429] With that comment, Michael Martin, firing the starting pistol for the moves that were to bring about his downfall, invited a motion of no confidence in his Speakership. His challenge to David Winnick made him look arrogant and that he thought himself to be untouchable. By the Sunday, the leader of the Liberal

Democrats, Nick Clegg, announced on the *Andrew Marr Show* that he had:

> arrived at the conclusion that the Speaker must go. He has proved himself over some time now to be a dogged defender of the way things are, of the status quo, when what we need very urgently is someone at the heart of Westminster who will lead a wholesale, radical process of reform.[430]

The support of the leadership of the main political parties was crucial to Martin's survival and so Clegg's announcement was a clear indication that his days in the Chair were numbered. The Conservative MP Douglas Carswell seized on the opportunity to oust the Speaker:

> It wasn't just a sort of ad hoc response to the expense scandal. Some people talk about my campaign to remove the Speaker as though it was a consequence of the expense scandal. In fact, a year before the expense scandal broke [...] we had published a plan that set out what we wanted to do.

Indeed, in 2008, Carswell co-wrote a book with the Conservative MEP Daniel Hannan called *The Plan: Twelve Months to Renew Britain* in which they wanted to elect a new Speaker by secret ballot with a mandate to sort out Parliament's problems.[431] The expenses scandal was, however, the catalyst Carswell needed to bring about what he had proposed in his plan and so he set about putting together a motion of no confidence in Speaker Martin. Carswell explains:

> I spoke to the Table Office. I did a draft. I did a lot of it on the Internet. I blogged it and got a lot of suggestions [...] and was

able to sort of raise interest in the campaign through blogosphere in a way which would have been unimaginable pre-Internet.

At 3.30 p.m. on 18 May 2009, Martin made a statement to the House in which he apologised to the country on behalf of the Commons, 'We have let you down very badly indeed'. He added, 'We must all accept blame and, to the extent that I have contributed to the situation, I am profoundly sorry'.[432]

Despite calling for an emergency meeting with the Prime Minister and leaders of all the other political parties to agree a way forward, this was not good enough for many MPs who had expected some indication of when Speaker Martin would step down. Martin clearly wanted to cling on to office and hoped that his statement would at least appease enough MPs to help him achieve this. Labour MP Gordon Prentice immediately rose after the Speaker's statement asking whether a motion of no confidence in Martin would be debated and voted upon the following day.[433] When the Speaker told Prentice that his question was not a point of order, the Labour MP defied the Chair by exclaiming, 'Oh yes it is'.[434] The next to speak was Douglas Carswell who talked about his substantive motion, one which takes a decision, to remove the Speaker. Carswell recalls:

On several occasions during interviews before I tabled it, I allowed the interviewer [...] to refer to it as an Early Day Motion because that meant they were underestimating the significance of it and it had a rather fortuitous consequence in that, in the crucial moment in the debate in the chamber, the Speaker showed he was unaware as to the precise state of the motion and a row ensued, lots of shouting, that I think made for visibly ceding that he was out of his depth.

Indeed, when Martin argued with Carswell over whether his motion was a substantive motion or an Early Day Motion, the Speaker remarked, 'Please give me credit for having some experience in the Chair'.[435] Martin was immediately made to look inadequate when the Conservative MP Richard Bacon called out, 'It is a substantive motion. The Deputy Leader of the House just told me that it is a substantive motion.'[436] Despite having been an experienced chairman of committees, a Deputy Speaker and a long-serving Speaker, Martin felt compelled to consult the clerks in front of him. This public show of uncertainty prompted David Winnick to ask: 'Will you bear in mind that it would be very useful for the reputation of this House – I say this with reluctance, but I say it all the same – if you gave some indication of your own intention to retire? Your early retirement would help the reputation of the House.'[437]

For a Labour MP to say this was a crippling blow to Martin who, after all, had become Speaker thanks to the support of backbench Labour colleagues. Shortly afterwards, the veteran Conservative MP Sir Patrick Cormack likened the mood of the House to that of the country at the time of the Norway debate in 1940 which brought down Neville Chamberlain's premiership.[438] Martin's old ally, the Labour MP Sir Stuart Bell attempted to support the Speaker but, as Mullin recorded, his intervention 'attracted only mild hear-hearing (all from the Labour side)'.[439] Winnick's response to Bell's call for support for Martin was 'What world is he living in?'[440] Such open criticism and defiance of the Chair was unprecedented. Vince Cable commented: 'The day when he defied the growing clamour to go and was shouted down in the House ranks as perhaps the most excruciatingly embarrassing in my memory of the place.'[441]

Martin's stumbling on procedure and his failure to maintain order during the debate clearly displayed that his time was up as Speaker. He now looked more of a liability than a man who could lead the Commons out of the expenses scandal. The result of this was that additional MPs were now prepared to sign Douglas Carswell's motion of no confidence. One of these MPs was Charles Walker, the Conservative Member for Broxbourne:

> The reason I signed it was that I was in the chamber the day that everything just seemed to deteriorate and fall away […] that day when he was heckled and booed and I couldn't bear to see someone I actually like very much being treated in such a way. It was just appalling and I signed that motion because, clearly, the end had been reached and it was just unfair for a man such as Speaker Martin, who really just wanted to do good, to be treated in such a way and it wasn't fair, in my view, to allow it to continue.

In the end, Carswell had twenty-four signatures although he maintains he could have obtained many more if necessary. Martin's fate was now in the hands of the government who had the final say over whether time would be given to debate the motion of no confidence. However, the political historians Anthony Seldon and Guy Lodge note that the Secretary of State for Culture Ben Bradshaw was ready to publicly demand Martin's resignation and they conclude that '[Gordon] Brown was not in control of events'.[442] Rawnsley explains that shortly after Martin's mauling in the Commons, the Prime Minister, Gordon Brown, paid him an unexpected call and made it clear that the government could no longer shield him from the no confidence motion tabled by backbenchers. The following day, at the end of the Cabinet meeting, an official passed the Prime Minister a note stating that the Speaker would resign that afternoon.[443]

Following prayers on 19 May 2009, at 2.34 p.m., Michael Martin made a statement to the House:

Since I came to this House thirty years ago, I have always felt that the House is at its best when it is united. In order that unity can be maintained, I have decided that I will relinquish the office of Speaker on Sunday 21 June. This will allow the House to proceed to elect a new Speaker on Monday 22 June. That is all I have to say on the matter.[444]

The second longest-serving Speaker of the post-war period bowed out abruptly. Dr Horace King had been pushed out quietly behind the scenes in 1970 but Michael Martin was the first Speaker to be forced to resign publicly since Sir John Trevor was voted out of office in 1695 for accepting 1,000 guineas from the City of London to push through the Orphans' Bill.[445] Martin presented himself as a King Lear figure sacrificing himself for an ungrateful brood of MPs who he had tried so hard to protect. In an interview with his old colleague, the former deputy leader of the Labour Party, Roy Hattersley, Martin insisted, 'if I had fought, I would have won', stating the reason for his resignation as the hurtful press stories saying that the Speaker's wife was not fit for the task because she had been a factory worker.[446] It is difficult to see how he could have survived without causing a constitutional crisis in Parliament. If the government had shielded the Speaker then there would have been uproar and even if Martin had survived the motion of no confidence he would have no longer enjoyed the support of a large section of the House. Considering his wife, Mary, had come under constant criticism during his Speakership, Martin once again believed that he was a victim of snobbery. Matthew Parris believes:

Michael Martin was just a disappointment. It was partly because Michael Martin couldn't be that sort of modern Speaker that he so conspicuously failed. [He] wasn't by historical standards

a particularly bad or a particularly good Speaker and he would
have been an entirely unremarkable Speaker in a pre-television,
pre-radio age.

Martin stepped down on 21 June 2009 after nearly nine years
as Speaker. The manner of his departure meant that even the
customary peerage for a retiring Speaker was questioned. The
former Chancellor of the Exchequer, Lord Lawson of Blaby, led
calls by peers for Martin to be blocked from joining the House
of Lords saying that he had 'let parliamentary democracy down'
and did not deserve the honour.[447] Even the independent House
of Lords Appointments Commission warned that Martin's presence could 'diminish' the upper chamber.[448] There were also
calls for Martin to break with convention and stay on as an MP
because Labour had recently lost the Glasgow East by-election
and could not afford to lose the former Speaker's neighbouring
seat.[449] But Martin did resign his seat and the tradition of a retiring Speaker being elevated to the House of Lords was upheld
when he was raised to the peerage as Lord Martin of Springburn
and introduced on 13 October 2009. Labour comfortably won
the resulting by-election, beating the Scottish National Party
challengers by over 8,000 votes. This result was a testament to
all the work that Michael Martin had done in his part of the city
and a real boon for the Labour Party. Despite the manner in
which he left office, Lord Martin has not hidden away and he is
a regular attendee of the House of Lords.

Michael Martin had an extremely troubled Speakership that
always appeared doomed. The tribalism that saw him elected to
the Chair left him open to accusations of bias towards the Labour
backbenchers and old Scottish colleagues who had put him there.
Despite these accusations and question marks over his expenses,
however, Martin is generally spoken of with affection by fellow

MPs and those who worked with him. Martin was undoubtedly the victim of regular negative press stories, the magnitude of which was unprecedented for any Speaker. The press no longer reported what the Speaker had done; it now passed judgement on what had become an increasingly public office.

Martin also suffered from class snobbery, which was only exacerbated by the laboured promotion of his humble origins. Martin's attempts at the end to sort out the expenses crisis might possibly have worked and prevented his resignation but for his previous actions. Martin went back to his roots and behaved like a trade union shop steward trying to protect his members but in the end those members turned against him when they realised that an alternative route had to be taken. Martin might well have survived in the period before Parliament was televised but now the Speakership was accountable to the wider British public who could see the events unfolding live from their homes.

Fortunately, the office itself was not greatly damaged by Martin's downfall although it undoubtedly became a slightly devalued currency from its heyday under the previous three incumbents. Martin was elected to office with little enthusiasm and in the end he had to deal with one of the biggest scandals of recent years. Even the strongest of Speakers would have found this difficult to overcome. Perhaps his greatest problem was taking over from Betty Boothroyd who had embodied the Speakership, set a high standard and was such a hard act to follow. He also remained in office for too long. If he had only served six or seven years like Speakers King, Lloyd or Thomas he would have retired with his head held high rather than in disgrace, having lost control of the House. As it was, Speaker Martin will always be remembered as being the fall guy for the expenses scandal and as the first Speaker to be publicly forced from office in over 300 years.

Eight

The Controversial Reformer:
John Bercow (2009–)

*His undoubted merits as a Speaker and reformer of parliament's prac-
tices in a fast-changing world would be better appreciated if the Bercows
ceased to make themselves the story – and concentrated instead on the office
he holds.*

– Michael White, Associate Editor of *The Guardian*, 2012

John Bercow became Speaker following the expenses scandal
that rocked Westminster and brought about the resignation
of his predecessor in the summer of 2009. Bercow's political
journey from the right wing of the Conservative Party to a more
liberal, centrist viewpoint, plus the manner he was elected to the
Chair and the way he has carried out the job have made him a
somewhat controversial figure.

John Simon Bercow was born on 19 January 1963 at Edgware
General Hospital in north-west London. His father, Charles,
came from a Jewish-Romanian family originally called Bercowitz
and Charles's father had come to the United Kingdom in
1900. His mother, Brenda, converted to Judaism on marrying
Charles in 1956. Charles Bercow owned a car dealership with
his brother Ralph, and Bercow Motors flourished until the early
1970s when it started to struggle and was forced to close. From

then on, Charles Bercow worked as a taxi driver to provide for his family.

Living in nearby Hendon, John Bercow attended Finchley Manorhill Comprehensive School and most of his youth was spent becoming Britain's No. 1 junior tennis player as a member of the Finchley Manor Lawn Tennis Club. Bercow was, therefore, well-placed to see the rise of the local MP and Conservative leader, Margaret Thatcher. During the 1979 general election campaign, whilst Bercow was studying for his O levels, he went to a local school to hear Mrs Thatcher give an address. Bercow recalls talking to the future Prime Minister afterwards and being told to join the Conservative Party.[450]

Bercow's other political hero was the former Conservative and Ulster Unionist MP, Enoch Powell. Concerned about the impact of mass immigration, Bercow joined the right-wing Monday Club in 1981 and became secretary of its Immigration and Repatriation Committee. By February 1984, however, he had left because he opposed the views of other members. Bercow remained active within the Conservative Party during his time as a student of government at Essex University and, after having graduated with a First, he was elected the last National Chairman of the Federation of Conservative Students in 1986. The organisation was disbanded the following year, with the help of Bercow, by the then Chairman of the Conservative Party, Norman Tebbit, who wrote that the FCS was being taken over 'by a coalition of people, some of whose views and actions were incompatible with Conservatism'.[451] Having started off with an interest in the Monday Club and Conservative student right-wing politics, Bercow had begun his move towards the centre ground.

In 1986, Bercow was elected as a Conservative councillor for the St Leonard's ward of the London Borough of Lambeth

where he served for one term. The following year, he became
the youngest deputy leader of a Council group in the country.
This experience was a training ground for a future career at
Westminster and so Bercow put himself forward as a potential
parliamentary candidate. The same year, at the age of only
twenty-four and despite being a Londoner and an Englishman,
he was selected to contest the safe Labour seat of Motherwell
South. Although Mrs Thatcher won convincingly overall at the
1987 general election, the Conservatives managed to lose eleven
seats in Scotland and Bercow was pushed out of second place in
Motherwell by the Scottish Nationalists.

In 1988, Bercow became a political lobbyist when he was
employed by the public affairs company, Rowland Sallingbury
Casey. He also remained on the candidates list and, believing
that he would not get a safe Conservative seat, decided to go
for constituencies which were held by Labour with only a slim
majority. In 1989, he was selected to fight Bristol South which had
a Labour majority of just 1,404 and whose MP, Dawn Primarolo,
would later become one of Bercow's Deputy Speakers. Even
though John Major managed to pull off a surprise win at the 1992
general election, there was a swing to Labour and so Bercow
failed to take Bristol South. Following his disappointment in
Bristol, Bercow returned to political lobbying and worked for a
division of the advertising company Saatchi & Saatchi. In 1995,
he was appointed special adviser to the Chief Secretary to the
Treasury, Jonathan Aitken. Within a few months, Aitken had
resigned from the Cabinet in order to pursue a futile libel case
against *The Guardian* and Granada Television for accusing him of
doing arms deals with Arab businessmen. Bercow then became
special adviser to Virginia Bottomley, the Secretary of State for
National Heritage.

Still determined to enter Parliament, Bercow paid £1,000 in

1996 to hire a helicopter so that he could attend the selection meetings in Surrey Heath and Buckingham which fell on the same day. With both seats being staunchly Conservative, they were a guaranteed route to Parliament. In the end, he was selected to contest Buckingham and he has described the hiring of the helicopter as 'the best £1,000 I have ever spent'.[452] The following year, despite Tony Blair's landslide victory, Bercow achieved his goal and was elected to the House of Commons with a majority of 12,386.

John Bercow first made the front bench in June 1999 when he was made an opposition spokesman on Education and Employment. A year later, he was moved to speak on Home Affairs and then, following the election of Iain Duncan Smith as Conservative Party leader, Bercow joined the shadow Cabinet as shadow Chief Secretary to the Treasury. In July 2002, he was demoted to shadow Minister for Work and Pensions and resigned in November when he sided with Labour over the introduction of allowing gay and lesbian couples to adopt children. Bercow had already voted for an equalisation of the age of consent for gay people in February 2000 and this was a further significant step in Bercow's emerging political journey from right-wing Monday Clubber to centrist libertarian.

When Michael Howard became leader of the Conservative Party in November 2003, Bercow found himself back on the opposition front bench as shadow Secretary of State for International Development. Bercow's return to the shadow Cabinet was, however, short lived and he resigned shortly after the 2005 general election thanks to his disagreements over the contents of the Conservative Party manifesto and, in particular, his belief that the immigration policy was 'repellent'.[453] These disagreements had started to bubble to the surface in late 2004 and Lord Spicer, the former Conservative MP for West

Worcestershire and Chairman of the 1922 Committee, records in his diaries that he was

> 'invited in' by the Chief Whip to witness John Bercow threatened with having the whip withdrawn. In the event he surrenders and agrees to apologise for being publicly rude about the party, especially in Monday's *Independent*, and also to declare he will 'never' cross the floor of the House.[454]

Bercow's move towards the left of the Conservative Party became even more apparent during the leadership election that followed Michael Howard's resignation. Bercow chose to support the more left-wing and pro-European former Chancellor of the Exchequer, Kenneth Clarke. Bercow recalls that if Clarke had won the leadership contest then he would have been willing to have returned to the front bench.

David Cameron, the newly elected leader of the Conservative Party, chose not to appoint Bercow to his shadow team. Having been left out, Bercow had to consider what to do with his political career:

> I didn't want to be a minister. I wasn't sure that I would be a particularly good minister. I didn't think it was very likely that I'd be asked to be a minister. After all, I'd not been appointed to David Cameron's front bench so was it particularly likely that if the Conservatives won he would suddenly ask me to serve in government? Not really, no. Not very likely. In fact, I'm pretty sure he wouldn't have done and yet, like a lot of politicians, I felt I had got a contribution to make. So, I decided, sort of as long ago as late 2005, that as and when the opportunity arose, if and when the opportunity arose, i.e. there was a vacancy; I'd have a go [at becoming Speaker].

This was not an unnatural decision for Bercow to take because, after all, he loves Parliament and he loves the House of Commons chamber. Bercow is more of a parliamentarian than a member of the executive, which makes the Speakership the ultimate job. He undertook, therefore, to do what was necessary to make him a viable candidate for the office.

Bercow joined Speaker Martin's Panel of Chairmen immediately after the 2005 general election and started to chair the standing committees which examine bills. As has been seen, this is usually the start of the traditional route to the Chair because Speakers Martin, Boothroyd, Thomas, King and Clifton Brown had all served on the Chairmen's Panel earlier in their parliamentary careers. Bercow admits that:

> I joined the Chairmen's Panel in July 2005 and the idea [of becoming Speaker] was already in my mind, it was – (a) I quite fancied doing a bit of chairing anyway and (b) the idea was in my mind but it was only finally formed after the leadership election.

Bercow had already set about making himself a real 'House of Commons man', spending a great deal of time in the chamber. From the moment he had been elected to the Commons in 1997, he had always enjoyed sitting in the chamber and contributing to debates. In February 2005, Bercow won the Channel 4/Hansard Society Political Award for 'Opposition MP of the Year' and in the December he was also voted the Backbencher of the Year in *The House Magazine* awards. Winning such awards, which, after all, were voted upon by his peers in Parliament, showed that he was gathering recognition and support from his parliamentary colleagues; perhaps Bercow could win an even bigger prize.

The mellowing of Bercow's political views was also helpful in gaining support from other parties in the House. This change of

viewpoint had already begun before Bercow admits to thinking
about going for the Speakership and he argues that:

> First of all, the Conservative Party lost very, very, very badly in
> 1997 but it lost almost as badly four years later and it may seem
> strange […] but my political views weren't hugely influenced by
> the loss of the 1997 election but after four years we got smashed
> again […] and that did cause me to think about the Conservative
> Party's approach to lots of issues.

Bercow also admits that, 'I'm sure that marrying my wife played
a role' in his move towards the centre ground of British politics.
In December 2002, Bercow married Sally Illman who he had
first met at a Conservative student conference in 1989. Sally
Bercow, as she became, had been a member of the Oxford
University Conservative Association but had switched her political allegiance to Tony Blair's New Labour in the mid-1990s. The
two had been seeing each other on and off for over a decade and,
despite their now differing political views, finally decided to get
married in 2001. Bercow himself believes that:

> Of course, I think if people live together and are in a relation-
> ship and so on, they influence each other up to a point but my
> shift politically towards the centre, and I never wanted to be a
> member of any other Party than the Conservative Party, but my
> shift towards the centre pre-dated my marrying Sally.

Despite Bercow's comment that he did not want to leave the
Conservative Party, rumours were rife that he would defect
and join Gordon Brown's 'government of all the talents' in
late 2007. Indeed, following the defection of the pro-European
Conservative MP Quentin Davies, the new Prime Minister had

his sights set on Bercow. In the end, Bercow did not cross the floor but he did agree to lead a review of support for children with speech, language and communication special needs on behalf of the Labour government. Sam Coates, the Chief Political Correspondent of *The Times*, argues that this move 'sealed the divorce with the Tories in the view of many colleagues'.[455] It is no wonder that Chris Mullin would later record that his side would support Bercow's candidature for the Speakership 'as a way of getting back at the Tories'.[456]

In November 2008, Bercow was appointed as a member of the Speaker's Conference on Parliamentary Representation. He had distanced himself from the front bench and signalled his interest in matters associated with the House.

Despite Bercow's election to the Speakership on the back of the 2009 expenses scandal, there were question marks over his own use of the system. The *Daily Telegraph* journalists Robert Winnett and Gordon Rayner, who were instrumental in bringing the expenses scandal into the public eye, at first assumed that Bercow did not have any excessive claims because: 'Clearly, anyone who believed they could restore the public's trust in politicians must have been supremely confident that their own expenses would not attract any adverse comment.'[457]

Some further investigation, however, uncovered that Bercow had flipped his second home designation between his constituency house in Buckingham and a £540,000 flat in London, and then back again. In 2003, Bercow had sold his house in Buckingham and his flat in central London and then bought other properties. It later transpired that Bercow had not paid Capital Gains Tax on either of the two properties and so, in response to this, he announced he would pay more than £6,500 to HM Revenue & Customs. The *Sunday Telegraph* also exposed the fact that Bercow claimed nearly £1,000 over two years in order to reimburse himself for paying an accountant to complete his self-assessment tax return.[458] Such facts should have damaged Bercow's chances of the Speakership but, because some of the other contenders for the office were also embroiled in questions over their expenses, in the end it did not seem to matter. Bercow has argued that:

> I am not saying I am some sort of saint but I am certainly saying that it is possible for all of us to put the past behind us by accepting responsibility and committing to thorough and immediate change.[459]

Perhaps not being a saint was appealing to all those MPs who were themselves guilty of excessive claims. Bercow's election, however, came about because it was accepted that it was the turn of a Conservative to hold the office and Labour wanted to return one who was of their choosing. Bercow's shift to the left, his marriage to a Labour-supporting wife, his unpopularity among fellow Conservatives and finally his experience as a dedicated parliamentarian all combined to make him the front-runner for the Chair. Finally, Bercow's assertion during his speech to the chamber that he was the 'clean break' candidate was just what was needed to propel him into office.[460]

On 22 June 2009, John Bercow became the 157th Speaker of the House of Commons after seeing off nine rivals. His long-term plan and strong election campaign for the office had paid off. What was evident was that Bercow's election had mainly been thanks to a large amount of support on the Labour benches with very few Conservatives prepared to vote for him. The following day, a leading article in *The Times* argued that: 'Mr Bercow now needs to work to ensure that he acts as a Speaker for all the House rather than a practical joke played on David Cameron by Labour MPs.'[461]

The right-wing press immediately set about making it clear that Bercow would be put under the spotlight when it came to checking his impartiality. Quentin Letts, the parliamentary sketch writer for the *Daily Mail* who had consistently criticised Speaker Martin, gave his article the heading, 'Impossible! They voted for someone worse than Gorbals Mick'.[462] In the same way that Letts had given Speaker Martin the nickname 'Gorbals Mick', from the outset the new incumbent was called 'Squeaker Bercow'. Letts explains that this nickname for Bercow 'seemed to chime with his smallness, both physical and moral'.

The front page of the *Daily Mail* the day after Bercow's election read, 'So much for a fresh start' and stated that the 'New Speaker is a Tory hated by his party, tainted by expenses furore and already facing a plot to unseat him'.[463] This plot did surface less than a year later, in May 2010, when a very small handful of Conservative MPs, led by Nadine Dorries, called out 'No' on Bercow's re-election at the beginning of the new Parliament. The tiny number of Conservative MPs who were prepared to show their dissatisfaction with Bercow demonstrates that, for most, he had established himself as a competent Speaker. He had overcome some of the instant criticism that his initial election to the Chair had brought. It also showed some of Bercow's biggest critics were not prepared to ditch another Speaker within a year of getting rid of the last one.

The manner in which Bercow had managed to get himself elected in June 2009 had not won him many friends in the right-wing press and the *Daily Mail* in particular meant to scrutinise Bercow's every move. The immediate criticism dished out by the *Daily Mail*, which was in keeping with its stance on Speaker Martin, showed that twenty-first century Speakers had far greater expectations placed upon them than their predecessors had ever faced.

The press has seen fit to criticise Bercow wherever the possibility has arisen. Particular attention has been paid to the Speaker's finances and the way he has used public funds whilst exercising his duties. In this respect the Speaker is treated no differently from any other politician; the holder of the office is no longer considered as someone special and beyond reproach. In April 2011, for example, the *Daily Mail*, exposed the fact that taxpayers had footed a bill of £1,400 to pay for washing machines in the Bercow household.[464] This had followed on from the £45,000 that had initially been spent on refurbishing Speaker's House when the Bercow family first took up residence. This cost was significantly lower than the money spent by Bercow's predecessor on work that needed to be done to make the apartments more appropriate for his family. Nevertheless, it was just after the expense scandal and every penny of public money spent was meticulously scrutinised.

In October 2011, the Speaker was again criticised by the press when it turned out he was not reducing his pension in line with the decision taken by MPs to introduce a new, less generous scheme for parliamentarians.[465] At the same time, Bercow was also accused of saving himself thousands of pounds by delaying a pay cut for nearly a year and then only applying it to the Speakership element of his total salary.[466] In September 2012, he finally agreed to take his pension when he reaches sixty-five rather than at the conclusion of his Speakership.

The impact of the expenses scandal and the global recession even caused the press to question the amount of money spent by the Speaker on foreign travel. In December 2011, the *Daily Telegraph* revealed that the Speaker had spent more than £30,000 in order to attend nine visits to foreign parliaments. In the same article it is, however, pointed out that Speaker Martin spent nearly £150,000 over a similar period.[467] Whilst the

Speaker could travel economy class in order to make further savings, the same newspapers would then accuse Bercow of demeaning the office. Travelling to foreign parliaments and representing the House of Commons abroad is now firmly part of the overall job of being Speaker and so it has to be accepted that there is a cost associated with this function.

Bercow was also criticised for the official portrait he had commissioned, which was unveiled in November 2011. The portrait, which cost £37,000, was hailed as 'A Waste of Monet' by *The Sun*.[468] Despite the fact that every other Speaker has had an official portrait, Bercow was rebuked by the TaxPayers' Alliance for commissioning something which was 'very excessive at this time of public sector austerity'.[469] Whilst this is true, Speaker's House is full of portraits of the people who have held the office and Bercow was only following that tradition. What was more controversial was the simultaneous unveiling of his coat of arms which included rainbow colours and pink triangles to represent Bercow's championing of gay rights. This was certainly an overt political statement by Speaker Bercow and something which his predecessors would have avoided for fear of jeopardising the impartiality and reputation of the office. It does, however, symbolise the kind of 'new Speakership' that Bercow seems to be creating because, whilst the occupant of the Chair still has to remain completely impartial in terms of party politics, he or she is now expected to take on a much wider role. The present Speaker has taken this even further.

Bercow had assumed an office that had far more expectations placed on it and its holder than at any time during its entire history. A month after Bercow had become Speaker, he stated that:

My overriding objective is to try to strengthen Parliament, if necessary, at the expense of the power of the Executive. I want a stronger, a more dynamic, a more assertive Parliament in which backbenchers have greater opportunities and in which the legislature holds the executive more effectively to account in the future than it has done in the past.[470]

Moreover, in his speech to the chamber during the Speakership election on 22 June 2009, Bercow argued that the 'House must seize back control of its own core functions by making a number of changes'.[471] One of these changes, he said, should be that 'Urgent Questions must be more readily granted', and in his first two-and-a-half years as Speaker he allowed eighty-three. Bercow has explained the rationale behind this massive increase on the number granted by his immediate predecessor:

> The Speaker's role is not to be in the government's pocket or indeed for that matter in the opposition's pocket. The Speaker's role is to be on the side of Parliament. If matters where I think there ought to be a government statement, there isn't, ministers choose not to offer an oral statement to the House but a Member applies for permission to ask an Urgent Question [...] well, then I am generally inclined to grant it.[472]

Bercow admits that 'we get lots of UQ applications that we reject' but the effect of allowing far more means that it 'has changed the terms of trade in Parliament. It has made Parliament much more topical and interesting'. Bercow also believes that his 'reactivation or reinvention of a long-established power of the Speaker' has:

> been a really good thing because [...] they [Urgent Questions] have actually spurred an improvement in government performance. The very fact that a minister might be subject to a

rearranged timetable and a demand to appear in the House to respond to an Urgent Question has tended to cause ministers to think a bit more carefully, 'Well, perhaps I ought to offer a statement here'.[473]

Bercow has caused a renaissance in the use of the Urgent Question in order to bring about greater scrutiny of the government and to reduce the number of times ministers neglect Parliament in favour of the media. Bercow also gives ministers the following warning: 'If they get the judgement wrong or they're inconsiderate and they just don't think of offering a statement and I think it's important and I think it's urgent, I think it warrants scrutiny, the minister has to come.'[474]

This is most definitely a sign of Parliament, through the limited powers of the Speaker, fighting back and reclaiming some of the initiative over what has become an overmighty executive. In this case, Bercow has not been reluctant to use the power to grant Urgent Questions in the way that perhaps some of his predecessors have and has instead followed the tradition of Speakers Weatherill and Lloyd who were far more inclined to make sure ministers were brought to account.

Bercow is also not afraid to allow Prime Minister's Question Time to overrun if it means allowing as many backbenchers as possible to ask their questions. The Speaker has given his rationale for this stance:

I'm not as a matter of policy making Prime Minister's Questions longer but I do think that it's important that there should be a full opportunity to question and probe the Prime Minister. If, for example, there is an important announcement, including of the number of fatalities, to make at the start of Prime Minister's Questions, it's absolutely right that that announcement should be made [...] but I think it's important that it shouldn't eat into the time available for backbenchers.[475]

With only thirty minutes available, announcements made by the Prime Minister at the commencement of Question Time can seriously reduce the amount of time that backbenchers have to put their questions. Bercow is continually thinking of ways to improve the backbencher's lot and this move also helps to ensure that Parliament has the full opportunity to scrutinise the head of the executive.

On 29 November 2011, Speaker Bercow punished the Chancellor of the Exchequer, George Osborne, with a three-hour session at the despatch box because much of the Autumn Statement on the economy had been leaked to the media. On the BBC's *The Record Review*, the Speaker admitted that:

> It is absolutely true that I was displeased that the contents of the statement had been brazenly leaked and chatted about in the public domain long before Parliament got to hear about them, and to question the Chancellor. And apart from anything else I thought, well, let's have a very full airing of the issues, not least so I can hear whether the Chancellor of the Exchequer has anything to say in the chamber about these matters that he hasn't already said in the media.[476]

Previous Speakers, such as Speakers Boothroyd and Weatherill, have complained about ministers speaking to the media before addressing Parliament but none have actually taken such direct action to punish a minister for doing so. Bercow's predecessors had simply announced their displeasure in a statement to the Commons and then tried to improve matters with discussions behind the scenes. The present Speaker has shown that he is prepared to take far more obvious steps in order to make ministers think again the next time they go to make an announcement in the media before they have had occasion to inform Parliament.

Of course, the downside of being the champion of Parliament and the backbenchers is the almost inevitable accusation of bias against the government. Even Bercow's greater use of the Urgent Question has been seen as a way of undermining the Conservative led coalition rather than as a method of better scrutiny. On 30 April 2012, Speaker Bercow granted an Urgent Question to the Leader of the Opposition, Ed Miliband, regarding the ongoing affair of the Secretary of State for Culture, Jeremy Hunt's handling of the BSkyB deal, requiring the Prime Minister, David Cameron, to break off campaigning for the local elections and come to the House of Commons to answer the question.[477] Quentin Letts wrote in the *Daily Mail* that it was 'possibly the lamest Urgent Question in parliamentary history'.[478] As the Prime Minister pointed out: 'I answered questions on this issue at Prime Minister's Questions last Wednesday, and the Culture Secretary made a full statement, but let me set out the position again.'[479]

David Cameron was clearly annoyed with the Speaker for forcing him to come to Westminster and having to cancel part of his campaign trail. As the Political Editor of the *Daily Mail* commented: 'The Prime Minister insisted voters would rather be talking about jobs, clearing Britain's debts and kick-starting growth, taking an extraordinary public swipe at the Speaker for ordering him to the Commons.'[480]

Bercow has defended his decision by arguing that new information regarding Lord Justice Leveson's inquiry and evidence given by the Permanent Secretary at the Department for Culture, Media and Sport, Jonathan Stephens, opened up further questions for MPs to debate in Parliament.[481] Nevertheless, the

Speaker's decision to grant the Urgent Question would have done nothing to improve the relationship between himself and the Prime Minister.

Bercow only granted twenty-three Urgent Questions during his first year when the Labour Party was still in government. In contrast, he granted over fifty UQs within the first eighteen months of the Conservative led coalition. He has been correct to grant such questions when matters have arisen that need to be debated in Parliament. For example, on 16 July 2012, he granted Yvette Cooper, the shadow Home Secretary, an Urgent Question on security arrangements for the Olympic Games in light of the inability of G4S to deliver on its contract.[482] This was a topic which needed to be debated on the floor of the House of Commons.

Bercow is, however, accused of further bias against his old side. Conservative MP Rob Wilson, has researched the number of times Speaker Bercow has reprimanded Conservative MPs compared to opposition MPs since the 2010 general election. Wilson's statistics, which were taken over a one-and-a-half year period, show that the Speaker had aggressively intervened 375 times against Conservative MPs whereas he had only done so 160 times against Labour MPs, seventy-seven times against Liberal Democrat MPs and fifteen times against MPs from the smaller parties.[483] What constitutes 'aggressively' intervening is, of course, highly subjective and Bercow dismisses this argument by saying:

It has sometimes been said, 'Oh well, he is biased against the Conservatives', and the evidence advanced to try to justify this, in my view, ridiculous line of attack was that I had called to order Conservative Members more times, or rebuked them, than I had called to order Labour Members. The answer to that is that you don't prove impartiality by statistical equality. What the Speaker has to do is to keep order and intervene to restrain people or admonish them when they're guilty of an abuse.

Speaker Bercow then went on to say that, 'I really genuinely believe that the people who are trying to make a point here are people who start from a position of hostility and then desperately scurry around to try to justify it'. The problem for Bercow is that he appears to relish barking, 'Order! Order!' at the Conservative benches when they are either being too noisy or are giving lengthy responses.

Bercow does seem to have an uneasy relationship with the Conservative front bench and his rebukes fuel the resentment created by the way in which he made it to the Speakership. Since the 2010 general election, Bercow has not been afraid to admonish Cabinet ministers, the government Chief Whip and even the Prime Minister in the chamber. On 7 July 2010, the Speaker halted David Cameron when he was about to quote from Tony Blair's former Director of Communications, Alistair Campbell's published diaries with, 'Order. No, we will not bother with that.'[484] A year later, on 29 June 2011, Bercow again decided to cut short the Prime Minister's answer with a curt, 'We are very grateful'.[485] The Speaker was not satisfied with that and later he reminded Cameron that, 'Prime Minister's questions is principally for backbenchers', which appeared to be criticising the length of the answers.[486] Speaker Bercow's drive towards ensuring greater pace and so allowing more questions does not spare any quarter. He is prepared to reprimand even the Prime Minister in order to achieve this goal.

On 6 December 2010, Bercow had a stand up row with the government Chief Whip, Patrick McLoughlin, following objections raised to a procedural motion regarding Higher Education.

McLoughlin accused the Speaker of prompting Labour MPs to call out 'object' at the right time.[487] Bercow was having none of it and immediately reprimanded the Chief Whip: 'Order. The government Chief Whip has absolutely no business whatsoever shouting from a sedentary position. He– *[Interruption.]* Order. The right hon. Gentleman will remain in the Chamber. He has absolutely no business scurrying out of the Chamber. *[Interruption.]* Order. The Chief Whip has absolutely no business–.'[488]

McLoughlin, however, did not back down and he accused the Speaker of helping the Labour benches by telling the chamber, 'We all saw you'.[489] It was an extraordinary scene and a slanging match between the Speaker and the Chief Whip on the floor of the House of Commons was totally unprecedented in the post-war period.

Speaker Bercow has also seen fit to chastise other ministers. The day after Bercow's joust with the Chief Whip, the Speaker cut short Simon Burns, the Conservative Minister of State for Health: 'Order. The Minister will resume his seat. His answers have been excessively long-winded and repetitive and it must not happen again. I have made the position clear and I hope that the Minister will learn from that.'[490]

Again, this kind of admonishment by the Speaker was very unusual although Burns and Bercow had already had a spat in the summer of that year. On 29 June 2010, the Speaker had made a point of reminding the Health Minister to face front and address his answers to the whole House rather than continually turning to his Conservative colleagues. In the end, Burns, who must have felt bruised by the constant chastisement, muttered under his breath that Bercow was a 'stupid, sanctimonious dwarf'.[491] Later that day, Ian Paisley Jnr, the Democratic Unionist MP, asked the Speaker whether 'it is in order for a Member on the Front Bench to berate, scoff, scold and hiss at the Chair when a Member is trying to ask a question?'[492] Bercow answered that 'respect for the Chair is important'.[493]

Simon Burns is not the only minister to have been told off in the chamber. During Prime Minister's Question Time on 13 July 2011, Tim Loughton, the junior Education minister, was publicly rebuked by the Speaker. During a loud and rowdy question time, Bercow stopped the proceedings and singled out Loughton: 'Order. I say to the Children's Minister: try to calm down and behave like an adult, and if you cannot – if it is beyond you – leave the Chamber and we will manage without you.'[494]

When the noisy behaviour continued, Bercow went as far as to name Loughton, 'No, it is not funny. Only in your mind, Mr Loughton, is it funny. It is not funny at all; it is disgraceful.'[495] Whilst Bercow is not there to be liked by all MPs, and he certainly has to show that he is capable of rebuking unruly Members, he has to be careful not to alienate too many of his colleagues. The problem is that he does seem to like singling out ministers and making a public example of them. On 13 June 2012, Bercow called to order Michael Gove, the Secretary of State for Education, and announced that, 'In the average classroom, he would have been excluded by now. He must calm down.'[496] The reforming mandate with which Bercow was elected has given him the zeal to take on members of the government as part of his quest to reinvigorate the House of Commons and allow backbenchers to be heard.

All these events have produced a seemingly difficult relationship between the Speaker and the Prime Minister. In late 2010, David Cameron told a joke at the expense of Bercow during a speech to a group of lobby journalists. The Prime Minister told his audience an apocryphal tale about Simon Burns's driver inadvertently backing his ministerial car into the Speaker's official limousine in one of the courtyards in Parliament. According to Cameron, the Speaker told the Health minister, 'I'm not happy!' to which Burns responded, 'Well which one [of the seven dwarves] are you?'[497] Bobby Freidman, Bercow's biographer, argues that Cameron's willingness to tell the joke in front of an audience of journalists who would undoubtedly report it 'shows not only that there is no love lost between the pair, but also that Cameron is not afraid to show it'.[498]

There were signs of Cameron trying to get his own back on Bercow in the summer of 2011 when it was mooted that the Speaker would swap places with the Afghan Speaker as part of an exchange. The idea had been floated by Downing Street officials following a visit by David Cameron to Afghanistan during which he met with Abdul Rauf Ibrahimi, the Speaker of the Afghan Parliament. It transpired, however, that no one had consulted Bercow about this proposal and the Speaker's Office announced, 'The Speaker has not received an invitation to go to Afghanistan and has no plans to go to Afghanistan'.[499] This curt response shows that Bercow had no intention of allowing the Prime Minister to dispose of him temporarily. A prolonged absence could well have given Bercow's critics the opportunity they needed to plot against him.

The Prime Minister also showed his annoyance at the Speaker during Bercow's address at a special event in Westminster Hall to mark the Queen's Diamond Jubilee. In his speech, the Speaker called the monarch a 'kaleidoscope Queen of a kaleidoscope coun-try'.[500] David Cameron was caught on camera giving the Speaker a frown and glare when Bercow praised the Queen for reigning over a country in which people are 'respected regardless of how they live, how they look and how they love'.[501] This appeared to be a political message on gay rights; Bercow is President of the Kaleidoscope Trust, a gay rights pressure group. Even though the Prime Minister is in favour of gay marriage, he appeared to not favour the Speaker raising such controversial matters on this important occasion. Again, Bercow was making a political point albeit at a time when he was not chairing the House of Commons. On occasion, he appears unable to restrain the political campaigner inside him and this did nothing to improve his relations with Cameron. When asked about his relationship with the Prime Minister, the Speaker has said: 'I think that he does his job and I do mine. If you're asking me, "Are we bosom pals?" No, we're not but we don't need to be and we shouldn't be.'[502]

This is entirely true because otherwise the Speaker could be accused of being in the pocket of the Prime Minister and the government of the day. Bercow does, however, believe that he has a 'professional and constructive' working relationship with David Cameron which is, of course, what is needed for Parliament to function properly.[503] Any serious breakdown in that relationship would mean certain trouble for Bercow because no Speaker can survive if the Prime Minister completely turns on him.

Even though Bercow is constantly being criticised for chastising Conservative MPs, he does, of course, also rebuke opposition Members when they go on for too long. On 7 December 2010, the Speaker cut short the shadow Secretary of State for Justice and Labour MP Sadiq Khan, announcing:

> Order. I am loath to interrupt the shadow Secretary of State, but he is getting towards the point where his questioning has been longer than the Secretary of State's pithy statement, so he really does now need to bring it to an end. He can have another sentence, but he must then bring it to an end.[504]

On 16 July 2012, Bercow also cut short Maria Eagle, the shadow Transport Secretary, during her response to a government statement on rail investment telling her that 'she had well and truly had her time'.[505] Bercow will intervene when opposition frontbench spokesmen go on for too long in the same way that he would stop a minister. The fact that Bercow stops Conservatives more often is most probably down to the fact that they have greater opportunities to speak. Former Labour MP Martin Salter, who led Bercow's campaign for the Chair, believes that the Speaker will stop lengthy front bench speeches because he wants to make sure 'that backbenchers are heard and called more often'. This move has gained him respect and support among backbenchers from both sides of the House.

Bercow nevertheless seems to have annoyed some Conservative MPs and, on occasion, this has caused some lack of deference to the office of Speaker. For example, in January 2011, Conservative MP Mark Pritchard clashed with the Speaker in one of the corridors at Westminster. Bercow had refused to allow Pritchard to ask a question only minutes before, wrongly claiming that the MP had not been present in the chamber at the beginning of proceedings.[506] The aggrieved Conservative MP had a confrontation with the Speaker when Bercow pointed at Pritchard and accused him of not complying with a tradition of the House and standing aside for him when he passed by. According to James Chapman, the Political Editor of the *Daily Mail*, Pritchard told the Speaker not to point at him; Bercow told the MP that he must respect the courtesies of the House. With that, Pritchard told Bercow that, 'You're not f***** royalty, Mr Speaker', and then walked off. The Speaker, determined to have the last word, called back, 'Well, a good morning to you, sir'.[507] Such a scene is incredible and would have been unthinkable in the days of previous Speakers. Even Michael Martin, who was forced from office, did not have to put up with this kind of disrespect and defiance. This episode shows that the mystique of the Speakership has been stripped away over the years so that some MPs are no longer prepared to bite their tongues in front of the Speaker.

One episode which seems to have damaged Bercow's reasonably good standing among Conservative backbench MPs took place on 13 June 2012 during an Opposition Day debate on the Secretary of State for Culture, Jeremy Hunt's handling of the Rupert Murdoch bid for BSkyB. During the debate, Labour MP Chris Bryant, said in his speech that Hunt 'had lied to Parliament'.[508] *Erskine May*, the parliamentary rule book, quite clearly states that 'charges of uttering a deliberate falsehood' are not permitted and constitute unparliamentary language.[509] As already seen, Betty Boothroyd had banished Dr Ian Paisley for the use of the word 'falsehood' back in 1993. Speaker Bercow, however, immediately rose and ruled that Bryant's accusation was permissible:

> Let me say to the House that the substantive matter under consideration reflected in the terms of the motion is whether the House of Commons has been misled in any way. That is the thrust of the matter under debate and the Secretary of State is making a very clear defence of himself, so when Members cavil and inquire whether what we have heard is legitimate, I am guided by advice and I operate on the basis that there is a substantive motion, which is what the whole debate is about and in relation to which the Secretary of State is speaking.[510]

Bercow had taken the advice of the clerks and this rather convoluted justification derives from a footnote in *Erskine May* which states that 'The suggestion that a Member is deliberately misleading the House is not parliamentary [...] and the proper course, if such an allegation has been made, is to table the appropriate motion'.[511] That is, of course, what the opposition had done and so Bercow was merely following advice based on this footnote. The ruling caused uproar among the Conservative benches. Sir George Young, the Leader of the House of Commons, questioned the Speaker's judgement.[512] For such a senior MP and former contestant for the Speakership to do such a thing is quite a serious occurrence in the chamber. Nevertheless, Bercow stuck by his ruling. He was sticking to the rules but he was not gauging the mood of the House as all Speakers need to do. Bercow was not obliged to follow the advice of the clerks and he could have ruled that Bryant's language was too strong. For many Conservative MPs this would have been a clear sign of bias.

Sir George Young followed up what he had said in the chamber with a letter to the Speaker in which he recounted that 'Members continue to raise their concerns with me, and their disquiet that such a direct accusation was allowed to take place on the floor of the chamber'.[513] Clearly, Bercow's action has been a setback in terms of the goodwill that he had been building up with Conservative backbenchers. He obviously realises this because, in his reply to Sir George Young, Bercow wrote that there 'were aspects of the debate that I found regrettable and upsetting' and he insisted that his ruling had not set a new precedent.[514] The problem with that is that every ruling given by a Speaker can be used as a precedent and many of the rules governing the House of Commons are based on rulings given by Bercow's predecessors in the Chair. Bercow had based his ruling on a footnote in *Erskine May* and so what he did could form the basis of a footnote in a future edition. Whilst this is probably unlikely, because the clerks who write *Erskine May* could choose not to include it, a Speaker must be so careful when making controversial rulings. What is clear is that by allowing a Labour MP to call a Conservative Cabinet minister a liar yet again causes Bercow to be subject to further accusations of bias.

His course of action has certainly done nothing to improve his relations with the Conservative side and has probably created a few more doubters among those who had, up until then, been pleased with his pro-backbencher stance.

In contrast three months later, on 18 September 2012, Speaker Bercow proved that he was prepared to discipline a Labour MP for accusing a government minister of lying. Labour MP Paul Flynn, and a friend of Bercow, called the Secretary of State for Defence, Philip Hammond, a liar during a debate on Afghanistan. Bercow asked Flynn to withdraw his allegation but the Labour MP refused. The Speaker then named Flynn and MPs voted to suspend him from the House.[515] This was an important signal because it showed that Chris Bryant's accusation was tolerated because of its particular circumstance and that that episode was the exception rather than the rule.

Conservative MPs were again unhappy with the Speaker on 29 November 2012 when he allowed Deputy Prime Minister, Nick Clegg, to give a statement opposing David Cameron's response to the Leveson report. Cameron rejected calls for legislation to regulate the press but Clegg did not agree and so made a separate statement in which he made common cause with Labour. A government spokesman making a different and opposing statement from the same despatch box as another had not been seen since the National Government of the 1930s and is an innovation of coalition politics. Nevertheless, the Conservative MP Peter Bone tried to prevent Clegg's statement from taking place by proposing the adjournment of the House. Bercow did not accept this motion and so Clegg proceeded with his statement.[516] Despite the fact that Bercow ruffled a few more feathers on the Conservative benches, the Speaker has to see that minority opinion is heard even if that minority opinion is from within the government.

Another reason why Speaker Bercow faces constant criticism is thanks to the activities of his wife, Sally. Mrs Bercow has turned herself into a minor media celebrity on the back of her husband's position and those who wish to attack the Speaker have used this against him. In May 2010, Sally Bercow stood as a Labour candidate in the St James ward of the City of Westminster. Commentators and critics immediately questioned this action querying whether this broke the strict impartiality of Speaker's House.[517] What they had all forgotten, or not bothered to check, was that Dr Horace King's wife had been a Labour member of Southampton City Council at the beginning of his Speakership in the mid-1960s. Whilst unusual, Mrs Bercow's wish to serve on a local council was not therefore totally unprecedented. What was different was that the Kings had both been Labour supporters whereas the Bercows sat on opposite sides of the political divide.

Sally Bercow has now gone beyond simply seeking public office, enjoying a high profile in the media with a regular column in the *Daily Star*. A particularly embarrassing episode for the Speaker was in February 2011 when his wife appeared in the *London Evening Standard* wearing nothing but a bedsheet with the Houses of Parliament in the background. The article, which was part of a feature for Valentine's Day, caused one Conservative minister to announce that Mrs Bercow should 'shut up and cover up'.[518] Sally Bercow reacted to this furore by saying that:

> The trouble is, because I'm married to the Speaker, whatever I do is put in the media and used to get at him and I think Ann Widdecombe [the former Conservative MP], apparently, I've just been told [...] was saying that it's not in keeping with the dignity of the office. Well, sorry, I'm not the Speaker, my husband is, and fortunately, he doesn't view my main role in life as to support him.[519]

Sally Bercow branded the entire incident as a 'storm in a bedsheet', however, it served to fuel criticism of her husband's Speakership. Whilst they could have been cause for further embarrassment, Mrs Bercow's appearances on the television programmes *Celebrity Big Brother*, *When Paddy met Sally* and *Paddy & Sally's Excellent Gypsy Adventure* have only served to boost the profile of both husband and wife. More and more people are aware of who the Speaker is thanks to Mrs Bercow, although her television appearances have potentially damaged her husband's position internally at Westminster. Indeed, thanks to the way in which Bercow was elected, the journalist Andrew Pierce told the BBC's *Daily Politics* programme that, 'They [the Conservatives] can't stand him anyway. That's the trouble and, because of her [Sally's] antics, it just hardens that bitterness towards him.'[520] A Speaker cannot survive long if he upsets too many of his parliamentary colleagues and so Bercow is clearly not keen for his wife to participate in such programmes. The Speaker has said that he told his wife that he was not in favour of her taking part in *Celebrity Big Brother* but in the end he respected her decision to go ahead.[521]

Sally Bercow is also outspoken in her criticism of the Conservatives in her regular tweets on the social media site Twitter. In 2009, she called the then Leader of the Opposition, David Cameron, a 'merchant of spin' and in 2010 she criticised the Foreign Secretary William Hague for the way he dealt with accusations about his private life.[522] All this led to the International Development minister, Alan Duncan, stating that Sally Bercow's tweets were 'becoming a pretty serious problem'.[523] Duncan, who was asked for his views on the BBC's *Daily Politics* programme, went on to say that:

> If the wife of the Chief of the Defence Staff, say, were a member
> of CND [the Campaign for Nuclear Disarmament] it would be

pretty awkward but she may be free to do that. The wife of the
Speaker is entitled to opinions of course but, you know, she's living
in the House, a grace-and-favour house, but then says, 'I have a
separate life' and a lot of it is personal attack on Conservative
politicians. She attacked William Hague. That's quite different
from saying, 'I want to stand as a Labour candidate in a local
council.' I think this is becoming a pretty serious problem.[524]

Alan Duncan's point was well made but Bercow defends his wife
and explains the position:

> One thing I do think is quite wrong and unfair is for somebody to
> say: 'Oh well, it's improper for the Speaker's wife to be engaged
> in acts of politics.' That's wrong. It may well add to the spice of
> life, it might well cause some difficulties in terms of press cover-
> age, but to suggest that it's somehow constitutionally improper
> is quite wrong. And the simple reason for that is that the obliga-
> tion for impartiality applies to me. It does not apply to Sally, and
> deep down I ask you to consider this, and hope you might even
> agree. It's a deeply sexist view based on the idea that the wife is
> my chattel.[525]

The fact is that it is the office of Speaker, and not just the holder
of the position, that has to be impartial and the partner (male or
female) of the incumbent is loosely affiliated to the overall office.
That being said, Speaker Bercow is quite right to say that his
wife's political involvement is not at all constitutionally improper.
After all, what constitution is that? Speaker Horace King's wife's
role as a Labour alderman in Southampton shows that there
is already a precedent in a job which relies entirely on conventions created by previous occupants of the Chair. The concept
of the husband, wife or partner of the sitting Speaker having

a far more prominent and talked about role is just part of the continuing evolution of the office of Speaker.

The problem is that Sally Bercow's political outbursts have caused commentators and parliamentarians to question her husband's impartiality. For example, in November 2010, Speaker Bercow appeared to have been influenced by his wife when he delayed calling a by-election following a court ruling which declared void the result in Oldham East & Saddleworth. The court had ruled that Mr Woolas had knowingly made false allegations about the Liberal Democrat candidate in the Oldham seat. Mrs Bercow announced on television that, 'I do think Phil Woolas [the Labour MP for Oldham East and Saddleworth] has the right to appeal and for that appeal to be heard.'[526] Rather than immediately declare that there was a vacancy and a by-election was needed, Bercow appeared to be taking his wife's advice because, in his statement on 8 November 2010, he announced that he would wait for the outcome of the judicial review.[527] Although it was portrayed in the media that Sally Bercow had influenced her husband's decisions, it was probably the right one to take. A decade earlier, in March 1999, Speaker Boothroyd had hastily announced that the Newark constituency was vacant because its MP was found guilty of election fraud. Fiona Jones was, however, reinstated by the Court of Appeal.[528] This was undoubtedly a very recent precedent for not rushing into calling a by-election and showed why Speaker Bercow did not have to take an immediate decision.

Apart from accusations of bias in the Commons chamber, Speaker Bercow has voiced some political opinions which have brought into question his own impartiality. Firstly, in October 2009, Bercow declared at the first ever UK Youth Parliament sitting in the Commons chamber that the far-right British National Party was 'a poison which we could well do without'.[529] Whilst this is a completely mainstream point of view, the Speaker is supposed to refrain from such political statements. Bercow argued that he was 'under no obligation whatsoever to be impartial between the forces of democracy on one hand and the forces of evil on the other'.[530] This is pretty powerful language for someone who is not supposed to express partisan views in public; at times, Bercow cannot restrain the political animal which still lurks inside him.

In January 2011, further controversy arose concerning the Speaker's neutrality when he wrote to a constituent in Buckingham stating that he supported banning foxhunting. Not only was Bercow changing a view he had held when he was first elected to Buckingham in 1997, he was also expressing a political opinion, something a Speaker usually avoids. A constituency spokesman for Bercow defended the remark stating that the Speaker's 'role is to be neutral in the chamber but not neutered as a constituency member'.[531] This, of course, opens up a huge debate on how far the Speaker's neutrality should reach and whether being Speaker restricts the holder's role as a constituency MP. Whilst Bercow did not state his views in the Commons chamber, he nevertheless did so on the Speaker's headed notepaper. Again, it is clear that Bercow finds it difficult to stop himself taking part in the political debates that had been part of his life for so long. In response to all the negative publicity he had received in the *Daily Mail*, the Speaker hit back and called it a 'sexist, racist, bigoted, comic cartoon strip'.[532] John Bercow demonstrates how tough it is for a very opinionated political campaigner to carry out a job in which you are supposed to keep your views to yourself.

John Bercow is very keen on the ambassadorial role of the Speakership in the same way that Betty Boothroyd was but he has taken it a step further. This is very much part of Speaker

Bercow's strategy for restoring confidence in Parliament following the expenses scandal:

> I try to act as an ambassador for the House and a robust advocate
> of democratic politics by getting out and about around the coun-
> try visiting schools, colleges, universities, charitable organisations,
> faith groups, voluntary bodies of one sort or another to talk about
> the role of the Speaker, the importance of democracy, the way
> in which Parliament is changing, the merit of people becoming
> involved in the political process.

This shows just how much the Speakership has developed in the post-war era. In the 1950s, Speaker Morrison would refuse such invitations and would only attend events that he was obliged to go to or were related to his capacity as a constituency MP.[533] The Clerk of the House, Robert Rogers, believes that Speaker Bercow has taken the role even further than his predecessors:

> I think that he [John Bercow] is approaching outreach on a much
> more co-ordinated, much more planned basis, but also a wider
> spectrum of things that he does. Now Betty [Boothroyd] was a
> great enthusiast for going to other Parliaments and that was her
> style. He is doing that too.

Rogers points to that fact that when Speaker Bercow visited the National Assembly for Wales in September 2009 he was also determined to go to a school in Cardiff and speak to some sixth-formers. Bercow has, therefore, extended the Speaker's role beyond the usual ambassadorial duty of visiting other Parliaments. He now goes out to meet the wider public rather than just confine himself to meeting parliamentarians and digni-taries from other countries. This move goes hand in hand with the much greater expectations placed on the Speaker thanks to the enhanced public awareness that the office now enjoys.

Speaker Bercow also receives lots of guests at Speaker's House and is carrying on the tradition established by George Thomas in the late 1970s. Bercow has described the number of events held in his apartments: 'I, so you've got a sense of the order of magnitude of it, would reckon to host somewhere between two and four, probably averaging at about three, charitable organisations every week here in the House.'

The fact that the Bercows have become something of a show-biz couple has also benefited the outreach work. They became the first Speaker and wife to do a joint television interview when they appeared together on ITV1's *Lorraine* programme and talked about their eldest son's autism.[534] The interview came across as a justification for why Sally Bercow went on *Celebrity Big Brother* (she earned £100,000 for the charity Ambitious about Autism) but, at the same time, it showed just how much the Speaker was reaching out to the masses and using his position to support good causes.

The most noticeable thing that John Bercow did when he became Speaker in June 2009 was to abandon the official regalia in favour of less formal attire. Bercow states that: 'I basically feel that on ceremonial occasions there is an argument for dressing up but on day to day business occasions I have made the change to wearing an ordinary business suit with a modest robe on top.'

His reason for this change is, as he puts it, that, 'My view is that the office is not defined by the dress but by the values'. This is reminiscent of Chris Patten's decision not to wear the full colonial uniform when he was made Governor of Hong Kong in 1992. Patten's reason for dispensing with the ceremonial dress was because he wanted to be 'more open and accessible and without some of the flummery'.[535] This is exactly the same rationale behind Bercow's decision not to wear the Speaker's traditional regalia.

As already seen, Bercow came under fire from one of his predecessors, Baroness Boothroyd, for the decision to downgrade the Speaker's dress; she thought he should 'be proud of your uniform. Be proud of what it represents.' In an interview with Radio 4's *World This Weekend*, she said that Bercow's decision to wear a suit was 'not good for Parliament' and that 'if you are doing a job, you wear the uniform of that job'.[536] For a former Speaker to criticise the current occupant of the Chair was very unusual and showed that Bercow had battles to fight on all fronts. There were those pining for reform and there were those who were jealous guardians of tradition.

Despite saying that he would wear the State Robe on ceremonial occasions, Speaker Bercow did not wear it for the State visits of Pope Benedict XVI and President Obama. When Heads of State, such as President Mandela, have previously addressed Parliament whilst on a State visit, the Speaker has worn the full regalia. When tackled on the reason why he did not wear the State Robe for President Obama's visit, Speaker Bercow recalled that:

I was personally rather keen to wear the State Robe on the occasion of the Obama visit and I got the message back that Helene Hayman [the Lord Speaker] wasn't minded to do so and I think I agreed that it was better either that we both did or that neither of us did and I think she felt as she did and, therefore, we didn't, neither of us did.

Bercow chose to wear the State Robe when the Queen addressed Parliament in Westminster Hall on the occasion of her Diamond Jubilee and so perhaps with the election of a new Lord Speaker, Baroness D'Souza, the tradition has been re-established. It certainly seems that it was not a deliberate decision for Bercow not to wear the State Robe and he has shown that he is quite willing to wear it on bigger, grander occasions.

Despite his desire for reform, in some ways Bercow is a traditionalist. For example, in February 2012, the Speaker insisted that parliamentary privilege meant that the prayers which take place at the beginning of each day in the House of Commons would not be affected by a controversial court ruling which outlawed them in town halls. Even the *Mail on Sunday*, a regular critic of Bercow, lauded the Speaker's stand on this matter.[537] Bercow has insisted that:

> Personally I would prefer to keep it as it is. Yes, I'm a reformer, but just because you are a reformer, it doesn't mean you have to change everything. I believe in changing to make the House stronger. I don't myself believe that getting rid of prayers would make the House stronger.[538]

Bercow takes a rather pragmatic approach to the Speakership and he will defend tradition where he feels it still has a place.

Previous Speakers have had matters of security of the House of Commons to contend with and John Bercow is no exception. In July 2011, the media mogul, Rupert Murdoch, was hit by a custard pie whilst giving evidence to a House of Commons select committee investigating the phone hacking scandal. Bercow has said that:

> The incident that took place in July when Rupert Murdoch was attacked was a very considerable embarrassment to the House [...] it was embarrassing. I commissioned an independent report on the subject which showed that mistakes had been made. That independent report made a number of recommendations for the future and all of those either have been or are in the process of being implemented.

It was reported in the press that one result of the Speaker's dissatisfaction with security was the premature retirement of the Serjeant-at-Arms, Jill Pay.[539] Mrs Pay denied this, however, during an interview on BBC Radio 4's *The Westminster Hour* although she was certainly not the first member of staff surrounding the Speaker to vacate their position prematurely.[540] John Bercow has seen two Speaker's Secretaries, Angus Sinclair and Kate Emms, leave the Speaker's Office showing that he is not reluctant to move people on if he deems it necessary.

Speaker Bercow has tried hard to win over his critics. His bias in favour of backbenchers has gained him additional support on the Conservative side even if he has alienated the front bench at the same time. Whilst Conservative ministers might grumble about the Speaker, Conservative backbenchers, such as Jane Ellison, welcome the fact that he 'has the interests of the back-benchers very much at heart'. Bercow's strongest critic, Quentin Letts, believes that the Speaker also 'uses his patronage to full effect' in order to win support. Letts argues that:

> Yes, he [Speaker Bercow] is good at getting through the Order Paper [...] This indeed earns him some popularity. He is also assiduous in greasing up to certain backbenchers – e.g. Chris Bryant, Douglas Carswell– who have a presence on Twitter and on the web. He has introduced Speaker's Lectures as a form of patronage to be dispensed to older backbenchers. He has dished out Speaker's Panel positions (which carry a financial premium) to not so obvious allies.

Bearing in mind the way in which Bercow was elected to the Chair, it is no wonder that he has had to employ strategies to strengthen his hold on his position. No Speaker can continue in office if he or she does not enjoy the support of a strong majority in the House, just as Bercow's immediate predecessor discovered.

In a similar fashion to Jack Weatherill in 1988, John Bercow is not afraid to use the media to defend his actions and take on his critics. On 14 August 2012, Bercow used an interview on BBC Radio 4's *World at One* programme to accuse his critics of being 'embittered and resentful' and frustrated about not doing as well in their own political careers.[541] He added that 'Just as I don't bear a grudge against anyone who did not vote for me, I would argue that if people are fair-minded they should not, three years on, be sulking about who won'.[542] Bercow's interview during the slow news post-Olympic Games summer season prompted articles in most of the major newspapers the following day. His timing was excellent in terms of achieving maximum media exposure. Unlike Weatherill, however, this tactic provoked a counter-attack from Bercow's arch-critic, Rob Wilson, who wrote in the *Mail on Sunday* that the Speaker was 'preening, partisan and pompous'.[543] Weatherill's critics had accused him of weakness in the Chair but Bercow's outburst in the media has provoked a direct personal attack on his own character.

Although Speaker Bercow has been instrumental in setting up the Independent Parliamentary Standards Authority (IPSA), such as appointing its Chief Executive, Andrew McDonald, he has nevertheless been critical of some its strict rules. Whilst Bercow has a mandate to 'clean up' Parliament and make the expenses system more transparent, he also has a duty to look after the interests of the Members of Parliament who elected him. In this he has to strike a balance because the public and the media would not take kindly to a Speaker who acted like a shop steward in the way that Michael Martin appeared to have done. Speaker Bercow admits that IPSA was hastily put together and that it needed a review. He put forward a submission which suggested changes in order to make it fairer for MPs.

Such a move would have made him popular among backbenchers because many were having to pay rent for constituency offices upfront and then wait several months to be reimbursed. Bercow managed to assist his constituency in the House of Commons and probably gained a few more supporters in the process.

In the same light, Bercow also attempted to protect MPs in October 2012 when, in response to a point of order from Conservative MP Julian Lewis, the Speaker stated that he had written to Sir Ian Kennedy, the Chairman of IPSA, to block the publication of the addresses of MPs' landlords.[544] This was because some MPs rented their flats to other MPs and publishing these addresses would constitute a breach of security. There was an immediate backlash from the press because MPs were claiming taxpayer-funded expenses to rent homes in London whilst at the same time letting property in the capital. The *Daily Telegraph* reported Sir Alistair Graham, the former Chairman of the Committee on Standards in Public Life: 'It would be unfortunate if the Speaker was seen to be involved in what looked like a potential cover-up.'[545] Bercow has to be careful not to fall into the trap of his predecessor. Nowadays the Speaker cannot protect MPs if it means preventing important information about the use of public money being released.

A month later, four members of IPSA stood down following the Speaker's decision to make them reapply for their posts. A row between Sir Ian Kennedy and John Bercow took place in a series of letters in which the chairman claimed that the Speaker's changes would allow 'placemen' to be appointed and risked exposing the authority to party political bias.[546] Bercow had set up a panel to vet the appointment of IPSA members which included the former Conservative MP Peter Atkinson. This was seen as the Speaker taking revenge on IPSA members for the crackdown on what MPs can claim.[547] Speakers must try to look after the interests of the MPs who elected them but at the same time they now have to be extremely conscious of how such actions are perceived by the wider public.

John Bercow's Speakership has seen something of a sea change. The expenses scandal and resulting public antipathy towards party politics have shaped how he has tackled the office of Speaker. Bercow has used his powers to allow far greater scrutiny of the government and at the same time given more opportunities to backbenchers to contribute in debates. This has made him very much a 'marmite Speaker': disliked by the government front bench and yet liked by the back benches. A coalition government rather than a strong majority government has helped Bercow's cause. A strong majority government might not have tolerated a Speaker who would cause them difficulties in the House. Bercow is also fortunate in that there would be great reluctance to get rid of another Speaker following the downfall of Michael Martin.

Thanks to a combination of increased interest in the office and its personalities, and the Bercow family's own self-publicity, Bercow has found himself in the media spotlight far more than any of his predecessors. Speaker Bercow has given more television and press interviews than any of his predecessors and his wife's media profile has led to unprecedented media interest in the 'First Family' of Speaker's House. John Bercow has increased the role of the Speakership thanks to his outreach work and his crusade to improve the standing of Parliament post-expenses-scandal fallout. Whilst Sally Bercow's actions are not always as sympathetic to her husband's position as they should be, they have still given the present Speakership an added interest that has made the job even more notable. Together, they have certainly made the Speakership into an office that the public and the media see as just as important as any senior ministerial position. As a consequence, the holder of that office now enjoys the same level of media exposure as any Cabinet minister. Bercow's ability to use the media to his benefit and his confident use of the Speaker's powers constitute a success story: he has made the Speaker's office far more able to ensure that the government is held to account.

Conclusion

Wider Still and Wider: The Post-War Evolution of an Ancient Office

As Labour Members have said, the role of the Speaker has changed and continues to change. When the right hon. Member for Chesterfield [Tony Benn] and I first came to the House, the Speaker was like a High Court judge. One did not speak to him or see him socially.

– Sir Peter Emery, former Conservative MP, 2001[548]

Whilst the essential elements of the Speakership have remained intact since 1945, the role has also witnessed a continuous reshaping thanks to the different occupants of the Chair and the events and parliamentary reforms that have coloured their tenures. But, are the changes merely minor adaptations and natural evolution or has the office seen a major transformation since 1945?

In 1951, William Shepherd Morrison was invited up to Downing Street to be offered the Speakership by the Prime Minister, Winston Churchill, as if it were a ministerial position in the government. Indeed, the political scientist, Peter G. Richards, wrote in the late 1950s that when a vacancy occurs in the Speakership 'the selection is made by the Cabinet'.[549] Speaker King wrote in the early 1970s that: 'The choosing of a Speaker is now a House of Commons matter. For centuries it was so in theory only.'[550] King was a bit premature in this assumption because he was most definitely the agreed choice of the two front benches and his successor, Selwyn Lloyd, was the government's chosen candidate. It was not until Jack Weatherill's election as Speaker in 1983 that what King described became the case. Weatherill was most definitely the choice of the backbenchers because he was not the preferred candidate of the Prime Minister, Margaret Thatcher. From that moment on, the backbenchers have asserted their right to choose their own Speaker rather than have a government-backed candidate forced upon them. Neither Betty Boothroyd, Michael Martin nor John Bercow were the preferred frontbench candidate and this went in their favour and gave them the Speakership. Having the support of the government and opposition front bench is now no longer an advantage when it comes to electing a Speaker as it was in the first half of the post-war period. It is often a disadvantage.

A significant change in the previous clout of the Speaker has occurred since the war: the House now prefers professional backbenchers rather than former ministers. Six out of the ten post-war Speakers have served as a Deputy Speaker before they were elected to the main job and John Bercow had experience of chairing the House in committee as a member of the Chairmen's Panel. Out of these seven, only George Thomas had served as a minister before going on to become a Deputy Speaker and Speakers Weatherill and Boothroyd had both been whips. Nevertheless, it has become a distinct advantage, if not a necessity, for a potential Speaker to have had experience chairing the Commons. The controversy surrounding the election of former ministers Morrison, Hylton-Foster and Lloyd as Speakers demonstrates the House's reluctance to have a convenient choice parachuted in by the government who might not be the best person for the job. Backbenchers want the Speaker to be their champion and not the placeman of the executive.

The last two Speakership elections have seen a perverse twist away from backbenchers choosing a mutually acceptable champion towards a competition to see which side could get one over on the other. Labour backbenchers elected Michael Martin in order to ensure that one of their own was in the Chair even though he did not enjoy the approval of the Conservative opposition or indeed the backing of the government front bench. In 2009, Labour backbenchers again used their numerical superiority to elect John Bercow who, despite being a Conservative, was not the preferred candidate of that side of the House. Bercow's transformation from a right-wing Conservative into a more liberal parliamentarian married to a Labour supporting wife meant that the *Daily Mail*'s parliamentary sketch writer, Quentin Letts, went as far as to say that the 'Commons' Labour majority voted for Bercow to spite the Tories'.[551] This was undoubtedly the case and it seems that although backbenchers have seized the power to choose a Speaker they are now prepared to abuse that power in order to score party political points.

Previously, the judicial nature of the Speakership had meant that the office had gone to those from a legal background. Speakers Morrison, Hylton-Foster and Lloyd had all been lawyers and so had the vast majority of their predecessors since the 1700s. Any requirement for legal expertise has ceased and being a backbencher with experience in the Chair is clearly now more preferable. A Speaker's ability to give clear rulings on complicated issues has now become less important than the ability to be a fair chairman. Robert Rogers, the Clerk of the House of Commons, explains why:

The House itself is less procedurally minded. You very rarely see Members getting hold of a copy of [*Erskine*] *May* and looking things up [...] but in the past, I think, many more Members have had an instinctive understanding of how the House works and the rules and what lies behind them. That's far less the case now.

The role of an MP has changed because the public expect their local representative to be a community champion working hard in the constituency rather than a skilled parliamentarian who spends all his or her time at Westminster. The office of Speaker has, therefore, evolved with that change. Rather than learning all the rules, a modern Speaker has got to be more conscious of allowing Members the opportunity to raise the concerns of their constituents on the floor of the House.

Perhaps the most quantifiable change has been to the workload of the Speaker:

I think Speakers have become increasingly busy people. I doubt if Speaker Morrison spent anything like the hours on the job, studying upstairs what he was going to do, as recent Speakers under whom I served have had to do. I don't think that older Speakers under whom I served did nearly as much real work outside the Chamber of the House as current Speakers have had to do.[552]

One of Sir Donald Limon's colleagues, Robert Rogers, confirms this by saying, 'I don't think George Thomas would recognise the job that John Bercow does in chairing the House of Commons Commission'. The *House of Commons (Administration) Act 1978* certainly added to the workload of the Speaker because it invested all the responsibility for running the parliamentary estate in the office. The change to the Speaker's job is summed up by Lord Martin when he said that:

I had been a Deputy Speaker for some time but being a Deputy
Speaker and being Speaker are light years apart because as
Deputy Speaker what you did was you took your share in the
Chamber whereas you soon learned when you became Speaker,
and I have described the Clerk as the Chief Executive of the
organisation, as Speaker you are like the Chairman of the organisation, and therefore you deal with all sorts of things. There is
security [...] there is maintenance, and it is a caring organisation
because there are many thousands of people employed here in
the precincts of this Parliamentary Estate.[553]

At the beginning of the post-war era, the gap between the
amount of work undertaken by the Speaker and one of his
deputies would not have been so great. Most of the Speaker's
time, just like a Deputy Speaker, would be spent in the Chair.
Now, this role is just the tip of the iceberg with the real work
going on behind the scenes in meeting rooms and offices beyond
the chamber.

This administrative burden has placed great financial responsibility on the holder of the office of Speaker. He or she is now in
overall charge of all the budgets which finance the running of the
House of Commons. It is, of course, this duty which got Michael
Martin into trouble because even though the expenses scandal
affected many MPs, in the end the buck stops with the Speaker.
In Australia, the Speaker of the House of Representatives has
been called 'The House's "Minister"'.[554] The responsibility of
overseeing all the departments which manage the House of
Commons is very similar to the job of a government minister
and so the Speakership has grown to encompass this role. This
additional undertaking has made the Speaker even more open to
scrutiny and media attention as more and more people become
interested in the way public funds are administered.

The Speakership has assumed a more ambassadorial role commensurate with its increased profile. This has grown gradually throughout the post-war period ever since Colonel Clifton Brown became the first Speaker to travel abroad and represent the House of Commons at international functions. Horace King was described by Robin Turton, the veteran Conservative MP, as having 'gained the reputation of being the most travelled Speaker of the House of Commons' thanks to all the official visits abroad he undertook.555 Betty Boothroyd was, and still is, a strong advocate of the Speakership's representative role and boasts, 'I left the Speaker's job with nearly twenty invitations still outstanding [...] because I was in such demand to go abroad'.

The Westminster Speakership is a model that has been adopted by the countries of the Commonwealth within their Parliaments. The newer parliaments and assemblies of the Commonwealth look to Westminster for advice and guidance thanks to its long established procedures and precedents. Robert Rogers has commented that 'It is fairly frequent that I get e-mails, or other colleagues get e-mails, saying, "We've got this problem..." I had one from the Caribbean last week.' The office of Speaker in the United Kingdom is, therefore, influential in shaping how other parliaments create institutions to carry out the same or similar functions. It is a testament to the history and strength of the office of Speaker that so many countries have sought to emulate it in their own parliaments. Even after independence, the countries of the Commonwealth have retained this institution.

The antiquity of the Speakership means that Commonwealth countries have not, however, found it possible to re-create the totally non-partisan element that is present at Westminster. Commonwealth Speakers do not resign from their political parties in the way that the British Speaker does. Canada tried to copy this model in the late 1960s and early 1970s when Speaker

Lucien Lamoureux was re-elected as an Independent rather than continuing with his Liberal Party affiliation. However, this move has not continued and Lamoureux's successors have returned to being re-elected on their party tickets. It is not uncommon for former Speakers in Commonwealth countries to return to the back benches or even become ministers after having served in the Chair. At Westminster, a retiring Speaker continues to give up his or her seat in the House of Commons and does not attempt to restart a political career.

Even the Scottish Parliament and the Welsh and Northern Ireland Assemblies have not managed to replicate this important gesture of impartiality. The only two Speakers to continue beyond an election are Dafydd Elis-Thomas in Wales and William Hay in Northern Ireland, and both men retained their party affiliations when standing for re-election to their respective assemblies. Being a presiding officer does not preclude people from returning to party politics in the devolved legislatures like it does at Westminster. Indeed, Lord Elis-Thomas and Alex Fergusson, the former Presiding Officer of the Scottish Parliament, have both returned to the benches of their party grouping after giving up the chairmanship of their respective legislatures. Lord Elis-Thomas even stood for the leadership of his party, Plaid Cymru, after having been Presiding Officer. That these newer legislatures within the United Kingdom cannot emulate a Westminster tradition shows what a unique position the Westminster Speakership is in. Even long-established institutions such as the Canadian House of Commons cannot embed the complete impartiality that is so important to the British office.

It is interesting how, to some extent, the Speakerships of all the Commonwealth countries are all intertwined. Whilst on most occasions it is the precedents and practices set by the Westminster Speakership which are adopted by other Commonwealth countries, it is also possible for the older office to learn from the newer ones. For example, the precedent set by Sir Norman Stronge, who was Speaker of the Northern Ireland House of Commons, when he was allowed to return to the Chair having been absent from Stormont through disqualification, could easily be used at Westminster. The case of the Speaker of the Australian House of Representatives, Peter Slipper, who in April 2012 decided to 'step aside' to clear his name of personal and financial allegations rather than resign, is also something which could be used as a precedent at Westminster. Robert Rogers believes that, in such circumstances, it would be 'a choice for Members rather than dictated by precedent'. This is, of course, because there is no precedent but the Australian example could well be used. The Speakership of the United Kingdom is actually part of a much bigger institution of Speakerships around the Commonwealth and each can learn from the other.

The growing nature of the ambassadorial role of the Speaker is linked to increased public awareness of the job thanks to the introduction of radio and then television broadcasting in the 1970s and 1980s. Radio made George Thomas a household name and television made the job of Speaker much more identifiable during Jack Weatherill's time in the Chair. Television also made Betty Boothroyd, as the first Madam Speaker, into a world famous political personality. The downside of this spotlight on the Speakership, as Peter Riddell has commented, is:

A Speaker who is not very effective in the Chair, like Michael Martin, is immediately exposed because what he says and does is so much more in the public eye. I think that's the crucial difference with the past, because of radio and TV, the whole club is opened up to exposure from outside. I think that's the biggest change.

It is doubtful whether Sir Harry Hylton-Foster or Dr Horace King
would have survived very long as Speaker if Parliament had been
televised during their time in the Chair. Hylton-Foster's failure to
stand up to unruly MPs and King's fondness for sherry would have
been quickly exposed if proceedings were broadcast on television.
As it was, any shortcomings in a Speaker could be easily covered
up because they were not open to the instant scrutiny that their
successors in the Chair would have to deal with. The additional
prestige and importance bestowed on the Speakership thanks to
radio and television broadcasting is a double-edged sword because
that new prominence also means that anyone not up to the job
might not last. Michael Martin did well to continue in the role for
as long as he did but, in the end, he could not survive. The new
found prominence of the Speakership can propel a lesser-known
backbench MP into political stardom; it can also ruin the reputation of someone who cannot cope with the pressures of the job.

The biggest visible change to the Speakership in more recent
years is the increasing informality of the Speaker's uniform.
Speaker Boothroyd decided not to wear the traditional full-
bottomed wig when she was elected in 1992 and her successors,
Michael Martin and John Bercow have chosen not to reinstate
what was the most prominent part of the regalia. Lord Weatherill
disapproved of the abolition of the wig and commented that:

> George Thomas ... regularly would say in my day, 'There is going
> to be a very difficult debate: the old wig will protect me.' And
> there is no doubt, and I found this myself, that the 'old wig' of the
> Speaker in the Chair has an authority which the Deputies who
> don't wear wigs don't have.[556]

Boothroyd disagreed with her predecessor and said, 'I felt that,
if you didn't have the personality and the confidence yourself,

you shouldn't be in that Chair relying on props to do the job for you'.[557] Discontinuing the wig is symbolic of the change to the Speakership. When proceedings were first televised it was the Speaker's uniform that made the office stand out. Now the media focus on the personalities and so the regalia has become less important. The retirement of the tricorn hat after Dr Horace King does not seem to have caused a media outcry but then the Speakership was not so much in the public eye in the early 1970s and so the change would not have been of great interest at that time.

Not only has John Bercow decided not to re-introduce the wig, he has also chosen to wear a simple black academic gown over a normal business suit rather than the more formal regalia. Despite this downgrading of the uniform at Westminster, there are at least ten countries or overseas territories (the Bahamas, Bermuda, the Cayman Islands, Isle of Man, Kenya, Malawi, New Zealand, Papua New Guinea, Sierra Leone and Zambia) whose Speaker still wears the wig. The degree to which it is used varies and the Speaker of the House of Assembly in the Bahamas, Dr Kendal Major, has only worn the wig once on the occasion of the opening of Parliament. The Speaker of the House of Keys on the Isle of Man, Stephen Rodan, however, wears the wig and gown all the time in the chamber as does the Speaker of the House of Assembly in Bermuda, Stanley Lowe. Speaker Rodan has explained why he still wears the traditional regalia: 'I wear the full bottomed wig both to emphasise the historic nature of the office of Speaker, and to draw attention that it is the office and not the identity of the individual which is important. Individuals come and go, but the office continues.'

The Commonwealth countries whose Speakers have retained the wig clearly still enjoy the pageantry and formality that the traditional uniform conveys. It could be that the British

Speakership has risen to such importance that it no longer needs a lavish outfit to project authority. On the other hand, this might be a token gesture of reform following the downfall of Michael Martin and it is symbolic of Parliament being less extravagant after the expenses scandal. What is clear is that, thanks to this change, the holder of the Speakership has become of greater interest than the office itself.

Despite having become such a high profile position, the Speakership has also become less formal over the years. This was encapsulated by the late Sir Peter Emery at the beginning of this chapter and, to this end, Quentin Letts believes that the Speaker 'has become a less Olympian figure, less judicial in flavour, less awesome in the proper sense of the adjective'. The Speaker is undoubtedly not such a distant figure now as he was at the beginning of the post-war period. Speakers Clifton Brown, Morrison and Hylton-Foster would not have socialised with fellow Members or conducted visits around the country to anywhere near the extent that more recent holders of the office have done. Of course, the introduction of television broadcasting has made the Speaker the focus of proceedings as he or she holds court from a throne-like chair in the centre of the chamber. Letts's comment only really comes from the fact that Michael Martin was not of the same ilk as his predecessor and because John Bercow has chosen not to wear the traditional court dress. The Speakership is now a job to aspire to and many parliamentarians embark on their career doing just that. Journalists are now far less deferential than they used to be. This phenomenon traces its origins to Andrew Alexander's *Daily Mail* article of 23 April 1988 in which he badly criticises Speaker Weatherill for weakness in the Chair.[558] Negative press stories about Speaker Martin were commonplace and were started by Quentin Letts with his 'Gorbals Mick' label.[559] Ever since, the Speaker has been fair game and subject to the same amount of criticism as any government minister. The Speaker is no longer untouchable since the office now has much wider ownership and is as accountable to the general public as it is to the House of Commons.

Although there have been many changes to the Speakership, in the main there has been continuity. Robert Rogers thinks that: 'in the chamber it has changed very little because the pattern of tensions, activity, aspirations may have changed but the constituent parts remain the same'.

The impartiality of the Speakership is still closely guarded by parliamentarians and the way the Speaker presides over the debates in the Commons chamber remains unchanged. The office has grown and developed but the underlying concept of the Speaker being the neutral, fair umpire endures as the sacrosanct tenet of the office.

The office has faced many challenges, changes and threats during the post-war period but has managed to overcome them all so that it has remained the highest and most prestigious parliamentary position. At the very beginning of the period of this study, on 1 August 1945, Winston Churchill, said on Clifton Brown's re-election to the Chair that he was part of a 'long and distinguished line of Speakers who have maintained the reputation of the First Commoner of England'.[560] Although the Speaker had lost this rank in 1919 and was now behind the Prime Minister and Lord President of the Council, it shows what high esteem the office still held at the end of the Second World War.[561] Political changes and differing priorities during the post-war era have not changed this view of the office. In fact, thanks to the radio and television broadcasting of the House of Commons, the Speakership is now one of the most high-profile roles in British political life. The dynamics and influence of the role have shifted as the House of Commons can no longer shelter weaker

Speakers in order to protect the institution. This was shown so
clearly with Speaker Martin and, although this episode temporarily made the office a devalued currency, the fact that ten MPs
put themselves forward to replace him demonstrates that it is still
a job to which politicians aspire.

At that election on 22 June 2009, Nick Clegg, the leader of the
Liberal Democrats, urged John Bercow 'to reinvent the role of
Speaker as a catalyst for radical change'.[562] Whether this is the
next stage of the evolution of the Speakership is yet to become
clear. What is the case is that each holder of the office can have
a very personal impact on the role. The Liberal Prime Minister
H. H. Asquith's famous comment that, 'the office of the Prime
Minister is what its holder chooses and is able to make of it'
equally applies to the Speakership of the House of Commons.[563]

The personality of the Speaker has been a key variable in
their performance of the post and those who have been stronger
and more capable of gauging the mood of the House and of the
country have undoubtedly been more successful. A successful
Speaker must be someone who has the strength of character to
command the House of Commons but at the same time listen
to its collective viewpoint. He or she must be able to get to grips
with all the administrative responsibilities that are placed on the
office and he or she must be an excellent host as well as being
an effective ambassador and diplomat. A modern Speaker must
now also be capable of dealing with the media and think about
how his or her actions will be interpreted by a much wider circle
than just those at Westminster.

As the champion of the Commons, the Speaker is central to
ensuring that the legislature is not by-passed by an overmighty
executive. In the past thirty years, this has manifested itself
when Speakers have complained about successive governments
announcing policy changes via the media rather than at the

despatch box. Speakers Weatherill and Boothroyd fought hard to ensure that governments with large majorities did not forget about Parliament in favour of making announcements on television or on the radio.

Linked to the struggle between the executive and legislature are the debates stimulated by political scientists Philip Norton and Bernard Crick. Norton's question 'Does Parliament Matter?' and Crick's look at the decline of Parliament both involve the office of Speaker and its role in representing and leading the House of Commons.[564] Certainly the Speakership plays a part in this wider debate about parliamentary reform. The office's greater public exposure means that it is crucial to the process of bringing about change. Norton argues that Parliament needs to strengthen its relationship with the citizen; clearly the Speaker's role in determining matters for urgent debate and in which MPs get to ask questions is important in achieving this. Bernard Crick wrote in 1970 that: 'The power of Parliament was never great, so cannot be restored; but its authority influence and prestige was [sic] once greater, and should be greater again.'[565]

This is still true more than forty years later and particularly in light of the damage caused by the expenses scandal. The 2009 Speakership election certainly made it clear that MPs, and a public prompted by media pressure, expected the new Speaker to take the lead in improving the way Parliament works and to make it even more accountable to the electorate. The Speaker is fundamental in making Parliament more powerful because, thanks to the spotlight now on the office, the general public, the media and MPs expect the incumbent to encourage and facilitate such a stance.

The Speaker is no longer an anonymous bureaucratic parliamentarian in the way that he was at the beginning of the post-war era. The office as an institution has always remained respected and prestigious but it is now the Speaker who determines whether or not that status is enhanced. The halcyon days for the Speakership were the 1980s and 1990s when George Thomas, Jack Weatherill and Betty Boothroyd were in the Chair. This saw the Speakership at the height of its prestige and authority because it gained the public recognition that had eluded it thanks to the introduction of radio and television broadcasting of Parliament. These three individuals were respected and effective parliamentarians and so they could rise to the challenge of greater media exposure. This could not be said of all their predecessors who managed to survive in a pre-broadcasting age precisely because they were not under a constant spotlight. Only W. S. Morrison and, to a lesser extent, Selwyn Lloyd seem to have had attributes such as presence and command of the chamber that would have allowed them to fulfil the role of the Speaker in more modern times.

The rise in status of the Speakership is proven by the fact that so many MPs now aspire to the office. Becoming Speaker is now most certainly on a par with becoming a Cabinet minister in terms of a politician's career aspirations. Although the Speakership does not carry political power, the public recognition and profile that comes with the job is no less than that enjoyed by any member of the Cabinet. Moreover, the Speaker is probably more well-known than the holders of some of the more junior Cabinet posts. This is especially pertinent to Speaker John Bercow: 'It was as though he [Bercow] said to himself, "Well, look, I'm not going to be Home Secretary, Chancellor, Prime Minister, so let's do something different but no less prominent. Let's have a shot at being Speaker."'[566]

The Speakership has transformed from a revered internal parliamentary job into a very high-profile, much sought after role that enjoys much greater recognition beyond the confines of Westminster – a greater recognition that brings with it greater scrutiny from increased media attention. The Speakership is similar to the role of a school teacher in that, like a teacher, the Speaker now has to earn the respect of those with whom he or she works rather than just rely on the authority that comes with the office. Gone are the days when the 'old wig' will save the Speaker because MPs and the public at large expect him or her to be up to the job and not have to fall back on the trappings of office. He or she cannot appear to be weak or indecisive in the Chair. The Speaker is, however, no longer simply the parliamentary referee; he or she has to be a skilled administrator and diplomat who can rise to the challenge of holding a high-profile public position. This spotlight has meant that there are even greater expectations on the Speaker when it comes to ensuring that Parliament remains a strong, democratic institution relevant to the British people and fully capable of scrutinising the government of the day. The Speakership remains the greatest honour that the House of Commons can bestow on any Member but it has become an even more crucial component of an effective modern parliament.

Notes

Introduction

1 All references in this chapter to Laundy from Philip Laundy, *The Office of Speaker* (London: Cassell, 1964), in this instance p. 7.

2 *The Speaker of the House of Commons*, House of Commons, 2009, p. 2.

3 Laundy, p. 211.

Chapter One

4 All references in this chapter to Boothroyd from Betty Boothroyd, *The Autobiography* (London: Century, 2001), in this instance p. 316.

5 Statement on the Speaker's Pension, 13 September 2012.

6 Lord Maybray-King, *The Speaker and Parliament* (Birmingham: Tom Stacey, 1973), p. 27.

7 HC Deb 22 March 2001 c. 511.

8 HC Deb 29 October 2001 c. 647.

9 Melissa Kite, 'Speaker breaks neutrality rule', *The Times*, 30 October 2001.

10 HC Deb 30 October 2000 c. 753.

11 Ibid.

12 Maybray-King, *The Speaker and Parliament*, p. 25.

13 Special Collections, University of Kent, Weatherill Papers, WEA/PP V13 Video of 'Mr Speaker, Sir', 28 March 1991.

14 Interview with former Deputy Speaker Baroness Fookes.

15 Quoted in Graham Cawthorne, *Mr Speaker, Sir*, (London: Cleaver-Hume Press Ltd, 1952), p. 81.

16 Special Collections, University of Kent, Weatherill Papers, WEA/PP V13 Video of 'Mr Speaker, Sir', 28 March 1991.

17 All references to Erskine May from Erskine May, *Parliamentary Practice*, 24th Edition, 2011, in this instance p. 420.

18 All references in this chapter to Thomas from George Thomas, *Mr Speaker: The Memoirs of Viscount Tonypandy*, p. 150.

19 Erskine May, p. 420.

20 HC Deb 22 July 1993 c. 606.

21 House of Commons Select Committee on Procedure, Second Report 2000–01, *Election of a Speaker*, HC 40, p. 51.

22 HC Deb 16 April 1980 c. 1215.

23 Lloyd, *Mr Speaker, Sir*, p. 60.

24 Thomas, p. 142.

25 Ibid., p. 143.

26 HC Deb 2 July 1992 c. 956.

27 Boothroyd, p. 246.

28 See Robert Rogers & Rhodri Walters, *How Parliament Works*, 5th Edition, (Harlow: Pearson Education Ltd, 2004), p. 45.

29 Maybray-King, *The Speaker and Parliament*, p. 22.

30 Tony Benn, *Free at Last! Diaries 1991–2001*, (London: Hutchinson, 2002), diary entry for 26 October 1993, p. 209.

31 Tony Benn, *Years of Hope: Diaries, Letters and Papers 1940–1962*, (Hutchinson: London, 1994), p. 375.

32 HC Deb 3 May 1923 cc. 1623–5. This matter is discussed in Peter Rose, *How the Troubles Came to Northern Ireland*, (Basingstoke: Macmillan, 2000), p. 20.

33 Laundy, p. 63.

34 HC Deb 5 April 2000 c. 975.

35 Peter Hennessy, *The Hidden Wiring: Unearthing the British Constitution*, (London: Indigo, 1996), p. 142.

36 Rogers & Walters, *How Parliament Works*, 5th Edition, p. 48.

37 Ibid., p. 45.

38 Erskine May, p. 441.

39 See Parliamentary Archives, HC/SO/2/58, Correspondence and papers relating to the Lunacy (Vacating of Seats) Act 1886 and affecting the Members of the House of Commons, 1918–1958.

40 Boothroyd, p. 262.

41 Erskine May, p. 649.

42 Laundy, p. 97.

43 The National Archives: CAB 128/24, C. C. (52) 11th Conclusions, 6 February 1952.

44 *Call Me Madam: A Profile of Betty Boothroyd by Michael Cockerell*, first broadcast on BBC2, 16 December 2000.

45 Michael Ryle, in 'The Role of the Speaker of the House of Commons', seminar held 25 February 2002, (Institute of Contemporary British History, 2005, http://www.icbh.ac.uk/icbh/witness/speaker), p. 72.

46 Boothroyd, p. 277.

47 Lloyd, *Mr Speaker, Sir*, p. 126.

48 Lord Weatherill in 'The Role of the Speaker of the House of Commons', p. 77.

49 Sir Donald Limon in 'The Role of the Speaker of the House of Commons', p. 77.

50 Thomas, p. 161.

51 Lloyd, *Mr Speaker, Sir*, p. 125.

52   Thomas, p. 162.

53   *Call Me Madam*, BBC Television.

54   Boothroyd, p. 165.

Chapter Two

55   Robin Oakley, describing the Speakership election of 23 October 2000 in
     Inside Track. (London: Bantam Press, 2001), p. 385.

56   Philip Laundy, 'The Speaker and his Office in the Twentieth Century', in
     S. A. Walkland (ed.), *The House of Commons in the Twentieth Century* (Oxford:
     Clarendon Press, 1979), p. 139.

57   Labour Party Archive, Parliamentary Labour Party Minutes, 'Minutes
     of the Party Meeting held on Saturday 28 July 1945', Labour History
     Archive and Study Centre [LHASC].

58   Laundy, 'The Speaker and his Office in the Twentieth Century', p. 139.

59   Harold Macmillan, *Tides of Fortune, 1945–1955*, (London: Macmillan,
     1969), diary entry for 28 October 1951, p. 365.

60   Philip Laundy, *The Office of Speaker in the Parliaments of the Commonwealth*,
     (London: Quiller Press, 1984), p. 74.

61   Janet Morgan (ed.), *The Backbench Diaries of Richard Crossman* (London:
     Hamish Hamilton and Jonathan Cape, 1981), diary entry for 31 October
     1951, pp. 28–9.

62   Peter Catterall (ed.), *The Macmillan Diaries: Prime Minister and After, 1957–
     1966*, Volume 2 (London: Macmillan, 2011), diary entry for 18 October
     1959, pp. 252–3.

63   Harold Macmillan, *Pointing the Way, 1959–1961*, (London: Macmillan,
     1972), diary entry for 22 October 1959, p. 21.

64   HC Deb 20 October 1959 c. 7.

65   Laundy, *The Office of Speaker in the Parliaments of the Commonwealth*, p. 76.

66   Letter from Sir Robin Maxwell-Hyslop, 22 April 2005.

67   All references in this chapter to Benn from Tony Benn, *Out of the Wilderness:
     Diaries 1963–67*, (London: Hutchinson 1987), diary entry for 4 September
     1965, p. 315.

68   Harold Wilson, *The Labour Government, 1964–1970: A Personal Record*,
     (London: Weidenfeld and Nicholson and Michael Joseph, 1971), p. 135.

69   Benn, pp. 339–40.

70   John Boyd-Carpenter, *Way of Life: The Memoirs of John Boyd-Carpenter*
     (London: Sidgwick & Jackson, 1980), p. 225.

71   HC Deb 12 January 1971 c. 12.

72   Hugh Noyes, 'Mr Lloyd new Speaker as revolt fails', *The Times*, 13 January
     1971.

73   D. R. Thorpe, *Eden* (London: Chatto & Windus, 2003), p. 565.

74   HC Deb 12 January 1971 cc. 18–19.

75   Ibid., c. 20.

76   All references in this chapter to Lloyd from Selwyn Lloyd, *Mr Speaker, Sir*
     (London: Jonathan Cape, 1976), in this instance pp. 24–5.

77 Douglas Hurd, *Memoirs* (London: Little, Brown, 2003), p. 288.

78 Betty Boothroyd, *The Autobiography*, (London: Century, 2001), p. 124.

79 Julian Haviland, 'Weatherill elected without dissent', *The Times*, 16 June 1983.

80 Boothroyd, *The Autobiography*, p. 138.

81 Giles Radice, *Diaries 1980–2001: From Political Disaster to Election Triumph*, (London: Weidenfeld & Nicolson, 2004), diary entry for 27 April 1992, p. 272

82 HC Deb 27 April 1992 c. 2.

83 Radice, *Diaries 1980–2001*, diary entry for 27 April 1992, p. 272.

84 HC Deb 27 April 1992 c. 15.

85 Boothroyd, *The Autobiography*, p. 139.

86 Radice, *Diaries 1980–2001*, diary entry for 23 October 2000, p. 470.

87 HC Deb 23 October 2000 c47.

88 Oakley, *Inside Track*, p. 385.

89 HC Deb 23 October 2000 c. 5.

90 House of Commons Select Committee on Procedure, Second Report 2000–01, *Election of a Speaker*, HC 40, p. 22.

91 Ibid., p. xxiv.

92 Chris Mullin, *Decline & Fall: Diaries 2005–2010*, (London: Profile Books, 2010), diary entry for 16 June 2009, p. 346.

93 Mullin, *Decline & Fall*, diary entry for 22 June 2009, p. 349.

94 Andrew Gimson, 'Unlikely neighbours squeeze into their new seats', *Daily Telegraph*, 19 May 2010.

95 Simon Carr, 'Order! Order! Commons gets a fresh dose of Bercow', *The Independent*, 19 May 2010.

96 Laundy, *The Office of Speaker in the Parliaments of the Commonwealth*, p. 69.

97 Ibid., p. 70.

98 The National Archives: PREM 11/863. 'Possibility of Independent opposition at General Election of Speaker of House of Commons: PM's request for support from Clement Davies MP and Clement Attlee MP 1955.'

99 Lloyd, p 134.

100 Ibid., p 137.

101 HC Deb 11 May 2005 cc. 9–10.

102 Nigel Farage, *Flying Free*, (London: Biteback Publishing Ltd, 2011), p. 229.

103 Laundy, 'The Speaker and his Office in the Twentieth Century', p. 153.

104 See HC Deb 24 April 1963 cc. 229–34.

105 House of Commons Procedure Committee, *2010 elections for positions in the House*, Fifth Report of Session 2010–12, pp. 11–12.

106 Ibid., Ev 1.

107 Ibid., p. 12.

108 Lloyd, p. 141.

109 Ibid.

110 See Northern Ireland House of Commons, *Official Report*, 24 January 1956, cc. 3141–4.

111 Northern Ireland House of Commons, *Official Report*, 26 April 1956, c. 930.

Chapter Three

112 Philip Laundy, *The Office of Speaker*, (London: Cassell, 1964), p. 341.

113 Stuart Ball (ed.), *Parliament and Politics in the age of Churchill and Attlee: The Headlam Diaries 1935–1951*, (Cambridge: Royal Historical Society, 1999), diary entry for 3 March 1943, p. 358.

114 Peter Catterall (ed.), *The Macmillan Diaries: The Cabinet Years, 1950–1957*, (London: Macmillan, 2003), diary entry for 12–17 March 1951, p. 57.

115 Philip Laundy, 'The Speaker and his Office in the Twentieth Century' in S. A. Walkland, *The House of Commons in the Twentieth Century*, (Oxford: Clarendon Press, 1979), p. 141.

116 Obituary of Viscount Ruffside, *The Times*, 6 May 1958.

117 'Profile – Mr Speaker', *The Observer*, 18 March 1945.

118 All references in this chapter to Boyd-Carpenter from John Boyd-Carpenter, *Way of Life: The Memoirs of John Boyd-Carpenter*, (London: Sidgwick & Jackson, 1980), in this instance p. 77.

119 Boyd-Carpnter, p. 78.

120 Ibid.

121 HC Deb 4 March 1947 cc. 239–40.

122 Ibid.

123 Obituary of Viscount Ruffside, *The Times*, 6 May 1958.

124 *My Birthday Trip of 1944*, Private Papers of Viscount Ruffside (held by Anthony Clifton Brown).

125 Douglas Clifton Brown, 'The Speaker Describes a Trip to France', *Hexham Courant*, 6 December 1947.

126 Catterall, *The Macmillan Diaries: The Cabinet Years, 1950–1957*, diary entry for 12–17 March 1951, pp. 57–8.

127 Laundy, *The Office of Speaker*, p. 342.

128 Ibid.

129 Ibid.

130 Parliamentary Archives, HC/LB/1/131 (Part 1 of 2), *Journal as Speaker*, an unpublished first person account of his tenure by Lord Maybray-King, c. 1970, p. 300.

131 Obituary of Viscount Ruffside, *The Times*, 6 May 1958.

132 Sir Robin Maxwell-Hyslop (ed.), *Secretary to the Speaker: Ralph Verney's Correspondence*, House of Commons Library Document No. 22, (London: The Stationery Office 1999), p. 196.

133 Obituary of Viscount Ruffside, *The Times*, 6 May 1958.

134 Obituary of Lord Dunrossil, *The Times*, 3 February 1961.

135 Labour Party Archive, Parliamentary Labour Party Minutes, 'Minutes of the Party Meeting held on Thursday 24 April 1952', Labour History Archive and Study Centre.

136 Ibid., 'Minutes of the Party Meeting held on Tuesday 29 April 1952', LHASC.

137 Ibid., Parliamentary Labour Party Minutes, 'Minutes of the Party Meeting held on Tuesday 6 May 1952'. LHASC.

138 Ibid.

139 Portrait Gallery, 'The Speaker', *Sunday Times*, 12 October 1952.

140 Laundy, 'The Speaker and his Office in the Twentieth Century', p. 188.

141 *The Times*, 2 November 1956.

142 Anthony Howard, in 'The Role of the Speaker in the House of Commons', seminar held 25 February 2002 (Institute of Contemporary British History, 2005, http://www.icbh.ac.uk/icbh/witness/speaker), p. 52.

143 Obituary of Lord Dunrossil, *The Times*, 3 February 1961.

144 HC Deb 22 July 1957 c. 35.

145 Ibid.

146 Laundy, 'The Speaker and his Office in the Twentieth Century', p. 186.

147 National Army Museum, Accession 9103–119, Papers of Brigadier Sir Francis Reid, 323, diary entry for 31 March 1955 & 325, diary entry for 12 July 1956.

148 Gloucestershire Archives, D11936, Alasdair Morrison, political and family papers.

149 Obituary of Lord Dunrossil, *The Times*, 3 February 1961.

150 Gloucestershire Archives, D11936, Alasdair Morrison, political and family papers.

151 Michael Ryle, in 'The Role of the Speaker in the House of Commons', p. 35.

152 HC Deb 19 February 1959 c. 549.

153 Ibid. c. 550.

154 Gloucestershire Archives, D11936, Alasdair Morrison, political and family papers.

155 Ibid.

156 Ibid.

157 Ibid.

Chapter Four

158 Harold Wilson, *The Labour Government 1964–1970: A Personal Record*, (London: Weidenfeld & Nicolson and Michael Joseph, 1971), p. 128.

159 HC Deb 13 February 1961 cc. 1025–1075.

160 Ibid. c. 1061.

161 Parliamentary Archives, HC/LB/1/131 (Part 1 of 2), *Journal as Speaker*, an unpublished first person account of his tenure by Lord Maybray-King, c. 1970, p. 259.

162 Philip Laundy, 'The Speaker and his Office in the Twentieth Century' in S. A. Walkland (ed.), *The House of Commons in the Twentieth Century*, (Oxford: Clarendon Press, 1979), p. 194.

163 Tony Benn, *Years of Hope: Diaries, Papers and Letters 1940–1962*, (London, Hutchinson 1994), p. 359, extracts from interviews with David Butler.

164 Ibid., p. 359.

165 Ibid.

166 Erskine May, *Parliamentary Practice*, 24th Edition, 2011, p. 652.

167 HC Deb 9 July 1965 c. 1990.

168 Parliamentary Archives, HC/LB/1/131 (Part 1 of 2), *Journal as Speaker*, p. 246.

169 Parliamentary Archives, HC/LB/1/131 (Part 2 of 2), *A Boy Called Horace*, an unpublished biography of Mr Speaker Horace King by Minni Horton, c.1980, p. 85.

170 Parliamentary Archives, HC/LB/1/131, (Part 1 of 2), *Journal as Speaker*, p. 385.

171 Ibid.

172 Richard Crossman, *The Diaries of a Cabinet Minister, Volume One: Minister of Housing 1964–66*, (London: Hamish Hamilton and Jonathan Cape, 1975), diary entry for 16 November 1965, p. 381.

173 Parliamentary Archives, HC/LB/1/131 (Part 1 of 2), *Journal as Speaker*, p. 270.

174 Procedure Committee, *Questions*, April 1967, HC 410, p. vii.

175 HC Deb 6 June 1967 cc. 812–13.

176 Parliamentary Archives, HC/LB/1/131 (Part 1 of 2), *Journal as Speaker*, p. 604.

177 Philip Laundy, *The Office of Speaker in the Parliaments of the Commonwealth*, (London: Quiller Press, 1984), p. 83.

178 Laundy, 'The Speaker and his Office in the Twentieth Century', p. 187.

179 Letter from William Whitelaw to Speaker King, 17 February 1969, The Maybray-King papers, Southampton City Archives.

180 Selwyn Lloyd, *Mr Speaker, Sir*, (London: Jonathan Cape, 1976), p. 118.

181 See Box 6 of The Maybray-King Papers, Southampton City Archives.

182 Lord Weatherill, in 'The Role of the Speaker of the House of Commons', seminar held 25 February 2002 (Institute of Contemporary British History, 2005, http://www.icbh.ac.uk/icbh/witness/speaker), p. 32.

183 HC Deb 10 December 1970 c. 669.

184 Parliamentary Archives, HC/LB/1/131 (Part 1 of 2), *Journal as Speaker*, p. 556.

185 Laundy, 'The Speaker and his Office in the Twentieth Century', p. 186.

186 Parliamentary Archives, HC/LB/1/131 (Part 1 of 2), *Journal as Speaker*, p. 309.

187 Obituary of Lord Maybray-King, *The Times*, 4 September 1986.

Chapter Five

188 Edward Heath, *The Course of My Life: My Autobiography*, (London: Hodder & Stoughton, 1998), p. 282.

189 Selwyn Lloyd, *Mr Speaker, Sir*, (London: Jonathan Cape, 1976), p. 118.

190 See Anthony Nutting, *No End of a Lesson: The Story of Suez*, (London: Constable, 1967).

191 All references in this chapter to Thomas from George Thomas, *Mr Speaker, the memoirs of Viscount Tonypandy*, (London: Century Publishing, 1985), p. 156.

192 All references in this chapter to Benn from Tony Benn, *Office Without Power: Diaries 1968–72*, (London: Hutchinson, 1988), diary entry for 25 January 1971, p. 327.

193 Selwyn Lloyd papers, Churchill Archives Centre, SELO 5/103, 'Notepad with SL's Impressions of the 1971/72 session', 11 November 1972.

194 Benn, p. 401.

195 See HC Deb 31 January 1972 c. 33 & c. 41.

196 Benn, p. 401.

197 D. R. Thorpe, *Selwyn Lloyd*, (London: Jonathan Cape, 1989), p. 422.

198 Lloyd, *Mr Speaker, Sir*, p. 70.

199 HC Deb 1 February 1972, c. 239.

200 Lloyd, *Mr Speaker, Sir*, p. 71.

201 HC Deb 31 January 1972 cc. 40–41.

202 Ibid., c. 41.

203 See Selwyn Lloyd papers, Churchill Archives Centre, SELO 5/103, 'Notepad with SL's Impressions of the 1971/72 session', 11 November 1972.

204 Interview with Lord Parkinson, 17 January 2009.

205 Philip Laundy, *The Office of Speaker in the Parliaments of the Commonwealth*, (London: Quiller Press Ltd, 1984), p. 86.

206 See HC Deb 7 February 1972, cc. 975–8.

207 See Thorpe, *Selwyn Lloyd*, pp. 419–20.

208 Lloyd, *Mr Speaker, Sir*, p. 81.

209 Ibid.

210 Selwyn Lloyd papers, Churchill Archives Centre, SELO 3/67A, 'SL's notes (possibly for his autobiography) on the Speakership, mistakes, people etc.', 13 February 1972.

211 Thomas, p. 131.

212 Lloyd, *Mr Speaker, Sir*, p. 116.

213 Thorpe, *Selwyn Lloyd*, p. 427.

214 HC Deb 3 February 1976 cc. 1140–41.

215 Quoted in Thomas, *Mr Speaker, the memoirs of Viscount Tonypandy*, p. 88.

216 Thomas, p. 90.

217 Ramon Hunston, *Order! Order! A biography of The Rt. Hon. George Thomas*, (London: Marshalls, 1981), p. 122.

218 Thomas, *Mr Speaker, the memoirs of Viscount Tonypandy*, p. 130.

219 Bernard Donoughue, *Downing Street Diary: With Harold Wilson in No. 10*, (London: Jonathan Cape, 2005), diary entry for 3 February 1976, p. 654.

220 Thomas, p. 139.

221 Ibid., p. 140.

222 Ibid., p. 143.

223 Ibid.

224 Ibid., p. 142.

225 Ibid., p. 147.

226 Ibid., p. 148.

227 Michael Heseltine, *Life in the Jungle: My Autobiography*, (London: Hodder & Stoughton, 2000), p. 170.

228 Ibid., pp. 170–71.

229 Thomas, p. 149.

230 Quoted in Thomas, *Mr Speaker, the memoirs of Viscount Tonypandy*, p. 151.

231 Heseltine, *Life in the Jungle: My Autobiography*, (London: Hodder & Stoughton, 2000), p. 172.

232 Thomas, pp. 152–3.

233 E. H. Robertson, *George: A Biography of Viscount Tonypandy*, (London: Marshall Pickering, 1992), p. 241.

234 Thomas, p. 142.

235 Ibid., p. 203.

236 Ibid., p. 157.

237 Bernard Donoughue, *Downing Street Diary: With James Callaghan in No. 10*, (London: Jonathan Cape, 2008), diary entry for 1 March 1977, p. 155.

238 Viscount Tonypandy papers, File 553, Letter from Mr Speaker to the Prime Minister, 18 December 1980. By permission of Llyfrgell Genedlaethol Cymru/The National Library of Wales.

239 Margaret Thatcher, *The Downing Street Years*, (London: Harper Collins, 1993), p. 34.

240 See Robert Blackburn & Andrew Kennon with Sir Michael Wheeler-Booth, *Griffith & Ryle on Parliament: Functions, Practice and Procedure*, (London: Sweet & Maxwell 2003), 9-041, p. 503.

241 Ibid.

242 See Edward Pearce, 'Straight-talker Speaker finds knives are out', *The Sunday Times*, 1 May 1988.

243 Thomas, p. 12.

244 Ibid., p. 184.

245 Ibid.

246 Ibid., p. 185.

247 Ibid., p. 208.

248 Ibid., pp. 210–11.

249 Tony Benn, *Conflicts of Interest: Diaries 1977–80*, (London: Hutchinson 1990), diary entry for Wednesday 17 January 1979, p. 439.

250 Viscount Tonypandy papers, File 550, Letter from the Clerk of the House to Mr Speaker, 5 April 1977. By permission of Llyfrgell Genedlaethol Cymru/The National Library of Wales.

251 See Leo Abse, *Tony Blair: The Man Behind the Smile*, (London: Robson Books, 2001), pp. 47–59.

252 'Order! Order!', *The Times*, 26 February 1985.

253 'Mr Speaker's Memoirs', Letter from James Callaghan to the Editor, *The Times*, 27 February 1985.

Chapter Six

254 Obituary of Lord Weatherill, *The Daily Telegraph*, 8 May 2007.

255 Obituary of Lord Weatherill, *The Times*, 8 May 2007.

256 *Bernard and Betty Speak Out*, Part 1, BBC Radio 4, first broadcast on 13 May 2007.

257 Ibid.

258 Ibid.

259 Geoffrey Howe, *Conflict of Loyalty*, (London: Macmillan, 1994), p. 281.

260 J. A. G. Griffith & Michael Ryle, *Parliament: Functions, Practice and Procedures*, (London: Sweet & Maxwell, 1989), p. 262.

261 Edward Pearce, 'Straight-talker Speaker finds knives are out', *Sunday Times*, 1 May 1988.

262 Andrew Alexander, 'Sorry, there's a fault in the Speaker', *Daily Mail*, 23 April 1988.

263 Ibid.

264 Ibid..

265 Donald Macintyre, 'Why Tories can't get Speaker out', *Sunday Telegraph*, 22 May 1988.

266 Ibid.

267 Special Collections, University of Kent, Weatherill Papers, WEA/PP S18, Letter from Norman Tebbit to the Speaker, 16 June 1988.

268 Ibid., Draft letter from Mr Speaker to Mr Worsthome.

269 Macintyre, 'Why Tories can't get Speaker out', 22 May 1988.

270 *Weekend World*, London Weekend Television, first broadcast on 8 May 1988.

271 See Heather Kirby, 'Madam of an orderly House?', *The Times*, 9 July 1990.

272 Labour Party Archive, Parliamentary Labour Party Minutes, 'Minutes of the Party Meeting held on Wednesday 30 November 1988', LHASC.

273 Ibid.

274 Ibid., 'Minutes of the Party Meeting held on Wednesday 7 December 1988', LHASC.

275 HC Deb 27 October 1983 cc. 524–5.

276 Russell Johnston, 'Unfair, Mr Speaker, unfair', *The Times*, 10 November 1983.

277 Lord Weatherill, in 'The Role of the Speaker in the House of Commons', seminar held 25 February 2002, (Institute of Contemporary British History, 2005, http://www.icbh.ac.uk/icbh/witness/speaker), p. 60.

278 See HC Deb 27 April 1987 c. 48.

279 *Bernard and Betty Speak Out*, Part 2, BBC Radio 4, first broadcast on 20 May 2007.

280 Erskine May, *Parliamentary Practice*, 24th Edition, 2011, p. 233.

281 HC Deb 13 July 1987 cc. 706–7.

282 See A. W. Bradley, 'Parliamentary Privilege, Zircon and National Security', *Public Law*. (Winter 1987), p. 489.

283 Tony Benn, *The End of an Era: Diaries 1980–1990*, (London: Hutchinson, 1992), diary entry for 27 January 1987, p. 490.

284 Ibid., p. 491.

285 Special Collections, University of Kent, Weatherill Papers, WEA/PP H102, Letter from Speaker Weatherill to Tony Benn, 28 January 1987.

286 Bradley, 'Parliamentary Privilege, Zircon and National Security', p. 494.

287 See *First Report from the Committee of Privileges*, House of Commons (1986–87) 365, paragraph 17.

288 HC Deb 12 March 1992 c. 968.

289 Obituary of Lord Weatherill, *The Independent*, 8 May 2007.

290 Shirley Williams, *Climbing the Bookshelves*, (London: Virago, 2009), p. 341.

291 Obituary of Lord Weatherill, *The Daily Telegraph*, 8 May 2007.

292 *Bernard and Betty Speak Out*, Part 2.

293 Lord Weatherill, in 'The Role of the Speaker in the House of Commons', p. 59.

294 Ibid., p. 78.

295 *Call Me Madam: A Profile of Betty Boothroyd by Michael Cockerell*, BBC Television, first broadcast on BBC 2, 16 December 2000.

296 Ibid.

297 All references to Boothroyd in this chapter are to Betty Boothroyd, *The Autobiography* (London: Century, 2001) Boothroyd, *The Autobiography*, p. 21.

298 See *Call Me Madam*, BBC Television and Paul Routledge, *Madam Speaker: The Life of Betty Boothroyd*, (London: Politico's Publishing, 2000), pp. 57–71.

299 Boothroyd, p. 25.

300 Ibid.

301 *Call Me Madam*, BBC Television.

302 Ibid.

303 Boothroyd, p. 121.

304 *Bernard and Betty Speak Out*, Part 1.

305 Boothroyd, p. 135.

306 Ibid., p. 137.

307 Labour Party Archive, Parliamentary Labour Party Minutes, 'Minutes of a Special Meeting of the Parliamentary Labour Party held on Monday 27 April 1992', LHASC.

308 *Bernard and Betty Speak Out*, Part 1.

309 Boothroyd, p. 163.

310 HC Deb 2 July 1992 c. 956.

311 HC Deb 17 December 1992 c. 588.

312 Boothroyd, p. 181.

313 Ibid., p. 183.

314 HC Deb 29 June 1993 c. 830.

315 Gyles Brandreth, *Breaking the Code: Westminster Diaries May 1990–May 1997*, (London, Weidenfeld & Nicolson 1999), p. 189.

316 *Call Me Madam*, BBC Television.

317 Boothroyd, p. 188.

318 Open University Archives, Betty Boothroyd Collection, BB/1/1/6, Lecture to the Thirty Club, 11 November 1997.

319 Boothroyd, p. 189.

320 HC Deb 29 November 1993 cc. 789–93.

321 *Bernard and Betty Speak Out*, Part 2.

322 HC Deb 14 April 1994 c. 415.

323 Ibid.

324 Ibid.

325 Ibid.

326 Ibid., c. 432.

327 Open University Archives, Betty Boothroyd Collection, BB/1/1/6, Lecture to the Thirty Club, 11 November 1997.

328 Boothroyd, p. 246.

329 Ibid.

330 Ibid., p. 247.

331 *Bernard and Betty Speak Out*, Part 2.

332 HC Deb 5 April 2000 c. 976.

333 *Call Me Madam*, BBC Television.

334 *Straight Talk with Andrew Neil*, BBC Television, first broadcast on BBC News 24, 10 June 2006.

335 Robert Blackburn & Andrew Kennon with Sir Michael Wheeler-Booth, *Griffin & Ryle on Parliament: Functions, Practice and Procedures*, (London, Sweet & Maxwell 2003), p. 530.

336 HC Deb 2 July 1997 c. 297.

337 Giles Radice, *Diaries 1980–2001: From Political Disaster to Election Triumph*, (London: Weidenfeld & Nicolson, 2004), diary entry for 21 March 1994, pp. 315–16.

338 Ibid., diary entry for 22 March 1994, p. 316.

339 HC Deb 7 February 1996 c. 331.

340 Boothroyd, p. 230.

341 *Call Me Madam*, BBC Television.

342 Ibid.

343 Ibid.

344 Ibid.

345 Ibid.

346 Ibid.

347 Ibid.

348 Sam Macrory, 'People Profile: Sir Alan Haselhurst. Speaking Up', *The House Magazine*, 12 July 2010, p. 21.

349 HC Deb 12 July 2000 c. 869.

350 *Call Me Madam*, BBC Television.

351 Andrew Pearce, 'Ministers cared only for perks of power, says Boothroyd', *Daily Telegraph*, 20 May 2009.

352 Ibid.

353 *Straight Talk*, BBC News Channel, first broadcast, 16 January 2010.

354 Ibid.

355 HL Deb 21 June 2011 cc. 1172–4.

Chapter Seven

356 Giles Radice, *Diaries 1980–2001: From Political Disaster to Election Triumph*,

(London: Weidenfeld & Nicolson, 2004), diary entry for 23 October 2000, p. 470.

357 Vince Cable, *Free Radical: A Memoir*, (London: Atlantic Books, 2009), p. 316.

358 Chris Mullin, *A View from the Foothills: The Diaries of Chris Mullin*, (London: Profile Books, 2009), diary entry for 23 October 2000, p. 134.

359 Radice, *Diaries 1980–2001*, diary entry for 23 October 2000, p. 470.

360 Mullin, *A View from the Foothills*, diary entry for 23 October 2000, p. 134.

361 Ibid.

362 Ibid.

363 Peter Riddell, 'House falls into theatre of the absurb', *The Times*, 24 October 2000.

364 Quentin Letts 'Gorbals Mick was set up on the shy and his rivals had to knock him off', *Daily Mail*, 24 October 2000.

365 Roy Hattersley, 'Michael Martin: "It was when they started attacking my wife that I knew I had to go"', *The Observer*, 21 June 2009.

366 Robert Winnett & Gordon Rayner, *No Expenses Spared*, (London: Bantam Press, 2009), p. 26.

367 Quentin Letts, *Letts Rip!*, (London: Constable, 2010), p. 28.

368 *Politics Show*, BBC One, broadcast on 11 February 2007.

369 Robin Cook, *The Point of Departure*, (London: Simon & Schuster, 2003), diary entry for 1 May 2002, p. 145.

370 Sam Macroy, 'Sir Alan Haselhurst Profile: Speaking Up', *The House Magazine*, No. 1352, Vol. 36, 12 July 2010, p. 21.

371 'Timeline of Martin's Career as Speaker', *The Daily Telegraph*, 20 May 2009.

372 Ibid.

373 Andrew Pierce, 'Unforgettable for all the wrong reasons', *The Daily Telegraph*, 20 May 2009.

374 Greg Hurst, 'Speaker's class war claims latest upper-crust victim', *The Times*, 23 June 2007.

375 Simon Walters, 'Commons aide No. 3 quits over rows with Speaker', *The Mail on Sunday*, 19 December 2004.

376 *Politics Show*, BBC One, broadcast on 11 February 2007.

377 HC Deb 29 October 2001 c. 647.

378 Matthew Parris, 'Savage nuclear attack causes local fallout', *The Times*, 30 October 2001.

379 HC Deb 30 October 2001 c. 753.

380 Ibid., 1 November 2006 c. 291.

381 Ibid.

382 Greg Hurst & Anthony Browne, 'Speaker reprimands Cameron over clash with Blair', *The Times*, 2 November 2006.

383 HC Deb 1 November 2006 c. 292.

384 Cook, *The Point of Departure*, diary entry for 25 November 2002, p. 252.

385 Lord Weatherill, in 'The Role of the Speaker of the House of Commons', seminar held 25 February 2002 (Institute of Contemporary British History, 2005, http://www.icbh.ac.uk/uk/icbh/witness/speaker), p. 64.

386 HC Deb 10 February 2003 c. 643.

387 Cook, *The Point of Departure*, diary entry for 25 November 2002, pp. 251–2.

388 See HC Deb 29 October 2002 c. 842.

389 Ibid., 27 February 2006 c. 1.

390 Sam Macroy, 'People Profile: Sir Alan Haselhurst. Speaking Up', *The House Magazine*, 12 July 2010, p. 22.

391 HC Deb 22 July 2008 c. 659.

392 Simon Walters, 'Gorbalsgate', *Mail on Sunday*, 11 July 2004.

393 Ibid.

394 Simon Walters, 'Speaker quizzed over wife's £100,000', *Mail on Sunday*, 18 July 2004.

395 See House of Commons Committee on Standards and Privileges, *Conduct of Mr Speaker*, Ninth Report of Session 2007–08, HC 559, 14 May 2008, p. 15.

396 Ibid., paragraph 4, p. 6.

397 Ibid., paragraph 38, p. 14.

398 'Timeline of Martin's Career as Speaker', *Daily Telegraph*, 20 May 2009.

399 Simon Walters, 'Speaker's wife claims £50k for flights to "support" him', *Mail on Sunday*, 20 January 2008.

400 Peter Hain, *Outside In*, (London: Biteback Publishing Ltd, 2012), p. 362.

401 Ibid., p. 363.

402 House of Commons Committee on Issue of Privilege, *Police Searches on the Parliamentary Estate*, First Report of Session 2009–10, HC 62, 22 March 2010, p. 3.

403 William Rees-Mogg, 'An historic attack on liberty and democracy', *The Times*, 1 December 2008.

404 Robert Blackburn & Andrew Kennon with Sir Michael Wheeler-Booth, *Griffin & Ryle on Parliament: Functions, Practice and Procedures*, (London, Sweet & Maxwell 2003), p. 125.

405 HC Deb 3 December 2008 cc. 1–3.

406 Ibid.

407 Chris Mullin, *Decline & Fall: Diaries 2005–2010*, (London: Profile Books, 2010), diary entry for 3 December 2008, pp. 290–91.

408 Interview with Peter Riddell, 4 October 2010.

409 House of Commons Committee on Issue of Privilege, *Police Searches on the Parliamentary Estate*, First Report of Session 2009–10 , HC 62, 22 March 2010.

410 Ibid., paragraph 39, p. 68.

411 Heather Brooke, *The Silent State: Secrets, Surveillance and the Myth of British Democracy*, (London, William Heinemann 2010), p. 223.

412 Ibid., p. 232.

413 Winnett & Rayner, *No Expenses Spared*, p. 23.

414 Ibid., p. 39.

415 Ibid., p. 25.

416 Andrew Rawnsley, *The End of the Party: The Rise and Fall of New Labour*, (London, Penguin Viking 2010), p. 650.

417 Winnett & Rayner, *No Expenses Spared*, p. 26.

418 Brooke, *The Silent State*, p. 246.

419 HC Deb 3 July 2008 c. 1121.

420 Lord Foulkes, 'Lord Foulkes: Speaker won't stand down for hypocritical scapegoats', *Sunday Times*, 17 May 2009.

421 Brooke, *The Silent State*, p. 249.

422 Ibid.

423 Robert Winnett, 'MPs' expenses: how Brown and his Cabinet exploit expenses system', *Daily Telegraph*, 8 May 2009.

424 Peter Riddell, 'An apologist for MPs, not a champion for voters', *The Times*, 19 May 2009.

425 HC Deb 11 May 2009 c. 548.

426 Ibid., c. 549.

427 Mullin, *Decline & Fall*, diary entry for 11 May 2009, p. 328.

428 HC Deb 12 May 2009 c. 682.

429 Ibid., cc. 682–3.

430 *Andrew Marr Show*, BBC One, 17 May 2009.

431 Douglas Carswell & Daniel Hannan, *The Plan: Twelve Months to Renew Britain*, (London, 2008), p. 48.

432 HC Deb 18 May 2009 c. 1205.

433 Ibid.

434 Ibid.

435 Ibid., c. 1206.

436 Ibid.

437 Ibid.

438 Ibid., c. 1207.

439 Mullin, *Decline & Fall*, diary entry for 18 May 2009, p. 332.

440 Andrew Gimson, 'A gruesome disaster as he tried to save his own job', *Daily Telegraph*, 19 May 2009.

441 Cable, *Free Radical: A Memoir*, p. 316.

442 Anthony Seldon & Guy Lodge, *Brown at 10*, (London: Biteback, 2010), p. 267.

443 Rawnsley, *The End of the Party*, p. 650.

444 HC Deb 19 May 2009 c. 1323.

445 Philip Laundy, *The Office of Speaker*, (London, Cassell 1964), pp. 250–51.

446 Roy Hattersley, 'Michael Martin: "It was when they started attacking my wife that I knew I had to go"', *The Observer*, 21 June 2009.

447 Gordon Rayner & Rosa Prince, 'Michael Martin faces backlash over possible peerage', Telegraph.co.uk, 21 May 2009.

448 Nicholas Watt, 'PM warned that elevation of Michael Martin could damage Lords', *The Guardian*, 1 July 2009.

449 Gordon Rayner & Rosa Prince, 'Michael Martin faces backlash over possible peerage', Telegraph.co.uk, 21 May 2009.

Chapter Eight

450 Stuart Jeffries, 'The Saturday Interview – John Bercow', *The Guardian*, 23 July 2011.

451 Norman Tebbit, *Upwardly Mobile*, (London: Weidenfeld and Nicolson, 1988), p. 257.

452 Bobby Friedman, *Bercow, Mr Speaker: Rowdy Living in the Tory Party*, (London: Gibson Square, 2011), p. 125.

453 Friedman, Ibid., p. 183.

454 Michael Spicer, *The Spicer Diaries*, (London: Biteback Publishing Ltd, 2012), diary entry for 2 November 2004, p. 545.

455 Sam Coates, 'Burning ambition of man who won in spite of his own party', *The Times*, 23 June 2009.

456 Chris Mullin, *Decline & Fall: Diaries 2005–2010*, (London: Profile Books, 2010), diary entry for 19 May 2009, p. 333.

457 Robert Winnett & Gordon Rayner, *No Expenses Spared*, (London: Bantam Press, 2009), p. 287.

458 Ibid.

459 Iain Dale, 'In conversation… John Bercow', *Total Politics*, Issue 19, January 2010.

460 HC Deb 22 June 2009 c. 624.

461 'Triumph or Disaster', *The Times*, 23 June 2009.

462 Quentin Letts, 'Impossible! They voted for someone worse than Gorbals Mick', *Daily Mail*, 23 June 2009.

463 James Chapman & Kirsty Walker, 'So much for a fresh start!', *Daily Mail*, 23 June 2009.

464 Gerri Peev, 'Taxpayers' £1400 bill for Speaker's washing machines', *Daily Mail*, 16 April 2011.

465 Robert Winnett, 'Bercow ignores pleas to reduce his pension', *Daily Telegraph*, 18 October 2011.

466 'Speaker Bercow spares himself pay squeeze pain', *Mail on Sunday*, 18 December 2011.

467 Christopher Hope, 'Taxpayers spend £30,000 for Speaker to fly business class', *Daily Telegraph*, 12 December 2011.

468 Emily Ashton, 'A Waste of Monet', *The Sun*, 29 November 2011.

469 Christopher Hope, 'Bercow's £37,000 portrait, hushing ministers and hailing gay rights', *Daily Telegraph*, 29 November 2011.

470 Interview with Jude Crocker, UK Parliament Web Team, 31 July 2009, http://www.youtube.com/watch?v=VP8pjcES-NY

471 HC Deb 22 June 2009 c. 624.

472 Ibid.

473 *The Record Review*, first broadcast on BBC Parliament, 16 December 2011.

474 Ibid.

475 *Murnaghan*, Sky News, broadcast on 6 May 2012.

476 *The Record Review*, first broadcast on BBC Parliament, 16 December 2011.

477 HC Deb 30 April 2012 c. 1241.

478 Quentin Letts, 'Cameron performed rather brilliantly…Speaker Bercow, like Muttley the dog, had been foiled', *Daily Mail*, 1 May 2012.

479 HC Deb 30 April 2012 c. 1241.

480 James Chapman, 'Furious PM forced back to Commons to defend Hunt', *Daily Mail*, 1 May 2012.

481 *Murnaghan*, Sky News, broadcast on 6 May 2012. 482 HC Deb 16 July 2012 cc. 677–86.

483 Kirsty Walker, 'Point of order! Proof that Mr Speaker is picking on the PM', *Daily Mail*, 31 December 2011.

484 HC Deb 7 July 2010 c. 364.

485 Ibid., 29 June 2011 c. 948.

486 Ibid. c. 955.

487 Friedman, *Bercow, Mr Speaker: Rowdy Living in the Tory Party*, p. 239.

488 HC Deb 6 December 2010 c. 135.

489 Ibid.

490 Ibid., 7 December 2010 c. 161.

491 Friedman, *Bercow, Mr Speaker: Rowdy Living in the Tory Party*, p. 239.

492 HC Deb 29 June 2010 c. 719.

493 Ibid.

494 Ibid., 13 July 2011 c. 304.

495 Ibid.

496 Ibid., 13 June 2012 c. 318.

497 Friedman, *Bercow, Mr Speaker: Rowdy Living in the Tory Party*, p. 239.

498 Ibid.

499 Andrew Grice, 'I have no plans to work in Afghanistan, says Bercow', *The Independent*, 7 July 2011.

500 Jason Groves, 'Bercow hijacks Queen's speech', *Daily Mail*, 21 March 2012.

501 Ibid.

502 *Murnaghan*, Sky News, broadcast on 6 May 2012.

503 Ibid.

504 HC Deb 7 December 2010 c. 172.

505 Ibid., 16 July 2012 c. 691.

506 Ibid., 13 January 2011 c. 446.

507 James Chapman, 'You're not ****ing royalty, Mr Speaker', *Daily Mail*, 14 January 2011.

508 HC Deb 13 June 2012 c. 345.

509 Erskine May, *Parliamentary Practice*, 24th Edition, 2011, p. 444.

510 HC Deb 13 June 2012 c. 345.

511 Erskine May, *Parliamentary Practice*, 24th Edition, 2011, p. 444.

512 HC Deb 13 June 2012 c. 345.

513 Nicholas Cecil, 'Tories demand explanation from Speaker in "lying" row', *Evening Standard*, 3 July 2012.

514 Ibid.

515 HC Deb 18 September 2012 cc. 791–2.

516 Ibid., 29 November 2012 c. 469.

517 Sam Coates, 'Speaker's wife to contest ward for Labour', *The Times*, 13 November 2009.

518 James Kirkup, 'It's a storm in a bedsheet, says Speaker's wife', *Daily Telegraph*, 5 February 2011.

519 Sally Bercow talking to Victoria Derbyshire, BBC Radio 5 Live, 4 February 2011.

520 *Daily Politics*, BBC 1, 4 February 2011.

521 Paul Waugh & Sam Macrory, 'The independent iconoclast', *The House Magazine*, 23 February 2012, p. 22.

522 Jason Groves, 'Minister hits out at Bercow and wife over impartiality', *Daily Mail*, 20 January 2011.

523 Ibid.

524 *Daily Politics*, BBC 1, 19 January 2011.

525 Iain Dale, 'In conversation... John Bercow', *Total Politics*, Issue 19, January 2010, p. 18.

526 Holly Watt & Robert Winnett, 'Bercow delays by-election after his wife intervenes', *The Times*, 9 November 2010.

527 HC Deb 8 November 2010 c. 1.

528 Paul Routledge, *Madam Speaker: The Life of Betty Boothroyd*, (London: Politico's Publishing, 2000), p. 319.

529 Michael Savage, 'Bercow breaks convention to attack BNP', *The Independent*, 31 October 2009.

530 Ibid.

531 Sam Coates, 'Speaker hounded over anti-hunt letter', *The Times*, 19 January 2011.

532 Patrick Wintour, 'Bercow: Mail a "bigoted comic"', *The Guardian*, 8 June 2011.

533 Philip Laundy, 'The Speaker and his Office in the Twentieth Century' in S. A. Walkland, *The House of Commons in the Twentieth Century*, (Oxford: Clarendon Press, 1979), p. 186.

534 *Lorraine*, ITV1, 16 July 2012.

535 Quoted in Jonathan Dimbleby, *The Last Governor: Chris Patten & the Handover of Hong Kong*, (London: Little, Brown and Company, 1997), p. 3.

536 Simon Walters, 'Now Betty cuffs scruffy Mr Speaker', *Mail on Sunday*, 16 January 2011.

537 Simon Walters & Brendan Carlin, 'Defiant Speaker vows there will be no prayer ban in the Commons', *Mail on Sunday*, 12 February 2012.

538 Paul Waugh & Sam Macrory, 'The independent iconoclast', *The House Magazine*, 23 February 2012, p. 19.

539 Brendan Carlin, 'Jill, Serjeant-at-Arms, quit after bust-up over queues', *Mail on Sunday*, 16 October 2011.

540 *The Westminster Hour*, BBC Radio 4, 27 February 2012.

541 *World at One*, BBC Radio 4, 14 August 2012.

542 Ibid.

543 Rob Wilson, 'You're preening, partisan and pompous: hold your tongue Mr Speaker!', *Mail on Sunday*, 19 August 2012.

544 HC Deb 17 October 2012 c. 323.

545 Holly Watt & Claire Newell, '27 MPs let one home and claim another', *Daily Telegraph*, 19 October 2012.

546 Christopher Hope, 'Bercow's "revenge" on expenses', *Daily Telegraph*, 14 November 2012.

547 Ibid.

Conclusion

548 HC Deb 22 March 2001 c. 518.

549 Peter G. Richards, *Honourable Members: A Study of the British Backbencher*, (London: Faber & Faber, 1959), p. 71.

550 Parliamentary Archives, HC/LB/1/131 (Part 1 of 2), *Journal as Speaker*, an unpublished first person account of his tenure by Lord Maybray-King, c. 1970, p. 262.

551 Quentin Letts, *Bog-Standard Britain*, (London: Constable, 2009), p. 183.

552 Sir Donald Limon, in 'The Role of the Speaker in the House of Commons', seminar held 25 February 2002 (Institute of Contemporary British History, 2005, http://icbh.ac.uk/icbh/witness/speaker), p. 39.

553 See House of Commons Committee on Issue of Privilege, *Police Searches on the Parliamentary Estate*, First Report of Session 2009–10, HC 62, 22 March 2010, Ev 17.

554 See House of Representatives, Infosheet 3, *The Speaker*, May 2012.

555 HC Deb 29 June 1970 c. 3.

556 Lord Weatherill, in 'The Role of the Speaker in the House of Commons', p. 32.

557 Baroness Boothroyd in 'The Role of the Speaker in the House of Commons', p.33.

558 See Andrew Alexander, 'Sorry, there's a fault in the Speaker', *Daily Mail*, 23 April 1988.

559 See Quentin Letts, 'Gorbals Mick was set up on the shy and his rivals had to knock him off', *Daily Mail*, 24 October 2000.

560 HC Deb 1 August 1945 c. 12.

561 Philip Laundy, *The Office of Speaker*, (London: Cassell, 1964), p. 8.

562 HC Deb 22 June 2009 c. 638.

563 Earl of Oxford and Asquith, *Fifty Years in Parliament*, vol. 2, (London: Cassell, 1926), p. 185.

564 See Philip Norton, *Does Parliament Matter?*, (London: Harvester Wheatsheaf, 1993) & Bernard Crick, *The Reform of Parliament*, (London: Weidenfeld & Nicolson, 1964).

565 Bernard Crick, 'Whither Parliamentary Reform?' in A. H. Hanson & Bernard Crick, *The Commons in Transition*, (London: Fontana, 1970), p. 276.

566 *The Politics Show*, BBC 1, 30 January 2011.

Bibliography

Public and Institutional Records:
Gloucestershire Archives
Political and family papers of Alasdair Morrison (son of W. S. Morrison)
Southampton City Council Archives
Papers of Rt Hon. The Lord Maybray-King
Churchill Archives Centre, Cambridge
Papers of Rt Hon. The Lord Selwyn-Lloyd
National Library of Wales, Aberystwyth
Papers of Rt Hon. The Viscount Tonypandy
University of Kent at Canterbury, Special Collections
Papers of Rt Hon. The Lord Weatherill
Open University Library, Milton Keynes
Papers of Rt Hon. The Baroness Boothroyd of Sandwell
National Army Museum, Department of Archives, Photographs, Film and
    Sound
Papers of Brigadier Sir Francis Reid CBE
Labour History Archive and Study Centre, People's History Museum,
    Manchester
Minutes of the Parliamentary Labour Party 1945–1994
Boundary Commission Publications:
Fifth Periodical Review of the Boundary Commission for Scotland, December 2004.

Parliamentary Archive:
Speaker's Office Records:
HC/SO/2/58   Correspondence and papers relating to the Lunacy (Vacating
    of Seats) Act 1886 and affecting Members of the House of Commons,
    1918–1958.
Unpublished autobiography of Speaker Dr Horace King:
HC/LB/1/131 Parts 1 & 2 – Part 1 – *Journal as Speaker*
                            Part 2 – *A Boy Called Horace*

House of Commons Publications:

Procedure Committee, *Questions*, April 1967, HC 410.

Procedure, Select Committee on, First Report 1971–72, 'Election of a Speaker', Stationery Office, House of Commons Paper 111.

Committee of Privileges, Third Report 1971–72, HC 324.

Committee of Privileges, First Report 1986–87, HC 365.

Procedure, Select Committee on, Second Report 2000–01, 'Election of a Speaker', Stationery Office, House of Commons Paper 40.

Procedure, Select Committee on, Fourth Report 2002–03, 'Procedures for Debates, Private Members' Bills and the Powers of the Speaker', Stationery Office, House of Commons Paper 333.

Election of a Speaker of the House of Commons: Standard Note, House of Commons Library, 7 August 2000.

Election of a Commons Speaker, Research Paper 00/090, House of Commons Library, 29 November 2000.

Secretary to the Speaker: Ralph Verney's Correspondence, House of Commons Library Document No. 22, The Stationery Office 1999.

The Speaker, Factsheet M2, Members Series, House of Commons Information Office, Revised September 2003.

The Father of the House, Factsheet M3, House of Commons Information Office, Revised September 2003.

Divisions, Factsheet P9, House of Commons Information Sheet, Revised October 2003.

Standing Orders of the House of Commons, The Stationery Office, 2003, 2007 & 2010.

Deputy Speakers of the House from the start of the 1945/46 Parliamentary session to the present, compiled by the House of Commons Library, 2006.

House of Commons Committee on Standards and Privileges, *Conduct of Mr Speaker*, Ninth Report of Session 2007–08, HC 559.

Isobel White & Andrew Parker, *Speaker's Conferences*, House of Commons Library, 15 December 2008.

Serjeant for the Commons, House of Commons Library Document No. 13, Fourth Edition, 2009.

The Speaker of the House of Commons, House of Commons, 2009.

House of Commons Committee on Issues of Privilege, *Police Searches on the Parliamentary Estate*, First Report of Session 2009–10, HC 62.

House of Commons, *Speaker's Conference (on Parliamentary Representation)*, Final Report, 11 January 2010, HC239-I.

House of Commons Procedure Committee, *2010 elections for positions in the House*, Fifth Report of Session 2010–12.

House of Commons, Official Report:

Hansard columns of debates and rulings by the Speaker.

House of Lords, Official Report:

Hansard columns relating to Baroness Boothroyd's opposition to the Coalition government's plans for House of Lords reform.

Erskine May: 14th – 24th editions of Erskine May's *Parliamentary Practice*

Northern Ireland House of Commons Official Report:

Northern Ireland House of Commons Official Report from 1956 when Speaker Sir Norman Stronge was prevented from re-taking his seat following the election to the Stormont Parliament.

Australian House of Representatives Publications:

House of Representatives, Infosheet 3, *The Speaker*, May 2012.

The National Archives, Kew:

CAB 128/24. Cabinet conclusions, 6 February 1952.

PREM 11/863. Possibility of independent opposition at general election of Speaker of House of Commons: PM's request for support from Clement Davies MP and Clement Attlee MP, 1955.

Private Papers:

Private Papers of the Rt Hon. The Viscount Ruffside (held by his Great Nephew, Anthony Clifton Brown).

Interviews:

Jonathan Aitken, 29 November 2010

Rt Hon. Tony Benn, 19 September 2004

Rt Hon. John Bercow MP, 26 October 2010 & 27 October 2011

Sir Richard Body, 22 February 2007

Rt Hon. The Baroness Boothroyd OM, 5 April 2001, 24 October 2005 & 14 September 2010

Douglas Carswell MP, 30 June 2010

Sir Robin Chichester-Clark, 13 February 2007

Geoffrey Clifton-Brown MP, 23 November 2009

Rt Hon. Tam Dalyell, 14 March 2009

Mavis, Lady Dunrossil, 19 March 2005

Rt Hon. The Lord Elis-Thomas AM, 21 September 2004

The Baroness Fookes of Plymouth DBE DL, 25 October 2005

Rt Hon. Sir Alan Haselhurst MP, 29 July 2010

Lord Hooson QC, 25 April 2007

Rt Hon. The Lord Howe of Aberavon QC, 8 July 2009

Sir Donald Limon, 17 March 2001

Sir Robin Maxwell-Hyslop, 4 June 2007 & 18 August 2009

Sir William McKay KCB, 1 March 2001

The Hon. Dr Alasdair Morrison, 13 November 2004

Rt Hon. The Lord Naseby, 7 September 2004

Stanley Newens, 9 July 2007

Rt Hon. The Lord Parkinson, 17 January 2009

Matthew Parris, 5 October 2010

Edward Pearce, 22 October 2009

Rt Hon. The Lord Radice, 8 June 2010

Rt Hon. The Lord Renton, 1 March 2006

Rt Hon. Peter Riddell, 4 October 2010

Robert Rogers, 16 December 2010

Sir Roger Sands KCB, 29 July 2004
Dennis Skinner MP, 15 September 2008
Rt Hon. The Lord Steel of Aikwood KT, 15 March 2005
Sir Teddy Taylor, 26 October 2004
Charles Walker MP, 14 September 2010
Rt Hon. The Lord Weatherill, 3 June 2005

Memoirs, Autobiographies and Published Diaries:

Ball, Stuart (ed.), *Parliament and Politics in the age of Churchill and Attlee: The Headlam Diaries 1935–1951*, (Cambridge: Cambridge University Press, 1999).

Benn, Tony, *Years of Hope: Diaries, Papers and Letters 1940–1962*, (London: Arrow, 1994).

Benn, Tony, *Out of the Wilderness: Diaries 1963–67*, (London: 1987).

Benn, Tony, *Office Without Power: Diaries 1968–72*, (London: Hutchinson, 1988).

Benn, Tony, *The End of an Era: Diaries 1980–90*, (London: Hutchinson, 1992).

Benn, Tony, *Free at Last! Diaries 1991–2001*, (London: Hutchinson, 2002).

Benn, Tony, *More Time For Politics: Diaries 2001–2007*, (London: Hutchinson, 2007).

Blunkett, David, *The Blunkett Tapes: My Life in the Bear Pit*, (London: Bloomsbury, 2006).

Boothroyd, Betty, *The Autobiography*, (London: Century, 2001).

Boyd-Carpenter, John, *Way of Life: The Memoirs of John Boyd-Carpenter*, (London: Sidgwick & Jackson, 1980).

Brandreth, Gyles, *Breaking the Code: Westminster Diaries May 1990–May 1997*, (London: Weidenfeld & Nicolson, 1999).

Cable, Vince, *Free Radical: A Memoir*, (London: Atlantic Books, 2009).

Campbell, Alastair, *The Blair Years*, (London: Hutchinson, 2007).

Campbell, Alastair, *The Alastair Campbell Diaries Volume One: Prelude to Power 1994–1997*, (London: Hutchinson, 2010).

Campbell, Alastair, *The Alastair Campbell Diaries Volume Two: Power and the People 1997–1999*, (London: Arrow, 2011).

Campbell, Menzies, *My Autobiography*, (London: Hodder & Stoughton, 2008).

Castle, Barbara, *Diaries 1974–76*, (London: Weidenfeld & Nicolson, 1980).

Catterall, Peter (ed.), *The Macmillan Diaries: The Cabinet Years, 1950–1957*, (London: Macmillan, 2003).

Catterall, Peter (ed.), *The Macmillan Diaries, Prime Minister and After, 1957–1966*, Volume 2, (London: Pan Macmillan, 2011).

Cook, Robin, *The Point of Departure*, (London: Simon & Schuster, 2003).

Crossman, Richard, *Diaries of a Cabinet Minister, Volume One: Minister for Housing 1964–1966*, (London: Hamish Hamilton, 1975).

Dalyell, Tam, *The Importance of Being Awkward*, (London: Birlinn, 2011).

Donoghue, Bernard, *Downing Street Diary: With Harold Wilson in No. 10*, (London: Jonathan Cape, 2005).

Donoghue, Bernard, *Downing Street Diary: With James Callaghan in No. 10*, (London: Jonathan Cape, 2008).

Farage, Nigel, *Flying Free*, (London: Biteback, 2011).

Hain, Peter, *Outside In*, (London: Biteback, 2012).

Heath, Edward, *The Course of My Life: My Autobiography*, (London: Hodder & Stoughton, 1998).

Heseltine, Michael, *Life in the Jungle: My Autobiography*, (London: Hodder & Stoughton, 2000).

Howe, Geoffrey, *Conflict of Loyalty*, (London: Macmillan, 1994).

Hurd, Douglas, *Memoirs*, (London: Little, Brown, 2003).

Lawson, Nigel, *The View from No. 11: Memoirs of a Tory Radical*, (London: Bantam Press, 1992).

Lloyd, Selwyn, *Mr Speaker, Sir*, (London: Jonathan Cape, 1976).

Macmillan, Harold, *Tides of Fortune, 1945–1955*, (London: Macmillan, 1969).

Macmillan, Harold, *Pointing the Way, 1959–1961*, (London: Macmillan, 1972).

Maybray-King, Lord, *The Speaker and Parliament*, (Birmingham: T. Stacey, 1973).

Morgan, Janet (ed.), *The Backbench Diaries of Richard Crossman*, (London: Jonathan Cape, 1981).

Mullin, Chris, *A View from the Foothills: The Diaries of Chris Mullin*, (London: Profile, 2009).

Mullin, Chris, *Decline & Fall: Diaries 2005–2010*, (London: Profile, 2010).

Neill, Ivan, *Church and State*, (Belfast, 1995).

Nutting, Anthony, *No End of a Lesson: The Story of Suez*, (London: Constable, 1996).

Oakley, Robin, *Inside Track*, (London: Bantam Press, 2001).

Oxford and Asquith, Earl of, *Fifty Years in Parliament*, vol. 2, (London: Cassell, 1926).

Radice, Giles, *Diaries 1980–2001: From Political Disaster to Election Triumph*, (London: Weidenfeld & Nicolson, 2004).

Spicer, Michael, *The Spicer Diaries*, (London: Biteback, 2012).

Tebbit, Norman, *Upwardly Mobile*, (London: Weidenfeld & Nicolson 1988).

Thatcher, Margaret, *The Downing Street Years*, (London: HarperCollins, 1995).

Thomas, George, *Mr Speaker: The Memoirs of Viscount Tonypandy*, (London: Century, 1985).

Williams, Shirley, *Climbing the Bookshelves*, (London: Virago Press, 2009).

Wilson, Harold, *The Labour Government 1964–1970: A Personal Record*, (London: Penguin, 1974).

Secondary Sources:

Abse, Leo, *Tony Blair: The Man Behind the Smile*, (London: Robson Books, 2001).

Barker, Anthony & Rush, Michael, *The Member of Parliament and his Information*, (London: Allen & Unwin, 1970).

Blackburn, Robert & Kennon, Andrew, *Griffith & Ryle on Parliament: Functions, Practice and Procedures*, (London: Sweet & Maxwell, 2003).

Brivati, Brian, Buxton, Julia & Seldon, Anthony (eds.), *The Contemporary History Handbook*, (Manchester: Manchester University Press, 1996).

Brooke, Heather, *The Silent State*, (London: William Heinemann, 2010).

Campbell, John, *Edward Heath: A Biography*, (London: Jonathan Cape, 1993).

Carswell, Douglas & Hannan, Daniel, *The Plan: twelve months to renew Britain*, (London: Douglas Carswell, 2008).

Cawthorne, Graham, *Mr Speaker, Sir*, (London: Cleaver-Hume 1952).

Crick, Bernard, *The Reform of Parliament*, (London: Weidenfeld & Nicolson,1964).

Dimbleby, Jonathan, *The Last Governor: Chris Patten & the Handover of Hong Kong*, (London: Little, Brown, 1997).

Fair, John D., *British Interparty Conferences: A Study of the Procedure of Conciliation in British Politics*, (Oxford: Oxford University Press, 1980).

Friedman, Bobby, *Bercow, Mr Speaker: Rowdy Living in the Tory Party*, (London: Gibson Square Books, 2011).

Garrett, John, *Westminster: Does Parliament Work?*, (London: Gollancz, 1992).

Griffith, J. A. G. & Ryle, Michael, *Parliament: Functions, Practice and Procedures*, (London: Sweet & Maxwell, 1989).

Hanson, A. H., & Crick, Bernard (eds.), *The Commons in Transition*, (London: Fontana, 1970).

Hennessy, Peter, *Muddling Through: Power, Politics and the Quality of Government in Postwar Britain*, (London: Weidenfeld & Nicolson, 1996).

Hennessy, Peter, *The Hidden Wiring: Unearthing the British Constitution*, (London: Phoneix, 1996).

Hunston, Ramon, *Order! Order! A biography of The Rt Hon George Thomas*, (London: Marshall, 1981).

Jennings, Ivor, *Parliament*, Second Edition, (Cambridge: Cambridge University Press, 1969).

Kandiah, Michael D. & Staerck, Gillian (eds.), *The Role of the Speaker of the House of Commons*, Institute of Contemporary British History, ICBH Oral History Programme, (London: University of London, 2005).

Laundy, Philip, *The Office of Speaker*, (London: Cassell, 1964).

Laundy, Philip, 'The Speaker and his Office in the Twentieth Century' in S. A. Walkland (ed.), *The House of Commons in the Twentieth Century*, (Oxford: Oxford University Press, 1979).Laundy, Philip, The Office of Speaker in the Parliaments of the Commonwealth, (London, 1984).

Letts, Quentin, *50 People Who Buggered Up Britain*, (London: Constable, 2008).

Letts, Quentin, *Bog-Standard Britain*, (London: Constable, 2009).

Letts, Quentin, *Letts Rip!*, (London: Constable, 2010).

Marsden, Philip, *The Officers of the Commons 1363–1965*, (London: Barrie & Rockliff, 1966).

Norton, Philip, *Does Parliament Matter?*, (Hemel Hempstead: Prentice Hall/ Harvester Wheatsheaf, 1993).

Norton, Philip, *Parliament in British Politics*, (Basingstoke: Palgrave Macmillan, 2005).

Rawnsley, Andrew, *The End of the Party: The Rise and Fall of New Labour*, (London: Penguin, 2010).

Richards, Peter G., *Honourable Members: A Study of the British Backbencher*, (London, 1959).

Richards, Peter G., *Honourable Members: A Study of the British Backbencher*, Second Edition, (London: Faber, 1964).

Richards, Peter G., *The Backbenchers*, (London: Faber, 1972).

Riddell, Peter, *Parliament Under Blair*, (London: Faber, 2000).

Robertson, E. H., *George: A Biography of Viscount Tonypandy*, (London: HarperCollins, 1993).

Rogers, Robert & Walters, Rhodri, *How Parliament Works* (Fifth Edition), (London: Longman, 2004).

Rogers, Robert & Walters, Rhodri, *How Parliament Works* (Sixth Edition), (London: Longman, 2006).

Rose, Peter, *How the Troubles Came to Northern Ireland*, (London, Palgrave Macmillan, 1999).

Routledge, Paul, *Madam Speaker: The Life of Betty Boothroyd*, (London: Politico's, 2000).

Sampson, Anthony, *Who Runs This Place? The Anatomy of Britain in the 21st Century*, (London: John Murray, 2004).

Seaward, Paul (ed.), *Speakers and the Speakership*, (London: Wiley-Blackwell, 2010).

Seldon, Anthony & Lodge, Guy, *Brown at 10*, (London: Biteback, 2010).

Thorpe, D. R., *Selwyn Lloyd*, (London: Jonathan Cape, 1989).

Thorpe, D. R., *Eden*, (London: Pimlico, 2004).

Winnett, Robert & Rayner, Gordon, *No Expenses Spared*, (London: Bantam Press, 2009).

Pamphlets:

Benn, Tony, *The Speaker, The Commons and Democracy*, (Nottingham: Spokesman Books, 2000).

Briers, P. M., *The Speaker of the House of Commons*, Hansard Society Pamphlet No. 3, 1946.

James, Robin, *The Speaker of the House of Commons*, (London, 2006).

Times Guides to the House of Commons:

All *Times Guides to the House of Commons* (published by *The Times*) covering every general election from 1945 to 2010.

Printed Press:

'Profile – Mr Speaker', *The Observer*, 18 March 1945.

Douglas Clifton Brown, 'The Speaker Describes a Trip to France', *Hexham Courant*, 6 December 1947.

'Portrait Gallery: The Speaker', *The Sunday Times*, 12 October 1952.

Obituary of Viscount Ruffside, *The Times*, 6 May 1958.

Obituary of Lord Dunrossil, *The Times*, 3 February 1961.

'The Speaker Dies in London Street', *The Times*, 3 September 1965.

Hugh Noyes, 'Mr Lloyd new Speaker as revolt fails', *The Times*, 13 January 1971.

Julian Haviland, 'Weatherill elected without dissent', *The Times*, 16 June 1983.

Russell Johnston, 'Unfair, Mr Speaker, unfair', *The Times*, 10 November 1983.

'Order! Order!', *The Times*, 26 February 1985.

'Mr Speaker's Memoirs', Letter from James Callaghan to the Editor, *The Times*, 27 February 1985.

Obituary of Lord Maybray-King, *The Times*, 4 September 1986.

Andrew Alexander, 'Sorry, there's a fault in the Speaker', *Daily Mail*, 23 April 1988.

Edward Pearce, 'Straight-talker Speaker finds knives are out', *Sunday Times*, 1 May 1988.

Donald Macintyre, 'Why Tories can't get Speaker out', *Sunday Telegraph*, 22 May 1988.

Heather Kirby, 'Madam of an orderly House?', *The Times*, 9 July 1990.

Quentin Letts 'Gorbals Mick was set up on the shy and his rivals had to knock him off', *Daily Mail*, 24 October 2000.

Peter Riddell, 'House falls into theatre of the absurd', *The Times*, 24 October 2000.

Matthew Parris, 'Savage nuclear attack causes local fallout', *The Times*, 30 October 2001.

Melissa Kite, 'Speaker breaks neutrality rule', *The Times*, 30 October 2001.

Melissa Kite, 'Speaker denies remark betrayed political bias', *The Times*, 31 October 2001.

Simon Walters, 'Gorbalsgate', *The Mail on Sunday*, 11 July 2004.

Simon Walters, 'Speaker quizzed over wife's £100,000', *Mail on Sunday*, 18 July 2004.

Simon Walters, 'Commons aide No. 3 quits over rows with Speaker', *Mail on Sunday*, 19 December 2004.

David Cracknell & David Leppard, 'MI5 agent will build Fortress Westminster', *The Times*, 19 December 2004.

Greg Hurst & Anthony Browne, 'Speaker reprimands Cameron over clash with Blair', *The Times*, 2 November 2006.

Obituary of Lord Weatherill, *The Independent*, 8 May 2007.

Obituary of Lord Weatherill, *The Times*, 8 May 2007.

Obituary of Lord Weatherill, *Daily Telegraph*, 8 May 2007.

Greg Hurst, 'Speaker's class war claims latest upper-crust victim', *The Times*, 23 June 2007.

Simon Walters, 'Speaker's wife claims £50k for flights to "support" him', *Mail on Sunday*, 20 January 2008.

William Rees-Mogg, 'An historic attack on liberty and democracy', *The Times*, 1 December 2008.

Robert Winnett, 'MPs' expenses: how Brown and his Cabinet exploit expenses system', *Daily Telegraph*, 8 May 2009.

Lord Foulkes, 'Lord Foulkes: Speaker won't stand down for hypocritical scapegoats', *Sunday Times*, 17 May 2009.

Andrew Gimson, 'A gruesome disaster as he tried to save his own job', *Daily Telegraph*, 19 May 2009.

Peter Riddell, 'An apologist for MPs, not a champion for voters', *The Times*, 19 May 2009.

Andrew Porter, 'A very British revolution', *Daily Telegraph*, 20 May 2009.

George Foulkes, 'Michael was a reformer cut down by jittery MPs', *The Independent*, 20 May 2009.

Andrew Pearce, 'Ministers cared only for perks of power, says Boothroyd', *Daily Telegraph*, 20 May 2009.

Andrew Pierce, 'Unforgettable, for all the wrong reasons', *Daily Telegraph*, 20 May 2009.

'Timeline of Martin's Career as Speaker', *Daily Telegraph*, 20 May 2009.

Gordon Rayner & Rosa Prince, 'Michael Martin faces backlash over possible peerage', Telegraph.co.uk, 21 May 2009.

Roy Hattersley, 'Michael Martin: "It was when they started attacking my wife that I knew I had to go"', *The Observer*, 21 June 2009.

Patrick Sawer, 'Front runner claimed £1,000 for tax returns', *Sunday Telegraph*, 21 June 2009.

'Triumph or Disaster', *The Times*, 23 June 2009.

James Chapman & Kirsty Walker, 'So much for a fresh start!', *Daily Mail*, 23 June 2009.

Quentin Letts, 'Impossible! They voted for someone worse than Gorbals Mick', *Daily Mail*, 23 June 2009.

Sam Coates, 'Burning ambition of man who won in spite of his own party', *The Times*, 23 June 2009.

Nicholas Watt, 'PM warned that elevation of Michael Martin could damage Lords', *The Guardian*, 1 July 2009.

Michael Savage, 'Bercow breaks convention to attack BNP', *The Independent*, 31 October 2009.

Sam Coates, 'Speaker's wife to contest ward for Labour', *The Times*, 13 November 2009.

Angus Macleod, 'Labour poll victory in Glasgow as SNP challenge is crushed', *The Times*, 13 November 2009.

Obituary of Sir Robin Maxwell-Hyslop, *Daily Telegraph*, 26 January 2010.

Holly Watt & Robert Winnett, 'Bercow delays by-election after his wife intervenes', *The Times*, 9 November 2010.

Andrew Gimson, 'Unlikely neighbours squeeze into their new seats', *Daily Telegraph*, 19 May 2010.

Simon Carr, 'Order! Order! Commons gets a fresh dose of Bercow', *The Independent*, 19 May 2010.

James Chapman, 'You're not ****ing royalty, Mr Speaker', *Daily Mail*, 14 January 2011.

Simon Walters, 'Now Betty cuffs scruffy Mr Speaker', *Mail on Sunday*, 16 January 2011.

Sam Coates, 'Speaker hounded over anti-hunt letter', *The Times*, 19 January 2011.

Jason Groves, 'Minister hits out at Bercow and wife over impartiality', *Daily Mail*, 20 January 2011.

James Kirkup, 'It's a storm in a bedsheet, says Speaker's wife', *Daily Telegraph*, 5 February 2011.

Gerri Peev, 'Taypayers' £1400 bill for Speaker's washing machines', *Daily Mail*, 16 April 2011.

Patrick Wintour, 'Bercow: Mail a "bigoted comic"', *The Guardian*, 8 June 2011.

Andrew Grice, 'I have no plans to work in Afghanistan, says Bercow', *The Independent*, 7 July 2011.

Stuart Jeffries, 'The Saturday Interview – John Bercow', *The Guardian*, 23 July 2011.

Brendan Carlin, 'Jill, Serjeant-at-Arms, quit after bust-up over queues', *Mail on Sunday*, 16 October 2011.

Robert Winnett, 'Bercow ignores pleas to reduce his pension', *Daily Telegraph*, 18 October 2011.

Emily Ashton, 'A Waste of Monet', *The Sun*, 29 November 2011.

Christopher Hope, 'Bercow's £37,000 portrait, hushing ministers and hailing gay rights', *Daily Telegraph*, 29 November 2011.

Christopher Hope, 'Taxpayers spend £30,000 for Speaker to fly business class', *Daily Telegraph*, 12 December 2011.

'Speaker Bercow spares himself pay squeeze pain', *Mail on Sunday*, 18 December 2011.

Kirsty Walker, 'Point of order! Proof that Mr Speaker is picking on the PM', *Daily Mail*, 31 December 2011.

Simon Walters & Brendan Carlin, 'Defiant Speaker vows there will be no prayer ban in the Commons', *Mail on Sunday*, 12 February 2012.

Jason Groves, 'Bercow hijacks Queen's speech', *Daily Mail*, 21 March 2012.

James Kirkup, 'Did Speaker promote gay rights in speech?', *Daily Telegraph*, 21 March 2012.

Glen Owen, 'There goes another one, Mr Speaker', *Mail on Sunday*, 27 March 2011.

James Chapman, 'Furious PM forced back to Commons to defend Hunt', *Daily Mail*, 1 May 2012.

Quentin Letts, 'Cameron performed rather brilliantly...Speaker Bercow, like Muttley the dog, had been foiled', *Daily Mail*, 1 May 2012.

Nicholas Cecil, 'Tories demand explanation from Speaker in "lying" row', *Evening Standard*, 3 July 2012.

Rob Wilson, 'You're preening, partisan and pompous: hold your tongue Mr Speaker!', *Mail on Sunday*, 19 August 2012.

Holly Watt & Claire Newell, '27 MPs let one home and claim another', *Daily Telegraph*, 19 October 2012.

Christopher Hope, 'Bercow's "revenge" on expenses', *Daily Telegraph*, 14 November 2012.

Periodicals:

Bradley, A. W., 'Parliamentary Privilege, Zircon and National Security', *Public Law*, (Winter 1987).

Dale, Iain, 'In conversation… John Bercow', *Total Politics*, Issue 19, January 2010.

Macrory, Sam, 'People Profile: Sir Alan Haselhurst. Speaking Up', *The House Magazine*, No. 1352, Vol. 36, 12 July 2010.

Waugh, Paul & Macrory, Sam, 'The independent iconoclast', *The House Magazine*, 23 February 2012.

Broadcast Material

Weekend World, broadcast on London Weekend Television on 8 May 1988.

Call Me Madam: A Profile of Betty Boothroyd by Michael Cockerell, BBC Television, first broadcast on BBC 2 on 16 December 2000.

Straight Talk with Andrew Neil, BBC Television, first broadcast on BBC News 24 on 10 June 2006.

BBC Politics Show, BBC Television, broadcast on 11 February 2007.

Bernard and Betty Speak Out, Parts 1 & 2, BBC Radio 4, first broadcast on 13 May & 20 May 2007.

Andrew Marr Show, BBC One, broadcast on 17 May 2009.

Straight Talk, BBC Television, first broadcast on BBC News Channel on 16 January 2010.

The World This Weekend, BBC Radio 4, broadcast on 16 January 2011.

Daily Politics, BBC One, 19 January 2011.

The Politics Show, BBC One, broadcast on 30 January 2011.

Daily Politics, BBC One, broadcast on 4 February 2011.

Sally Bercow talking to Victoria Derbyshire, BBC Radio 5 Live, 4 February 2011.

The Record Review, first broadcast on BBC Parliament, 16 December 2011.

The Westminster Hour, BBC Radio 4, 27 February 2012.

Murnaghan, Sky News, 6 May 2012.

Lorraine, ITV1, 16 July 2012.

World at One, BBC Radio 4, 14 August 2012.

Electronic sources:

Interview with Jude Crocker, UK Parliament Web Team, 31 July 2009, http://www.youtube.com/watch?v=VP8pjcES-NY

http://www.johnbercow.co.uk/biog

Other sources:

Letter from the Rt Hon. The Lord Weatherill DL to Nicholas Winterton MP, 6 December 2000.

Letter from Philip Laundy, 1 March 2001.

Letter from Sir Nicolas Bevan, 5 March 2001.

Letter from Sir Clifford Boulton, 19 March 2001.

Letter from The Baroness Fookes of Plymouth DBE DL, 21 March 2001.
Letter from Rt Hon. Jonathan Hunt MP, Speaker of the New Zealand House of Representatives, 24 June 2004.
Letter from Philip Laundy, 15 July 2004.
Letter from Sir Philip Goodhart, 27 August 2004.
Letter from Sir Robin Maxwell-Hyslop, 5 January 2005.
Letter from Sir Robin Maxwell-Hyslop, 21 January 2005.
Letter from Sir Robin Maxwell-Hyslop, 22 April 2005.
Letter from Roger Sands, 27 May 2005.
'Duties of the Speaker on the death of a Sovereign', note produced by Roger Sands for the author, 4 November 2005.
Notes from Rt Hon. The Baroness Boothroyd OM, 6 December 2005.
Letter from The 9th Duke of Buccleuch, 19 March 2007.
Letter from Rt Hon. The Lord Morris of Aberavon KG, QC, 22 March 2007.
Letter from Rt Hon. The Lord Morris of Aberavon KG, QC, 24 May 2007.
Letter from Sir David Price, 3 June 2008.
Letter from Sir David Price, 16 September 2008.
Letter from Sir Robin Maxwell-Hyslop, 12 November 2008.
Letter from Rt Hon. Sir John Major KG CH, 10 February 2009.
Letter from Sir Robin Maxwell-Hyslop, 7 May 2009.
Letter from Sir Robin Maxwell-Hyslop, 10 August 2009.
Email from Professor Lord Alton of Liverpool, 31 March 2009.
Letter from Humfrey Malins MP, 28 October 2009.
Letter from Rt Hon. The Lord Ryder, 19 May 2010.
Email from Rt Hon. The Lord Martin of Springburn, 29 June 2010.
Email from Quentin Letts, 31 August 2010.
Email from Quentin Letts, 23 September 2010.
Email from Rt Hon. The Baroness Boothroyd OM, 12 October 2010.
Email from John Hall, Parliamentary Assistant to Jane Ellison, 22 July 2011.
Email from Martin Salter, 25 November 2011.
Email from Quentin Letts, 29 December 2011.
Email from Eric Janse, CSPOC Secretary, 28 February 2012.
Letter from Robert Rogers, 1 May 2012.
Email from The Hon. Dr Kendal Major MP, Speaker of the House of Assembly of the Bahamas, 9 August 2012.
Email from The Hon. Stephen Rodan SHK, Speaker of the House of Keys, 28 August 2012.
Email from Beryl Bright, Senior Private Secretary to Dr The Rt Hon. Lockwood Smith MP, 10 October 2012.
Email from Michael White, 9 November 2012.

Index